Ben
410-101-06-11

Fortress of Deceit

Fortress of Deceit

Fortress of Deceit

By

Bogdan Dzakovic

The Story of a 9/11 Whistleblower

Fortress of Deceit

Copyright © by Bogdan J. Dzakovic, 2016

ALL rights reserved, including the right to reproduce this book or portions of this book in any form.

Down&Out Press

ISBN-13: 978-1535033138
ISBN-10: 1535033134

This book is dedicated to federal government whistleblowers, who, despite the obstacles, do what is right. And to my brother Stefan, who never had a chance, but endured. And to the orphans.

Fortress of Deceit

CONTENTS

FORWARD By Steve Elson		8
INTRODUCTION The Green Room		16
1	A Credit to Holmes	34
2	Sea Duty	40
3	The Big Beach	56
4	A Hint of Warfare	65
5	A Hint of Crime Fighting	82
6	The Tombstone Agency	126
7	The Red Team	185
8	Analysis of the Threat	218
9	Jaws	228
10	The Predicted Attack	246
11	Retribution	248
12	A Gathering of Samurai	302
EPILOGUE		342
AFTERWORD By Tom Devine		358

Fortress of Deceit

ACKNOWLEDGEMENTS

I would like to thank all the misfits, miscreants, and morons that have crossed my life path, especially those applicable government managers and national elected officials, without whom the inspiration of this book wouldn't have existed. I would also like to thank the truly exceptional and patriotic individuals with whom I have had the fortune to have interacted and who [still] provide a glimmer of hope for the potentials of the future. I chose not to use the real names of most of the people who played a part in this story. Through experience, I learned that the government misfits, miscreants, and morons tend to get rewarded, especially when their malodorous behaviors are revealed in either internal government channels or the public spotlight. Unfortunately, I also learned that the exceptional individuals are punished or vilified by the government by excelling beyond the accepted norm and especially for fulfilling their oath of office to abide by the United States Constitution and to defend this country from ALL enemies both foreign and DOMESTIC. Some exceptions are those senior personnel whose governmental status is of public record and to those few persons who were astute enough to recognize the pre-911 terrorist threat and the vulnerabilities in aviation security, and attempted to prevent the attacks by waking up oblivious bureaucrats and politicians whose job was to prevent just such an attack. These individuals are clearly defined throughout the book.

Sections of this book are generalized and condensed to accommodate the above and to provide a smoother flow of information.

Fortress of Deceit

FOREWORD
+
By
+
Steve Elson

In having the honor of writing this foreword, I state up front that everything said here or in the past is the complete truth as far as we know. For my part, I invite, as I have for years, anyone who believes that I am lying or intentionally misrepresenting any issue to call me out and debate the issues in public. Additionally, if the government maintains that we are wrong or misrepresenting issues, then we once again challenge the government to authorize us to <u>prove</u> what we say. In writing and orally, we have named names and singled out the wrongdoers. Bogdan's book makes it patently clear where the blame for this government malfeasance resides.

As a rule, when talking about the battle Bogdan and I fought for several years to stop the lying/cover-up of the FAA/government regarding aviation security (AVSEC) there is no "I, MINE," or ME", only "WE, OUR or US." I had the opportunity to quit the FAA when I saw their "security" was leading to disaster; Bogdan remained on the job fighting the lying and corruption within the FAA and later the TSA.

Bottom Line: IF THE FAA/DOT AND GOVERNMENT HAD LISTENED TO US, 9/11 WOULD <u>NOT</u> HAVE OCCURRED! We have repeatedly proven this (to congress and interested public in movies, in books, in articles, and on TV). The US government, (including) the president, continues to lie, take money from PACs and waits out the American publics' short memory. We'll debate, in public, <u>anyone</u> who dares to lie and say that the US government cares about aviation security or the lives affected/lost in aviation terroristic attacks. We addressed the issue of cockpit security long before 9/11 to the Senior Executive Service personnel running the FAA. Realizing cost was always an issue, we geared our corrective measures to "Quick, Simple, Cheap, and Easy fixes using nothing more than cardboard, duct tape, sticks, strings, profiling, and a few simple procedures." Most people have had trouble understanding the statement we made that, *"9/11 could have been easily prevented by nothing more than some rope out of the garbage and a few simple procedures using already on-board equipment."* Again, we challenge **anyone** who doubts this to debate the issue.

Bogdan is one of the most honest and caring people anywhere. He is an enigma -- physically and mentally strong; a quiet man who when he talks or listens, his attention is totally on the person with whom he is conversing. Bogdan is one of a few in America that actually studied and understood the OATH he took when becoming a Coast Guard Officer, an NIS Agent, and an FAA Security Agent. His word is definitely his bond. In his book Bogdan reveals a little of his past. The reader should know that Bogdan's family came from the concentration camps in Europe. He was one of several children, all of whom were orphaned at a young age. The siblings were broken up and lived in orphanages and foster homes. Yet Bogdan rose from all this to become a servant of the people, an American Hero and definitely a Hero and brother-in-arms to me. Until his early 20's Bogdan did not even know his given name. He thought his name was John; when in an emergency room as a child, he was asked his middle name. He thought he was required to have one, looked around, saw a name and gave that name. As I recall, he learned that his name was "Bogdan" from relatives in his early 20s. There is no more perfect name for the meaning of Bogdan is "GIFT FROM

GOD." (This information can be found on sites like stuffaboutname.com.) Apparently his parents named him Bogdan to show gratitude for being able to come to America and having Bogdan in America. For me personally, I consider Bogdan as a "gift from God to me" and also to his America, that he has loved and fights for. If I were forced to describe Bogdan in one word, it would be Altruistic.

It did not take long working in the FAA, even in the regular FAA Security program to see that what we did was a farce, a façade, and would lead to peril; in the FAA Red Team, the failures, vulnerabilities, and corruption were overwhelming and frightening. FAA management did virtually nothing to correct these vulnerabilities. Once I quit the FAA, I had opportunities to do things that could not have been done inside the FAA. Bogdan and I worked together on everything we did with Bogdan assuming a great risk of being fired. For health reasons alone, Bogdan had to have medical coverage. Yet he literally risked it all because of his gratitude to America and her people but most of all because of his Oath to "protect and defend."

Coming from military backgrounds, Bogdan and I used the FAA Chain of Command to try to remedy these horrific and life threatening vulnerabilities – the FAA DIDN'T care. Once I quit, our efforts were still focused within the chain of command. Certain that the FAA did not care about AVSEC, we moved up to the Secretary of the Department of Transportation (DoT). DoT didn't care any more than the FAA. Though I moved from DC, we talked and coordinated several times a week. With Bogdan's input, I compiled large notebooks 2"- 4" of documentation and proof of which we spoke. Once the first one was done, I flew to DC and stayed with Bogdan for several days reviewing, organizing, ensuring factual information, and finally copying and distributing copies to both parties on both the senate and the house. This first book was entitled, The Big Blue Book of Death" (in a big blue notebook) and the second, "Better Read than Dead" (in a big red notebook). It took me two visits to Washington and a few months to get all this done, well before 9/11/01.

We made appointments by phones with congressional staffers who offered us a 20 – 30 minute appointment. Virtually all those appointments turned into 1½ to 3 hours; the staffers could not believe what they were seeing or hearing. Of course, as many Americans, they had seen media reports on AVSEC failures; they had never seen the overwhelming proof of failures in one such document. We began our presentation by telling each staffer that there is no way to stop all determined terrorists. The best we can do is to employ risk minimization strategies that are not necessarily tedious, invasive, or expensive. We acknowledged upfront that the odds of any one particular individual being killed by an air terrorist event was almost infinitesimally small. BUT those odds mean nothing to someone who had a family member killed by an air terrorism event. We noted that technology was only an adjunct to well- trained, highly motivated, and inspirationally led PEOPLE. Our goals were to reverse the FAA "Security" program which actually ensured the odds were in the favor of the terrorists rather than in favor of the flying public and flight crews."

Our presentation styles were pretty much opposites. Impatient and mad, I usually started in my loud voice, gesticulating, and animated in the attack mode. Following my "rants," Bogdan quietly, deliberately, intelligently, and authoritatively presented the similar information. One cannot dismiss the thoughtful, intelligent, and organized presentation of Bogdan. We left the staffers, mouths ajar, with our contact information and admonished them to take us to task if what we said was not true; there was no denying our proof. Unfortunately, once the staffers presented this incontrovertible information to their members (senators and representatives) the matter died. The members were willing to play the odds and risk the attacks we predicted in order not to alienate the airlines and PACs that gave them millions. NOTHING has changed as evidenced by the repeated and horrendous failures of over 95% by the over $7 Billion dollar/year TSA.

With Bogdan's continuous input and advice, I composed a white paper: "9/11, YES THERE IS A SMOKING GUN," Steve Elson, 04Sep03 (updated 28Sep04 for 9/11/04). (Copy available on the "9/11 Digital Archives.") Rather than include Bogdan's name, I dedicated it to him. He was not afraid of retribution but I was afraid -- for him. Bogdan took enormous chances in trying to warn an ignorant and often uncaring public of multiple air terrorism attacks in the near future. He did this even before he was granted the rare official Whistle Blower status. He certainly didn't want to be fired, but his Oath to the people of the country superseded all.

Over the years, before and after 9/11, we made many predictions, did many interviews, appeared in movies and on TV; we were joined by Brian "Sully" Sullivan after he retired from the FAA. Sully continues the fight to this very day and has done more than most any individual to archive the wrongs and the warnings that fell on the deaf ears of government that chose personal gain over the security of the American People. Though sidelined and ignored by the TSA, Bogdan, the most honest, valuable, and knowledgeable AVSEC person in the TSA, he continued a frustrating battle to daily honor his oath and "protect the flying public."

Fortress of Deceit

Shorty after 9/11, a friend set me up with an appointment with a congressional staffer. I flew to DC to join with Bogdan for the appointment. That staffer handed us off to a very bright and aggressive staffer on a House secret investigations committee; his reports were classified and went only to the House member tasking him with the study. Bogdan and I talked with this gentleman for over an hour. He told us that the new AVSEC organization, not yet named, would be unlike anything we had ever seen. We listened and then told him, "This new organization is virtually 100% guaranteed to fail." AND IT DID. When I found him a year later, he just hung his head and said, "Things didn't turn out as expected." Over the years, we wrote thousands of e-mails and I had the opportunity to do "security assessments" all over the Country with the media PROVING that as we had written and said –The TSA was worse than the FAA. None cared and no one cares today. Bogdan and I discussed some assessment protocols and in recent years; I repeatedly performed a very simple one entitled, "The Sock Bomb Assessment." The 100% success rates in proving how easy it is to get explosives through TSA Checkpoints (the failure being that of the government and TSA management rather than screeners) is nothing new. The assessment protocol demonstrated that a group of terrorists could blow 50, 100, 150, etc planes out the sky within an hour, destroying our economy and the National Aerospace System. The government knows and has acknowledged that we have middle eastern terrorists in this country. The administration is inviting more. The results of these assessments, in text and photos, were sent to the White House, DHS, TSA, and some in congress. NONE cared! The recent revelation that TSA had failed over 95.7% of their own tests validates what we have been saying and writing even before its inception. Despite the Billions of Dollars (over $7B last year to achieve a failure rate over 95.7% - Impressive!) spent on the TSA with its large group of unqualified Federal Security

Directors, the TSA has proven itself worse than FAA. Try to read Bogdan's book with a preconceived notion that it is all sour grapes and not true. You won't be able to do it! If you want validation of what we say, I present this quote from President Obama, please look up this link, http://townhall.com/tipsheet/katiepavlich/2015/11/04/surprise-tsa-is-still-sucking-terribly-n2075370 Note the President's quote, to wit: QUOTE *"It should be noted that after this failure, President Obama expressed full confidence in the agency (TSA). The President does believe the American people should feel confident in traveling airports all across the country because there are security measures in place to protect the traveling public," White House Press Secretary Josh Earnest said at the time. "The President does continue to have confidence that the officers of the TSA do very important work that continues to protect the American people and continue to protect the American aviation system."* UNQUOTE.

Easy words for someone (and his family) who hasn't flown on commercial airlines in the last 7 or 8 years and probably never will. His statement is the very visible proof that neither he nor the congress really gives a damn about AVSEC and the vulnerabilities present. If one believes these lies from the White House, DHS (TSA), then should the odds go against you and you lose family, don't say a damned word! You too knew and did nothing!

If the reader doubts our claims or wants to know more about us, feel free to use search engines for Bogdan Dzakovic, Brian Sullivan, Steve Elson. You may want to use other qualifiers after the name, e.g. "aviation security," to weed out others with the same name in other endeavors. Finally you should give thanks for Bogdan Dzakovic everyday; I do!

Steve Elson

Background. Retired Naval Special Warfare Enlisted/Officer. MA in National Security Affairs/Intelligence, focus on terrorism. Worked in counter-

/anti-terrorism and terrorism intelligence at national level. Executive Officer/Operations Officer Navy Red Team. DEA in Operation Snowcap in non-agent 1801 classification. FAA Security Agent/Red Team. Left FAA convinced that FAA was doing nothing to prevent air terrorism attacks and prepared briefs along with Bogdan for members of congress. Pre 9/11 interviews and TV Investigative reports. Fox 25 Boston's Deborah Sherman security assessment early spring 2001. Post 9/11 – Lead Story "60 Minutes" with Steve Croft 9/16/01. Interviewed for Numerous radio, TV (local, national, international) and print media articles and books. Along with Bogdan first national detractors of TSA, even before it was formed.

Fortress of Deceit

INTRODUCTION

The Green Room
+
The sword is the mind, if the mind is right, the sword is right.
Samurai
+
+

Contemptable!

That was my first thought on the morning of September 11, 2001 as the events unfolded. But my anger wasn't directed at the terrorists, it was directed at the politicians and bureaucrats who could have prevented the attacks. Fighting terrorism was easy compared to fighting bureaucracy and politics.

I began my thirty-two year government career as a young, ignorant, idealistic, go-getter, who was proud and even honored to serve my country. Never hesitated to put my life at risk for what this country stood for. I ended my career as older and wiser but with "contemptable" etched into my soul. Taking to heart the oath of office I took three times to abide by the United States Constitution and to defend this country from all enemies, both foreign and domestic; only to witness the gradual dissolution of honor in the federal government.

In its simplest rendition, the United States Constitution is designed to minimize the asinine behavior of our federal government. Most of the time this behavior may *only* result in a gross waste of tax dollars, but sometimes the system breaks under its own weight and innocent people die. And so, we had the preventable 9/11 terrorist attacks. The problem deliberately begins on Capitol Hill and is executed by the bureaucrats that run the agencies.

The 21st Century should have started off on a better footing, and would have if the politicians and bureaucrats acted on the warnings we gave them about 9/11. The "we" composed primarily of a couple members of the FAA Red Team, which was the only organizational unit in the entire federal government that actively tried to prevent the 9/11 attacks. In his gifted book *Red Team* (2015, which examines numerous civilian, federal government and military red teams), Micah Zenko reported from his interviewees that the best red team members "operate in another dimension" and were "inherently skeptical of authority and conventional wisdom". Maybe that's what it took.

The only thing that surprised me about the 9/11 attacks was that it took so long for the terrorists to execute the plan. As early as 1998 I suspected that this was in the making. That's the year I started working with like-minded colleagues to try to get the bureaucracy and Congress to do something about the dangerous culture of mismanagement within the Federal Aviation Administration (FAA). If we could determine that a major attack was imminent, what happened to the billions of tax dollars we threw away at the CIA, FBI and other federal agencies that failed to do so? Even in those days I believed that if you gave our combined federal law enforcement, intelligence and security agencies the task to predict the timing of the next sunrise, they couldn't do it without first spending a million dollars on contractors, then they'd have to debate the political consequences for a week, pass it through the lawyers, and make sure that whatever decision they would make wouldn't offend anybody in this mentally deranged, politically correct atmosphere. By the time they reached their conclusion – the moment would be history. I do believe the problems in the federal government are worse now than they were in the lead up to 9/11.

Fortress of Deceit

The federal government has elements of both Hollywood and a mafia or crime cartel. Hollywood in the sense that quite a bit of our tax dollars are wasted on pure illusion – to make it look like we're actually doing something productive when we're not. (I don't mean to besmirch Hollywood, they do a very good job at what they do. And I don't mean to offend the mafia either. In some context they have a higher sense of honor than what I've witnessed in the federal government.) Theater audiences make a conscience choice to pay money to see a movie, which you know is pure illusion. The government is like a cartel in that you don't have a choice but to buy into their illusion, refusal to pay taxes renders one subject to strong arm extortion type tactics. While the government may not break your legs (as sometimes depicted in organized crime movies), it will seize your property and take your liberty away, locking you away for years.

Suppose you find yourself morally repulsed by this government cartel miss-using our military by engaging in wars against countries that were not a threat to us – like our invasion of Iraq, falsely using the 9/11 attacks as a catalyst, destabilizing the entire area and resulting in the worst refugee crisis since World War II at the cost of thousands of our own casualties. You refuse to pay your tax dollars to fund these wars (which are still killing thousands of innocent people) – and you are now the criminal. Our government has killed more innocent people and destroyed more property, either directly or indirectly thru its destabilization programs, than the most psychotic of the crime cartels could ever hope too. And if you are a government employee who resists or even fights against this Hollywood type hype (IE: entertainment and illusion)/cartel/government *mental* comingling, you are treated similar to how political dissidents are treated in communist countries or fascist dictatorships. While they may not kill or incarcerate (yet), they effectively take away one's ability to make a decent living.

So this is a little story, describing my thirty-two years adventure in this very expensive, unaccountable, and illusion based governmental cartel:

My first direct exposure to Washington's illusion cartel occurred on a cold morning in February of 2002, a few months after the 9/11 attacks. Before sun up I found myself in a limousine on the way to the CBS news studio on M Street in Washington, D.C. Just days prior to this my name flashed in the news. I was the first of the 9/11 government whistleblowers whose story attracted the attention of the national and international news services.

During the ride, images of the fate of whistleblowers and similar folks who bucked the prevailing political and bureaucratic winds wafted through my mind. Karen Silkwood, the nuclear power whistleblower allegedly murdered; Frank Serpico, the New York City police detective was shot in the face; Buford Pusser, the Tennessee sheriff allegedly murdered; Galileo, one of the great intellectual minds of his time was persecuted just for opening up new doors of science; even Charles Lindbergh was vilified by the government for defying the political winds of his time, and a whole list of others whose careers and livelihoods were ruined for *blowing the whistle*. I'm not aware of any who lived happily ever after.

Thus, I became a messenger, bearing the news that the September 11, 2001 attacks could have been prevented; that we knew a terrorist attack of this nature was imminent, and aviation security wasn't up to the task of preventing it. I found myself in the middle of a situation that culminated in the deaths of nearly 3,000 innocent people, involving potentially billions of dollars in law suits (at least until the government bought off most of the victim's families), not to mention misguided and unconstitutional wars. So what did I have to worry about?

It wasn't that I was particularly fearful of any physical attack against me, I had routinely put my life at risk in service to my country and I looked at this as merely an extension of that service. Furthermore, the government spent a small fortune training me how to kill. I knew something of their dark little secrets and was comfortable and adept at applying them myself – had I chosen and needed to do so in my defense.

I also had an additional advantage of having spent the previous six years working as a Team Leader of the FAA's Red Team. This was essentially a "terrorist" team designed to replicate the tactics that terrorists would use in the commercial aviation environment. While in subsequent news articles this Red Team was described as an *elite* team, nothing could be further from the truth. The Red Team, however, was a *unique* team. It contributed greatly toward giving me an ability to get inside the mind of an adversary to anticipate his next move.

But, one can't stay awake indefinitely. Besides the limo driver, the only other person in the car with me was my good friend and colleague Steve Elson, who at this particular time also served as my bodyguard. I needed someone to watch my back, and Elson was the best. He is a retired Vietnam era U.S. Navy SEAL. The SEALS have gained much media attention primarily pertaining to the killing of Bin Laden and similar operations. But I've never been particularly impressed with their potential for causing mayhem. Amateurs are also extremely adept at killing and destroying things – all it takes is to cross a mental threshold to wield the sword; the rest, unfortunately, comes naturally.

SEALS are, of course, highly trained in killing, and I'm certainly glad they are on our side; but that's not what impressed me about Elson. Elson has an uncanny knack for keeping people from getting killed. I can't explain how he does this, but its second nature to him, an intuition of what and how the bad guys are going to operate and an innate ability to thwart those objectives. He once told me that his favorite type of mission in Vietnam was rescuing American POWs or those troops stranded behind enemy lines.

Long before my day in the news, Elson had already struggled against the odds trying to get the government bureaucracy to improve aviation security because he knew that terrorists were going to hit us hard. He also had previously been through the talking head TV news programs including *60 Minutes*, and he gave me pointers on how to deal with the news media without making myself appear like a total jerk.

After he retired from the navy he continued working for other government agencies doing classified work in various hotspots around the world. When I met him back in 1993 he was a Team Leader in the FAA Red Team. At that time, I was a Team Leader in the Federal Air Marshal service (which was also part of the FAA) and both of our offices were co-located in the same office space at Dulles Airport in Washington, DC. But I didn't have much interaction with him till the mid to late 90's. He did his secret stuff in the Red Team and I did my secret stuff in the Air Marshals and rarely did they overlap. Early on, however, I recognized the strength of his character and his fidelity to his country, his wife and kids, and his friends. Had Elson lived 200 plus years ago, he would be remembered in the same light as

Fortress of Deceit

Daniel Boone, Davy Crocket, Ethan Allen and Simon Kenton.

    I had spent my entire (top secret) career in the government working behind the scenes, not quite in the shadows, but certainly avoiding any public spotlight. Talking to the news media was anathema to me, but circumstances required that I take this step. By the time of that cold February limo ride, I had hardly eaten anything for days and had slept only a few hours. That morning I was exhausted and hungry but determined to follow this path that fate carved out for me.

    We arrived at the CBS News studio nearly an hour early and were escorted to the Green Room. My naiveté about Washington politics and national news syndication was as deep as my hunger and exhaustion. I rarely watched television and didn't even know what a Green Room was; but I discovered a nice sized living room type set up with several comfortable chairs, a couch, flat screen TV in the corner near the ceiling and a large coffee table in the middle festooned with a turntable of gourmet pastries and other breakfast foods. At another table several aromatic coffee pots were brewing, and half a dozen carafes of exotic juices on ice were waiting to be plundered. The lady that escorted me to the Green Room told me to sit in there and relax, help myself to the trove of food and drink and she'll come and get me when they're ready for me to go on camera.

    I poured myself a cup of gourmet coffee, a glass of some exotic juice, spun the food turntable around grabbing a French pastry here, some cheese and breakfast meat on the other side. Within the next few minutes I ate more food than I had in the previous three days.

Fortress of Deceit

I thought all this stuff was just for me. I'd take a bite out of some fruit pastry, put it back on the turntable, take a bite out of some other breakfast nodule and put the remains back on the table. Must have had three or four cups of juice going at the same time. This went on for about twenty minutes when another TV *guest* was escorted into the Green Room. "Oops", was the only thing that came to mind.

We introduced ourselves. I think he was a Pakistani physician, had a heavily accented English. He helped himself to a donut and some juice and made a comment about the mess on the table. I agreed and said that they don't do a very good job of cleaning this place up. The jungle side of me was rescinded and the sophisticated side – or as much of it as I had – started to take over. I sat back, sipped some coffee, took a bite of donut and engaged in small talk with my fellow guest.

We each explained what we were here to talk about, but I didn't have a clue what he was saying though, couldn't understand anything he said except for maybe every fourth or fifth word. I changed the subject and suggested that the half eaten rhubarb pastry was absolutely delicious.

After some ten minutes he was escorted out of the Green Room and in another fifteen minutes or so he was being interviewed live on the boob tube. Saw his whole interview on the TV set suspended in the corner ceiling of the room. I really felt sorry for the guy as he was terribly nervous even in the Green Room and I couldn't understand a word of what he was talking about on TV.

A few minutes later he returned and asked me how he did. "Excellent, Sir, you really got your point across." He thanked me and I was immediately escorted to the make-up room. And all I could think of was what the hell am I doing here?

It was my turn in the wringer.

In the make-up room I sat down in a barber shop type chair and some very attractive twenty something girl spent some ten minutes plastering a ton of make-up on my face and re-combing my hair. I don't ever remember having this much personal attention. When she was finished she spun the chair around and I saw myself in the mirror. I hardly recognized myself with all the makeup and made some comment to that effect and she provided a well-rehearsed explanation that under the glare of the stage lights and some technical stuff about the cameras that once on-camera I'd look normal.

All I could think of was that this was more appropriate for a clown convention – couldn't help but think of how these talking heads could keep a straight face on the boob tube when in the same room with the other talking heads. It also occurred to me that these make-up artists could totally destroy a person's credibility, no matter how serious their subject matter, depending on how much make-up they pasted on your face.

Finally I was escorted to the studio room where I was to be interviewed. This was a small *study* type room; on one side were the camera and lights and the other was my chair and a room out-fitted to look like a study. I had the opportunity before they hooked me up to the microphone, ear piece, and conducted a sound test, to observe the background. All the books and other accoutrements in the room were fake props. So I couldn't even pick up a book to read while I waited for the interview to start.

Fortress of Deceit

I sat there for another five minutes contemplating the situation, when a technician told me over the ear-piece that the interview would start in one minute, then counted down from ten seconds and I found myself introduced by and interviewed live by Bryant Gumbel on national TV.

I don't remember the bulk of the interview except near the end Mr. Gumbel made some comment that maybe I'm just a "disgruntled employee" and that's the root cause of my whistleblowing. Just one of the first of many hits I received concerning the attitude toward whistleblowers by many people. My response to Mr. Gumbel was, "If you use the *Webster's Dictionary* definition of disgruntled – it refers to a person that is dis-satisfied with the current state of affairs, and if that is the definition you are using, then yes, I am a disgruntled employee."

He thanked me for appearing on the show and the interview was over. After the technicians unhooked me from their equipment, I was escorted back to the make-up room where the makeup artist cleaned the pancake off my face. The limo driver was waiting for me outside, and I had the proverbial adrenal dump on the ride home and fell asleep.

After a few days, when I was acclimating to my status as a public figure and coming to terms with being on the government's hate list as a whistleblower, I was able to eat and sleep somewhat normally, Steve Elson went home – to his family; but we stayed in frequent contact. He continued doing his own news interviews and I continued doing mine.

Over the next few months I was interviewed on several talking head TV shows, countless print and internet news media and the radio. I couldn't possibly remember them all. During the first couple days I even had mini-van news trucks camped outside my townhouse near Washington, D.C.; much to the chagrin of my neighbors. But I refused to be interviewed by these mobile news crews at my home – effectively drawing a line between my professional public life and my private life.

Some of these interviews were particularly noteworthy, not so much for anything new that was presented but for one reason or another they stand out in my mind.

A few days later I had another limo ride, this to the Greta Van Susteren show and did a face to face interview with her. It was a similar type of set-up as before but I behaved a bit more dignified in their Green Room.

I was impressed with Ms. Susteren in that I felt she treated me with the same degree of respect that she did to all the other talking head power brokers that came across her camera lens. I was little more than some schmuck off the street but she was very gracious. She shook my hand after the interview and wished me luck for the ordeal that she knew lay ahead of me, demonstrating more insight into the situation than even I contemplated.

The only unusual part of the experience was that the make-up artist seemed to have spent an inordinate amount of time working on my face, trying to cover up a fresh scar.

The day before I had gone kayaking and running through the woods at the Occoquan Reservoir about twenty-five miles south of Washington. I call it "jungle therapy"; it was my way of blowing off steam, getting some exercise, and bonding with the ZEN aspect of nature.

When the opportunity presented itself and I discovered fresh large animal tracks I'd run them down –

just for the thrill of the chase. According to local game warden accounts there was at least one mountain lion in the vicinity. While I had come across large feline tracks before, I never did get close to the cat(s), so I'd normally run-down deer. It seemed like it was as much a game for the deer as it was for me, as they became more familiar with me being around – and would occasionally chase after me in a game of tag.

In this case I was stalking several deer through almost impenetrable underbrush (for a human) that they just seemed to zip right through, but I didn't duck quickly enough and a low hanging tree branch cut a small gash into the side of my forehead.

I always fancied myself as being something of a woodsman, having been weaned on the stories of frontier life in early American history. Even as a teenager I'd do survival camping during the winter break from school – meandering off into the local wilds with minimal equipment and just try to survive by living off the land.

When I explored out west, I spent two days and a night stalking a small herd of mule deer. They're particularly skittish, what with everything big enough around that would like to eat them. Spotted them on a distant hillside and spent the rest of the day tracking them. Followed them, more or less, throughout the night and continued the chase after I visually picked them up again after sun up.

I spent most of that day on my hands, knees and belly trying to snake my way close enough to them just to try to touch one. Even spent about fifteen minutes starring down a rattler that crossed my path as we both were crawling around on our bellies. I didn't carry a firearm, just a knife, a small backpack, and a walking stick. At one point in the late afternoon they all hunkered down in a hillside woods. I spent about two hours going the last twenty feet or so. When I was less than a yard from one of the deer he turned and saw me – we both were motionless for about five seconds, which doesn't seem like much time, but under the circumstances was something lasting and weird. It seemed a surreal moment. Like some acknowledgement of sentience and communication passed between us. I wondered which of the two of us was the most sentient. He then just slowly got up and walked away followed by the rest of the small herd. It was an unusual experience.

I never hunted animals after that, and never again deliberately put myself in such a stupid survival situation. Although I still engaged in the *thrill of the chase*, or, as Sherlock Holmes would have put it: getting into "The game is afoot" frame of mind. It did impress upon me the notion that life is so much simpler when survival is all one has to think about. I mention this little sidebar story merely to demonstrate that I applied this same mentality to my professional life. Like Sherlock Holmes – I lived for the thrill of the chase. Having an office job, and dressing up in a suit every day would have killed me. Working for money, no matter how much money, I considered boring and tedious. I was looking for a vocation. So I constantly pushed my professional bounds to the maximum extent possible.

Another interesting interview experience I had was as a guest of Wolf Blitzer. Same routine as before: limo drive, green room, make-up, etc. Unbeknownst to me, however, when the producer of the show asked me to do an interview she also asked a former Associate Administrator of the FAA (Cathal Flynn) to appear on the show with me.

So after I got set up in the Green Room I bumped into the former associate administrator who was in charge of the security division of FAA for most of the latter half of the 90's. Even before 9/11, FAA was known as the "Tombstone Agency" – meaning they never did anything to improve aviation safety or security until a lot of people got killed first (check that term out on the internet and one will be inundated with hits on FAA). Mr. Flynn didn't start this tombstone mentality, but the Administrator of FAA during most of this time frame was Jane Garvey and she had no interests in what the security division was up too, ignoring all the terrorist warning signs and the evidence that aviation security was a joke. I had even sent her a letter in August 1998 attempting to convince her that there was a dangerous culture of mismanagement within the security division of FAA and that the terrorist threat was increasing dramatically, hoping she'd initiate a major investigation (sent the letter thru Mr. Flynn). The Administrator didn't even have the courtesy to acknowledge receipt of my letter; but, expecting this non-response, I also sent a copy to the Secretary of Transportation Rodney Slater. He at least acknowledged receipt and copied me on a letter that he sent back to the Administrator – suggesting that she ought to look into my allegations. However, there was no follow up and Garvey did nothing. Her reward for doing nothing prior to 9/11 and keeping her mouth shut after 9/11 was that, according to press reports at the time, she was made head of security at the upcoming Democratic National Convention. This was the first of many such examples I came across of our elected officials rewarding failure prone individuals for their silence.

There was an inner circle of a few career bureaucrats that orchestrated this façade of security, but there were scores of other managers who readily bought into this nonsense. I'm not sure who they worked for but it certainly wasn't for the benefit of the majority of us Americans. Our tax dollars hard at work. Not one of these people were held accountable for their actions prior to 9/11.

So........, back to the Blitzer show:

After I had my makeup makeover, Mr. Blitzer approached me and asked if I would agree to be interviewed in the same room with Mr. Flynn so that we could have a three-way discussion with all of us at the same table – inferring that this makes for a more engaging interview for the TV audience. Without hesitating I stated, "Yes, I'll jump into the arena against anyone."

A few minutes later a producer escorted me to another small studio room with only one chair and a small table. Was hooked up to the usual gear and pointed toward the camera. I just assumed that some technical problem must have developed and didn't give this set-up a second thought.

The live televised interview progressed and Mr. Flynn made some glowing comments about me as an employee of the FAA Security Division. I took this as something of a joke, however, because when I worked for the FAA I was pretty much treated with contempt by most of the managers with whom I interacted. I tended to rock the boat whenever the opportunity presented itself and this conduct didn't exactly ingratiate me to becoming a member of their good old boys club. So his comments totally contradicted the reality I worked in. I would have been more comfortable with him trying to discredit me rather this gushy praise.

At any rate, the rest of the interview progressed normally and politely and pretty much skirted the main issues involved, I thought at the time.

Fortress of Deceit

The interview was over, I was disconnected from all the wires and as I was walking down the hall toward the make-up room Mr. Blitzer approaches me again and takes me off to the side. He shook my hand and stated that he knew before the interview started that I was the one in the right. I acknowledged and thanked him, and asked how he came to this conclusion.

I hope I'm not betraying any deep dark secrets of his show, but he stated that whenever there is a controversial subject (like this one), if he can get a party from both sides of the issue at his studio at the same time he always asks both persons if they would be willing to be interviewed with all parties in the same room. Invariably, he insinuated, the party that refuses to be interviewed in the same room is the one that has something to hide or is otherwise in the wrong; and conversely, the party that is willing to participate in a group session is the one in the right.

Wow, I thought, there actually is some higher brain functioning going on in this entertainment version of the national news talking head shows. I really was impressed with his insight. We chitchatted for a little bit and I told him that I was sitting a few seats behind him once on a commercial flight to Europe a few years back when I was a Federal Air Marshal. Small world at times.

After most of these TV and studio radio shows I participated in, the camera person and/or other technicians would shake my hand and thank me for my whistleblower activities. They were nice gestures and meant a lot to me at a time when the government just looked at me with its evil eye.

Fortress of Deceit

I left the studio and walked a few blocks to join Steve Elson and a few of his friends at a Capitol Hill restaurant. I tend to be somewhat observant of people and as I was walking down the street couldn't help notice that they seemed to be giving me strange looks. The chances of all these people watching the Blitzer show and recognizing me seemed remote.

When I arrived at the table of friends and colleagues, Steve pointed out that I still had my make-up on. Distracted, what with talking to Blitzer informally after the interview, I had forgotten to return to the make-up room to be cleaned up. In the evening darkness some of the neon lights of the restaurants and shops in the Capitol Hill area must have made me look like a cadaver from a zombie movie.

So much for my steps into Washington's entertainment media.

My interaction with the news media isn't what I would call a positive experience. The era of in-depth investigative journalism seems to have died off. With rare exception, all the news media were interested in were quick sound bites of stories that lasted about a minute or two. The rationale, it seemed, was that American's attention span was this short. Makes the whole process something of a disservice.

Still, I have to be grateful for the news media's interests in my story. The coverage I did receive, probably more than anything else, kept me from getting fired – or worse. The only bigger jokes are the laws Congress set up to protect federal government whistleblowers. More on both of these points later.

Over the next several years, I was featured in a number of TV and movie documentaries, all of which were interesting experiences. Eventually, a number of these journalists, TV producers and talking heads, mindful of their own institutional bureaucratic short-comings, strongly encouraged me to put pen to paper and write my story; and when things had settled down and I had more time on my hands, I did just that.

Here is my thirty-two year foray into the federal government wonderland, and the story behind the story of who knew what, when they knew it, and what they did about it in the lead up to 9/11, as well as its nefarious aftermath which continues to this day.

I should point out that this is not an expose' of classified information; nor is it a "how to" manual on how to breech airport security. I've always been very mindful of the fact that while there are a lot of good things and people in the government (particularly when held in the light of an increasingly bizarre world); when it goes bad, it goes very bad. And I've been very careful not to kill off the good with the bad. If any politicians and bureaucrats read this tome with an open mind, they might actually learn something, and discover a better way to fulfill their duty as public servants.

We the people, deserve a lot better than what we're getting from our government.

Fortress of Deceit

CHAPTER ONE
A Credit to Holmes

+

I abhor the dull routine of existence.
Sherlock Holmes

+

+

When I was about five I stumbled into the middle of a rock fight between groups of neighborhood kids in the slums where we lived – was hit in the left side of the head and nearly knocked out. About forty-five years later I developed a bleach white streak of hair in the same spot. Just reinforced a notion of cause and effect I understood and appreciated, and how predictable many things were if one learned to read the warning signs.

As it happened:

At my high school graduation, the Commencement Speaker challenged us to pick up the gauntlet and fight to make the world a better place. I picked up that gauntlet and ran with it. I earned my BA in Psychology from the University of Cincinnati in 1977. Took a number of Political Science courses focusing on the background and content of the Declaration of Independence, the Constitution and Bill of Rights, the Federalist Papers and other less well known developments that formed the basis of this great country.

In psychology we studied the usual giants in the field: Freud, Skinner, Jung, Maslov and others. What fascinated me about psychology wasn't the various theories, nor diagnosing psych health issues; rather, it was how to harness the power of the mind to make smarter, better, maybe even happy and moral persons. I looked at this particularly in light of the seemingly overwhelming examples of man's inhumanity to man I observed in studying the history of

World War II, as I tried to understand what my parents lived through; both of whom were in the middle of the conflict between the Germans and Russians. My studies of psychology and political science were intertwined (political science simply being psychology on a national and international level) and only reinforced my notion that the United States was the guiding beacon of light and hope in the world.

Technically, none of the psychology courses offered at the university covered my primary interests. But this didn't deter me. I sort of used reverse psychology in studying psychology. While the curriculum focused on the study of the various theories on how one's environment and genetics can skew a person's psychological mind set; why not turn the tables – how can one use these same influences to enhance the individual.

We studied the proverbial story of the ninety-eight pound woman whose child slipped beneath a car and she lifted the car long enough for someone to pull the kid out from underneath. What went on in the woman's brain and mind that allowed her to do this feat? I was convinced that there was something to this mind over matter phenomenon. It sparked my life-long interest in the general subject area.

While I can't boast of having any special skills in this area, I knew people who did: While in college I dabbled in the martial arts – primarily judo. My sensei was Lebanese and was built like how I imagined a cave man to be – solid muscle developed from surviving in a world where the odds were against him. He was the toughest individual that I knew personally. In sparring with him he would take me down nine out of ten times, but every once in a while I could slip in a move to trip him up. If his intent would have been to kill me, however, he could have done so with relative ease. My only advantage was that I could run faster than he could, and I wasn't really sure of that. But he wasn't the example I had in mind.

On a special occasion my sensei brought his sensei into the dojo along with five or six other black belt students of the *master* sensei, as well as their students. The Master Sensei was Korean, about six foot five inches tall. I thought this odd at the time, what with judo having originated in Japan combined with the traditional cultural differences between the two countries.

What was amazing to see was that the Korean Master Sensei was throwing around my sensei easier than my sensei could throw me around. It was a stunning display of technique, conditioning and sheer raw power. There must have been forty students in the dojo at the time and I'm convinced that the Master Sensei could have fought all of us at the same time and he'd be the only one to walk out of the dojo.

On another occasion an individual was invited into a different dojo I occasionally participated in. I don't recall him being a *master* in the traditional sense. A master implies that he has some students that he's training. This guy didn't seem to have any, he was a rogue. A slender white guy about five foot seven inches tall, his legs were knotted like a fireplug. He maxed out in the technique and conditioning of his chosen art and probably worked as a shoe salesman for his day job – there was a whole sub-culture of this community. This wasn't a *fight club* mentality, but rather individuals with a genuine interest in expanding the envelope of the physical and mental limitations they were born with and encouraged to accept by our traditional cultural norms.

Fortress of Deceit

He came into the dojo (which served as a basketball court at other times) and we made some polite introductions keeping within the traditional discipline of the dojo. Then we students backed off some twelve to fifteen feet from him forming a rough circle around him. He took off his shoes and socks and stood in a relaxed stance before us for about ten seconds. He then did a low squat and jumped vertically in the air well over the rim of the regulation height of the basketball hoop that wasn't too far from him, executed a round-house kick at the apogee of his jump, landed square on his feet and without interrupting his fluid motion repeated the jump another seven or eight times. He then put his shoes and socks back on and walked out of the dojo. First and last time I ever saw him. There was a long silence in the dojo as we students looked at each other trying to comprehend what we had just witnessed.

Ever since then I have always dabbled in the martial arts, not achieving anywhere near the capabilities of the individuals I described above, but what I did learn over time was that this *mind over matter* phenomenon that I was searching for can manifest itself in many different ways – not just in the martial arts.

An autistic high school girl I knew while I was in college would listen to a piano concert recital on the boob tube and a week later sit down in front of a piano in the school's recreation room and repeat the music note for note as far as I could tell. It was no less a marvel to witness this than it was the martial arts greats that I previously described. By my early twenties, I was just beginning to open my mind to the possibilities and learn not to put a limit on what the individual or groups of individuals could achieve. Pushing over sixty years old now, as I write this, I stumbled across many examples of these types of phenomenal people in my life – each in their own way. Some are mentioned in this tome.

So what does all this have to do with Sherlock Holmes? When I was in college, not wanting to be a financial burden on anyone, I became completely independent by age nineteen, and found myself in a situation where I had to pay all my school and living expenses on my own, couldn't even get a student loan. Determined to earn my degree in four years I did very little other than study, work, sleep, eat, work out, and study some more. Even the dojo's I trained at were piecemeal – if at the end of the month I had enough money left over from school and living expenses I'd pay for some martial arts instruction.

After college I was burned out from four years of full-time school and working between thirty-two and fifty-six hours per week at an endless series of menial jobs, took nearly a year off to recharge myself and figure out what I wanted to do with my life. Hitch-hiked extensively out west in Indian territory where I was first exposed to the *river of life* concept – a parallel theme (along with Holmes) though out my career. I then, and still do, read voraciously when I have the time. Between hitch-hiking adventures out west, I picked up the two volume set of the *Annotated Sherlock Holmes* and read all the stories.

Holmes was, of course, a fictional manifestation of one who used his gifts to an extraordinary degree to solve crimes and other mysteries. He used his own *mind over matter* abilities to observe details and applied deductive reasoning in ascertaining the who, what, where, when, how and why of a given mystery.

As incredible as his skills were in solving these mysteries, as I read these stories it occurred to me – could a person use these (and other to be developed skills) to identify a crime or mystery BEFORE it occurred AND prevent it. This, it seemed to me, to be a much greater service than just picking up the pieces after an incident occurred. A type of precognition, if you will, but not [necessarily] something in the paranormal, but rather a skill set that could be developed.

Sherlock Holmes turned out to be a mentor of mine. Someone that had, more-so than any other fictional or real person, the greatest impact on my career. Applying Holmes' methodology as well as a few tricks of my own, I was able to predict the 9/11 attacks (as well as other events) and attempted to prevent them. I jumped into the *river of life* and the [sometimes tumultuous] current has carried me through to this moment in time.

CHAPTER TWO
Sea Duty

+

We know more about war than we do about peace, more about killing than we do about living.
General Omar Bradley

+

+

So where to start on this track I set for myself. I didn't have any money, no business sense whatsoever. I figured law school would make a good foundation. But once in law school I found myself in a worse financial situation than I was as an undergraduate, once again couldn't even get a student loan. A promised job in a local law firm doing grunt work fell thru and I found myself still working menial jobs which couldn't pay my living expenses and my now nearly quadrupled tuition and wound up having to quit law school before the second semester. I couldn't really deal with the snobbish and arrogant attitude of the instructors and most of the students anyway.

Long before the days of the internet, one had to do legal research in a law library paging through books (at least for a person of my means). While conducting this homework research I'd find crucial pages missing out of the various references. In their own minds, law school was a very competitive atmosphere – but this wasn't competition, this was a problem with grown-ups that didn't have adequate potty training as kids. Some students would find a crucial citation for a homework assignment and rip the page out of the book so no one else would have access to it. A serious problem with ethics which was pretty much ignored. I quit law school and never looked back.

So my next logical step seemed to go into law enforcement itself – which was a close career path I envisioned anyway. What I discovered though – in those days the federal law enforcement community wouldn't even look at you unless you had prior local law enforcement experience or the military under your belt and the local law enforcement required near perfect vision. My vision was just under their minimum standards, which left me with the military option.

I interviewed with all the military services to narrow down my decision. The air force required perfect vision if one wanted to be a pilot; plus I had already parachuted out of a plane when I was in college and this didn't exactly feel like my natural element.

I gave serious thought to the Army or Marines, leaning more toward the army. The main reason was that the Army had a more forward thinking approach to warfare in the 20th century. I opined this based on the Green Beret's approach to warfare which involved working closely with the indigenous population of a stressed out country rather than just killing them. But the final deciding points with me were that I already taught myself most of the tricks of the trade of living off the land and surviving in wilderness environments on land (as much as I cared too anyway), but especially because I thought I would enjoy this work too much. I was ready for a different type of adventure – which left either the Navy or the Coast Guard.

I had a natural predilection toward the Navy's submarine service – what with my childhood obsession with Jules Verne's Nautilus – but compared to my educational background you practically had to be an Einstein to qualify for the Silent Service – which required one of the more technical and hard science backgrounds of any branch of the military. The submarine service did have a philosophy of preventing warfare on a massive scale, it was part of the

Fortress of Deceit

Triad of MAD (Mutual Assured Destruction) along with the nuclear armed B-52 bombers and our nuclear missiles scattered among various western states. However, threatening to annihilate the world to prevent a major act of violence wasn't exactly what I had in mind in extrapolating Holmes' methodology.

So that left the Coast Guard. Long before 9/11, before the hysteria and paranoia took over the psyche of the government, the Coast Guard was first and foremost known as the *life-saving service*. While the Guard was subject to the same Uniform Code of Military Justice (UCMJ) as the other services, its everyday job was not training or preparing for war but rather focused on maritime safety and law enforcement, and search and rescue at sea. It did have a wartime function but these were more in line with support roles to the Navy rather than actual combat roles – with some exceptions.

I was also a bit leery of military service. I really didn't have any interest in killing anyone, nor did I want to risk getting killed or maimed in some misbegotten adventure that had nothing to do with the Constitutional requirements of engaging in war. The Vietnam War wasn't quit history in my mind, what with having two older brothers who served there and hadn't fully recovered from the experience – one of whom was wounded and the other suffered PTSD. The wounded one would later die of a cancer that he claimed was due to his exposure to Agent Orange while a grunt in Vietnam; but that was years before the government even acknowledged Agent Orange ailments. History repeated itself after the Persian Gulf wars what with the government's denial of Gulf War Syndrome for years. Our government makes a big show of honoring our veterans but their treatment of them after a conflict is somewhat deficient. It wasn't the military itself that caused me to pause, but rather our political leaders who got us involved in these unnecessary foreign entanglements. I'm convinced the greatest contribution my generation has made to the history of the world was NOT engaging in all out nuclear war. Everything else pales in comparison. Unfortunately its been mostly down-hill since.

So I enthusiastically jumped into the Coast Guard's Officer Candidate School (OCS) in the summer of 1979 and almost just as quickly was bumped out. Since I didn't have any money – what with being stuck in menial jobs and even day laborer work - at the end of the month do I buy some toilet paper, a big bag of dried beans and a ton of broccoli or do I get a haircut from a real barber – I'd opt for the grocery shopping and cut my own hair with a scissors when it got too long.

So I showed up at OCS near Norfolk, VA with a head of hair that, when compared to my fellow officer candidates, made me look like a hippy freak. Why bother wasting money on a haircut ahead of time, I thought, when they're going to chop it all off anyway?

After graduation, one of my instructors told me that they always give two or three officer candidates a rougher time during OCS, just because, and my hair-do was enough of an incentive to peg me in this class on the first day.

Aside from the bull shit, the OCS course actually was a pretty good indoctrination to military life. Four months long, a month longer than the other services. Fifty percent of the course grade was academics which was a lot of math concerning fluid dynamics (how ships sink and stay afloat); navigation (how to get to where you want to go without having to test what one knows about fluid dynamics), which I was pretty good at; and other math which I still don't have a clue what it was for. It was really tough for me with my degree in psychology. Twenty-five percent was physical fitness of which I was average – what with nursing a couple of old broken bones which never healed properly, and the remaining twenty-five percent was military bearing. This included folding your underwear to specifications, marching around on the parade field, spit and polish uniforms and following the military chain of command and other similar protocols. I found that while I was already a very disciplined individual this didn't carry over very well in the military – it was a different mentality. I also had absolutely no sense of rhythm. When it was my turn to march the platoon around the parade field I couldn't count cadence. It was a sloppy mess. When I received my critique from my marching officer I told him that he should have hired people that were once marching band members rather than men that wanted to go to sea, rescue dumb civilians that couldn't handle a boat, and generally were eager to put their lives on the line to serve their country.

I received low marks for military bearing, and barely passed the academics, but I guess they felt that my enthusiasm made up for my shortcomings. Typically, first duty stations for new officers are dished out based on class standing, those who have the highest across the board scores are given first choice, and on down the line. I was so far down the totem pole I thought they'd station me in Utah. For my first tour of duty, however, I was given the most sought after ship type that was chosen by the academy graduates.

On graduation day in November of 1979 (when we received our Officer's Commission), aside from the usual military ceremonies involved, the most significant event was that we had to recite and swear an oath of office. Which basically went: "I do solemnly swear to abide by the

Constitution of the United States and to defend this country from all enemies both foreign and domestic." What I found unusual about this is that we were bound by oath to abide by the Constitution of the United States when we weren't even required to read the Constitution, not one second in OCS was spent studying this document that we were sworn to abide by. Having studied this extensively in college I found this to be a bit odd – especially since we were required to read and abide by a manual on how to fold our underwear, but not the Constitution. Furthermore, there were some un-resolved anomalies in this, namely that the Posse Comitatus Act of 1878 expressly forbade military involvement in domestic law enforcement. But at the time, I was just glad to have survived OCS and was looking forward to my first duty station and finally kick-starting my career.

My first tour of duty was as an Officer aboard the sea-going buoy tender Coast Guard Cutter Blackhaw which was based in San Francisco. A buoy tender was actually the best ship in the Coast Guard for a junior officer to get ship handling experience. It was small enough (a crew of 50), but large enough (180 feet long) to go anywhere and do almost anything a larger cutter could do.

The most interesting part of the job of being a junior officer aboard ship was serving as an underway Officer of the Deck (OOD). This was essentially the guy that, while the ship was at sea, was in charge of the ship subject only to the Captain's orders of the day and the Executive Officer's utterances. A whole book could be written about the duties and responsibilities of the OOD but that would take me away from the main theme of this tome. I do have a few bizarre observations of ship board life and sea duty in general, however.

Fortress of Deceit

On January 28, 1980 I was serving as the in-port OOD – the ship was tied up at the pier at its homeport at Yerba Buena Island in the middle of San Francisco Bay. In the late afternoon, one of the engineering crew, while doing his recurring ship inspections discovered several feet of water in the motor room of the ship. When he informs me I sound *general quarters* – which is an emergency condition in which the entire crew drops what they can safely drop and we collectively handle whatever the emergency may be.

In this case we had flooding in the ship, which, next to a fire is pretty serious. The ship wasn't in any danger of sinking – what with being tied up at the pier and in shallow water but it was a serious situation. The flooding had to be stopped and the leak repaired, the water pumped out and the situation secured. This was a very unusual situation on the ship but not a critical risk to life or the ships operational capability. Nothing similar to this occurred in the nearly two years I spent aboard her.

Later that evening, when the crew was mopping up the final details I turned on the evening news. Earlier that day the Coast Guard Cutter Blackthorn collided with a freighter off Florida and sank with the loss of about a third of its crew. A terrible tragedy in Coast Guard history especially for such a tiny service. Some of the casualties were friends of my fellow shipmates.

But here's an added feature. It turns out that the Blackhaw and the Blackthorn are sister ships and that this class of cutter was named after bushes and shrubs (don't ask why). The actual name of this plant is the *Black Hawthorn*. Going back to the earliest sailing days – sister ships always had a special connection with each other. They were typically constructed at the same ship yard, the exact same design down to the smallest nut and bolt, and similar names.

For lack of a better explanation sister ships seemed to have a spiritual connection with each other.

One of our engineers (who had a better understanding of fluid dynamics than me) calculated the rate of water flow though the broken valve with the volume of water in the motor room and concluded that both the sinking of the Blackthorn and the water leak in the Blackhaw could have occurred at the same time. Almost as if the Blackhaw was sobbing over the death of its sister ship.

On another occasion we were sent on a search and rescue mission (SAR) a hundred plus miles off the California coast during a severe storm. Some tugboat was having a rough time and radio'd in for some assistance. The Blackhaw was the nearest seaworthy vessel so we were sent. We were getting tossed about by the waves something fierce. Water breaking over the main deck and the ship getting bounced up, down, and sideways.

Mealtimes were a gymnastic feat. The tables were bolted to the deck but the chairs in the Officer's Wardroom had to be tied to each other and to the table to keep them from flying around the room. The cooks prepared meals like there was nothing unusual going on – usually soup followed by the main course. One had to eat the soup by coordinating the lurches with a brief pause where the ship was more or less level. The rest of the time one had to hold the bowl up in the air to keep the soup from splashing out as the room tilted from one side to the other. It took great effort just to keep from being thrown out of one's chair.

Beginning the second day, common sense set in and meals were reduced to sandwiches and other finger food. The crew was eating a lot less anyway as sea-sickness gradually started to spread though out the crew.

Later the second day we spotted the periled tugboat and established visual communication with it. But there was little we could have done if they started sinking. The sea was too rough. If they sank or the crew was washed overboard all we could hope to do is throw them a line before they disappeared in the sea. In the meantime all we could both do was ride out the storm as best as possible and slowly make our way toward a safe port.

One tried not to dwell on the fact that if our own ship started sinking we didn't have any lifeboats that would survive this pounding sea. Even our own life preservers didn't pass the Coast Guard's minimum standards. It ultimately wouldn't have made any difference anyway – the ice cold waters of this part of the Pacific would have killed a human within minutes anyway.

The ship itself saw service in World War II and wasn't exactly in the best sea-worthy condition. My stateroom (a large closet sized room which served as both an office and bedroom which I shared with another officer) was just above the water-line of the ship. When the ship rolled to the side my stateroom was in, the small porthole would submerge beneath the waves and a spit of sea water would shoot across the room from the loose fittings of the porthole and its frame.

Aside from not being able to eat, one couldn't sleep either. You had to strap yourself into the rack (bed) to keep from being thrown out.

Seasickness amongst the crew was so bad that one third of the ship's crew was totally incapacitated. We had to place corpsmen (*deputized* medical personnel) in the crew's quarters to make sure that no one asphyxiated on their own vomit as they were too weak to care for themselves. Suicide was also something to watch out for as seasickness was such a terrible experience it wasn't unknown for sailors to throw themselves overboard just to end the terrible ordeal.

On the third day I became seasick, joining about another third of the crew who were sick but could still stand their duty station. This is the first time I witnessed projectile vomiting, just like in that exorcist movie.

The *watch* schedule on our ship was eight hours off duty and four hours on duty as the OOD – a rotation that went on twenty-four hours a day. In this case I had the four to eight watch meaning that I stood duty as the OOD from four in the afternoon until eight in the evening and then again from four to eight in the morning. Sharing the shift schedule with two other junior officers. This may not seem like a heavy duty schedule but in the time off one had to eat, sleep and do all the other myriad administrative and operational chores required of sea going life. One rarely got more than two or three hours sleep at a time and during a heavy storm like this sleep was even less.

On my afternoon shift of the third day the storm was still a raging inferno of churning water. I got off shift at eight in the evening, had a small bite to eat, completed some chores, and hit the hay again near total exhaustion. I hadn't changed cloths in three days, even slept fully clothed including with shoes on. In the event of an emergency mere seconds delay could result in a calamity for the ship or the crew of the tugboat.

About three-thirty the following morning I was awakened by a crew member for my four to eight watch. The first thing I noticed was that the ship wasn't being beaten up anymore. The vibrations of the engines indicated the ship was moving at a good clip but there wasn't any of the normal rocking of an even mild sea.

Upon arriving at the bridge (pilot house) I was briefed by the off-going OOD – the storm abated a couple hours ago, the tug boat survived intact and went on its merry way, and we re-routed to our next duty assignment. I checked the radar, nothing around for miles and I walked around the bridge wing to get a feel for the night sea and air.

There was a feint veil of a thin fog and the sea was perfectly calm. Not even a ripple on the water, which was smooth as a sheet of glass except for the wake of the ship as it sliced through the water.

I couldn't help but be awed – as terrible as the sea was during the storm, this was yet another marvel to behold, a body of water this big, perfectly smooth. WOW, was all I could think of nature at its worst and best. It felt like you could just step out onto the water and walk around.

On another occasion the ship was cruising north in the vicinity of Point Reyes, California and I had been on the mid-watch (mid-night to four in the morning) for a couple of hours. I was out on the bridge wing doing a routine walk-about the bridge – looking and listening for any other ships or possible obstacles the ship might bump into and one couldn't help but be amazed at the crystal clear night sky some twenty miles from the lights of the nearest land lights.

My routine and reverie was interrupted by the radar operator who reported to me that there appeared to be something wrong with the radar. I examined the screen and observed that whenever the radar sweep passed due north of us the entire top edge of the screen would light up – as if we were heading right into a mountain. Our radar had various range settings from several hundred yards to scores of miles (although due to the curvature of the earth its effective range was significantly less). At the twelve mile range the radar indicated that some ten miles ahead of us we were fast approaching something big and solid.

    I adjusted the range of the radar and was grateful to see that the California coast was exactly where it was supposed to be, about twenty miles away to our starboard. Our compass was working fine and our LORAN navigation equipment (long before GPS) indicated we were right where we were supposed to be. I made some tests and adjustments of the radar sensitivity settings and everything seemed to be working the way it was supposed to.

    With everything working properly the next step was to ascertain what this was. I first assumed that this must be a massive tidal wave as the area around the west coast was an active fault line (I first learned this what with my research of the Nautilus' adventures years before), but whatever this was, it was dense enough and big enough to bounce the radar signal right back to us. I conducted a plot of the object and discovered it to be stationary – only the ships movement closed the distance.

    When the radar indicated the object was four miles away I had the lookout fire-up a huge search light located above the pilot house and sweep the area directly ahead of the ship.

    About two miles away the light started to reflect back to us a huge cloud formation, ie: fog.

    I turned on the ships fog horn and lights, routine procedure, in the hopes of warning any possible boats and ships that could be approaching the same point we were and couldn't see our ship's powerful search light which just bounced off the cloud bank and dissipated.

As the cloud rapidly closed in, the lookout manipulating the search light swept the beam up, down, sideways and all we could see was a perfectly smooth wall of fog ahead of us. There weren't any ruffles or bumps in the cloud, literally a perfectly smooth wall that extended beyond the effective range of the search light. At less than one hundred yards I could clearly see that this entire mass hovered about six feet above the water.

As we entered the fog bank we were enveloped in the thickest fog I have ever experienced. The visibility was less than the twenty-five foot width of the ship at the level of the bridge and you couldn't even see the other side of the interior of the bridge not twelve feet away – just a faint glow from the various lights and instruments in the bridge. The risk of collision with another ship was paramount in my mind and I slowed to half speed.

I ordered another lookout to the very bow of the ship and had him hooked up to the sound powered phones with instructions to keep in constant contact with the bridge and let me know if he could hear or see anything.

Once inside the fog the radar was marginally effective, but very grainy – there didn't appear to be any large vessels in the vicinity.

Off this area of the California coast it wasn't unusual to come across small fleets of local fishing boats, most thirty to fifty feet in length – small for any landlubber, so my next concern was making sure I didn't cross into one of these fishing groups. So I reduced the ships speed by half again, with the intention of making up the time when the fog lifted a bit.

    As the ship's navigator it was my job to receive the orders from the captain and make sure the ship arrived at the right location at the right time. There wasn't a whole lot of slack to play with. But the ship's safety was my paramount concern, not only the fifty lives on board but also the lives on any boat or ship we might collide with. So for the next hour or so I was totally occupied with a frenetic pace of quickly checking the radar screen, getting reports from the two lookouts and walking around the outside of the bridge looking for any lights, listening for any fog horns or sensing any change in the atmospherics or the smell of diesel fumes from other ships and zigzagging between boats that crossed our path. I was seasoned enough at this point that I didn't feel the least bit of panic or stress about this situation. It was just a very systematic series of steps an OOD takes on a routine basis given the job requirements of the moment. Was even joking around with the handful of crew members I had on watch with me and making sure everyone stayed focused and alert to their jobs. A healthy dose of adrenaline was certainly present though amongst the entire watch.

    So we're all diligently going about our duties. The radar scope was at the port side (left) of the inside of the pilot house immediately adjacent to the open bulkhead door which opened to the bridge wing. The bridge wing is essentially an outside walkway that surrounds the front and sides of the pilot house and the wing itself is surrounded by a solid steel wall about a half inch thick and about four and a half feet high. Its designed to help protect the bridge crew from the elements, but also from small arms fire should the ship find itself in such a situation. And the deck of the bridge wing is about twenty-two feet above the water level.

Fortress of Deceit

The port side running light was directly beneath the deck of the bridge wing causing an eerie glow as it lit up the fog.

I had just checked the navigation charts and gave the helmsman a minor course change, went to the radar scope and adjusted the range a few times to see if it detected anything around us – nothing for at least a few miles all around – and stepped out through the portside bulkhead door to do my usual walk around the bridge wing.

As soon as I stepped through the bulkhead door and walked a couple steps on the bridge wing, I looked up and saw the blurred figure of a man standing about eight feet outside the bridge wing at about a forty-five degree angle from the horizontal axis of the ship, in thin air. I was obviously startled and practically did a back flip back through the bulkhead door into the relative *safety* of the bridge. A moment later I looked back at the image and it faded away in about three seconds as if it was moving away, like a brownish shadow in the fog.

The operational demands of the moment didn't give me much time to contemplate what I had just seen so I just chalked it up to a trick of the ships running lights and the thick fog.

Once I got off watch I tried to rationalize what I saw but none of it made it any sense. Have no idea what it was and ruled out any tricks of the lights that might have caused my own reflection in the fog as the angle was all wrong plus the four and half foot high steel wall was between us and I clearly saw the legs and feet of the illusion, no other crewman was around.

My nearly two years aboard ship were soon up and it was time for a transfer. My collective experiences at sea were both another WOW moment as a well as a relief. Recognizing that I was outside my element, preferring solid ground beneath my feet, plus sea duty was taking me away from the current of the river of life that I felt I was destined for.

CHAPTER THREE
The Big Beach

+

The biggest big business in America is not steel, automobiles, or television. It is the manufacture, refinement, and distribution of anxiety.
Eric Sevareid

+

+

By the time I left my ship, I knew I wasn't going to make the Coast Guard a career. The Guard was a good outfit, but I didn't really adapt to the military life. For obvious reasons, the military is a highly regimented atmosphere. There are manuals for everything – everything from how to dress, how to pilot a ship, to military ships saluting each other when they pass on the high seas; you can find a manual for damn near anything. While this military regimentation serves a useful purpose allowing for a high degree of standardization and efficiency (I later learned through experience that this same acculturation occurs in the civilian federal government albeit not so blatantly), this mentality, unfortunately (I believe), also contributes to government wide failures of the applicable agencies (like the various intelligence, law enforcement and security agencies which allowed the 9/11 terror attacks to succeed with such ease). It's why the TV talking heads frequently say that whenever we get involved in a new war, that we're always fighting the new war with the last war's methodology and equipment – you fight the war using the latest manual as the bible until sufficient loss of life [of our own] forces the bureaucracy to change – note how long it took to field bomb resistant vehicles in Iraq. Some very bright people thrive in this environment, but I found it extremely stifling. It didn't allow one to think, but only to act according to established protocol. This may not be a totally fair assessment, but that's how I felt at the time. One can't argue the fact that the

Fortress of Deceit

United States has the most powerful military the world has ever seen.

I recall one of the military protocol theoretical debates we had in OCS: Suppose two large groups of officers are approaching each other on the sidewalk. Which group initiates the salute? Protocol is that a junior always initiates the salute to a senior officer. But suppose group [A] has a flag officer (admiral or general) as well as a lowly ensign (the lowest officer rank in the sea-going services). Does the ensign initiate the salute since he is the lowest ranking officer of the two groups, or does group [B] initiate the salute since their most senior officer is of subordinate rank than the senior officer of group [A]? While this debate was going on I was squeezing my head trying to keep out the pain, "you've got to be fucking kidding me" was my first thought. While all the officers are frantically scanning the rank insignias of the opposing group and trying to figure out what to do, some street kid would be doing a snatch and run pickpocketing venture and steal them blind. We spent more time debating this issue than we did discussing the meaning of our upcoming *oath of office* or what exactly our obligation was concerning abiding by the Constitution. I don't recall how that debate ended, nor did I care.

So for my second tour of duty I was looking for something different and found it in the desert. In 1981, I volunteered to participate in a multi-agency federal law enforcement drug interdiction task force. The headquarters was located in the desert on the Mexican border, which, as a sailor, I viewed as just a big beach.

The smuggling of narcotics into the US from Central and South America was a huge problem, even way back then; but it doesn't compare to the mayhem and utter insanity and frenzy of violence going on now in Mexico and elsewhere south of the border and starting to drip into the US.

I was privileged working with a great bunch of people, most were DEA agents, and some customs folks and others thrown into the stew – all pulling together in the same direction and watching each other's backs. This was my first introduction into a situation where a combination of good leadership, a handful of outstanding people, and few resources can combine to achieve incredible results.

Unfortunately, primarily because the drug war is an abysmal failure – I'd hate to give the bad guys any more advantage than they already have, but also to protect the lives and interests of the good folks involved in this effort – that I'm only going to generalize and highlight some of the more outrageous incidents in which I participated.

Having spent some of my childhood (and later a year when I was in college) living in the slums of a city I sort of grew up with the notion that drug smugglers and pushers were the scum of humanity. I've since changed my mind about this, but at the time that's how I felt.

The unit I was assigned to was tasked with stopping the shipment of marijuana via ships and boats from Columbia thru the Caribbean to the Gulf and Eastern Coasts of the US. Our group was composed of no more than seven or eight people at any given time split up on different round the clock shifts every day of the year. We effectively served as an intelligence and coordination center since we didn't have the command authority to order interdiction platforms around, but could only guide them toward the bad guys and advise the interdiction platforms on operational movements. While a small unit, we advised the resources of scores of aviation, sea borne, and land resources in this effort.

Fortress of Deceit

After the first nine months, we had seized so much marijuana that there wasn't any place big enough and secure enough to store the marijuana till it wasn't needed any more for the legal prosecutions. The marijuana was eventually delivered to the Marine Corps Base at Guantanamo Bay, Cuba.

A colleague later told me that when they finally collected a small mountain of marijuana that the only way to dispose of it was to burn it. Apparently the plume of smoke was so thick they closed down the air base for several days for fear of making the pilots high. This was multi-hundred tons of marijuana, maybe even multi-thousand tons burning all at once. The man in the moon could have probably seen the smoke plume.

I can't say that we totally stopped the spigot of marijuana coming into the US via sea, but we slammed the smugglers really hard (one doesn't know how much got through our little blockade). The problem was that we did our job too well and started getting the attention of the politicians and bureaucrats in Washington. This signaled the death knell of our efforts.

In our operations room we had a large wall chart of the Caribbean plotted with the positions of our interdiction platforms as well as the last known positions of the boats we were hunting and their projected routes.

We had a really close knit unit and humor was rampant. The real Coast Guard Cutters (CGC) we had on station in the Caribbean were the CGC Decisive, the CGC Diligent and like named cutters. The DEA agents put fake plots on the chart of Coast Guard Cutters with the names of CGC Delicious, the CGC Degenerate and the CGC Despondent. We even had the Delicious plotted in the Gulf of Maracaibo,

Fortress of Deceit

Venezuela. With our successes the local bureaucrats tolerated our little eccentricities.

Because of the *notoriety* we were receiving in Washington we started to get an influx of government bureaucrats and politicians coming into the unit for tours. As I recall, the highest level bureaucrat to visit the unit was the then Attorney General of the US (William French Smith).

None of us in the unit were impressed with any of our visitors – they were most often just an annoyance. Of course, when a VIP entered our shop none of us were allowed to brief them – rather it was some sycophantic ladder climber that escorted them around the facility and briefed the VIPs.

No one ever questioned what the CGC Delicious was doing in an inland waterway of Venezuela or why the Degenerate was paying Castro a visit in Havana Harbor. Whatever the illusion being presented – it apparently made a good enough impression with the politicians and senior bureaucrats from Washington that they decided to expand our operations around the entire coastal area of the US. They usurped our operational authority by organizing a dozen or so similar units around the country.

I have no idea how much money the tax payer wasted on this component of the drug war – it far exceeded the ten to twelve times multiplied by the expense of our little office. We went from fighting a drug war to building a bureaucracy, just because.

One of the worst situations that I was personally involved in concerned a *mothership* – a sizeable freighter that would meander its way up the eastern seaboard and at various points miles from the coast would off load portions of its marijuana to smaller boats for easy infiltration into the mainland. In this case I developed the *intelligence* which profiled a mothership off the eastern coast of Florida. According to our new rules, my office was prohibited from advising interdiction platforms; instead all I could do was relay the information to the Florida interdiction office and let them handle it. This occurred on a Friday afternoon.

When I returned the following Monday, I called the Florida office for a status report only to be told that they didn't have the operational units available to interdict the mothership and let it go. This type of thing wasn't any big deal and would occasionally happen. There were a lot more active smugglers than the good guys trying to stop them. I called the next most northern interdiction office explaining the situation and asked what they were doing about this mothership.

It evolved that the Florida office didn't even bother informing the next most northern office that there was a mothership entering their territory. The reason for this was obvious – the various interdiction offices competed with each other for brownie points in Washington and one office [occasionally] wouldn't inform another office of a mothership entering their area because they wouldn't want the other office to get credit for the bust.

I inquired about making a formal complaint about this through my own chain of command but was told to shut up and forget about it as what these other offices do is outside our bailiwick. Apparently, as I was learning, this type of nonsense was just a routine and acceptable way the government worked.

This was my first real clue that the drug war was more choreography than conflict. Sometimes the good guys would lead the dance steps and sometimes the bad guys would lead the dance – and sometimes the good guys would just sit the dance out. This was the first time that I thought if the Founding Fathers were alive today, they would have executed these bureaucrats for treason.

But this was just the beginning of my education into the dark side of government service.

On another occasion, a US Air Force Reserve pilot colleague was flying reconnaissance training flights over the New Mexican desert. Just taking reconnaissance photo's over a targeted area. It turned out that several of the photos showed a two engine propeller airplane parked at a dirt runway in which it appeared that large bales of something were being piled up near the plane with a couple of trucks nearby and a dozen or so people milling around. The aircraft also appeared to have military insignia on the wings, but they were too blurred to identify.

It took about a week after the photos were taken until delivered to my hands and I spent another week analyzing the photos and trying to find out exactly what type of plane it was and whom it may have belonged too. Sifted through a mountain of aircraft manufacturer guides to determine the make and model of the airplane, and then tracked which countries purchased this aircraft. Had to also figure out exactly where the photo was taken. I wrote up a report suggesting that there was a strong probability – based only on the available photographic evidence, that this airplane actually belonged to the military of a certain country south of the border and suggested that we need to examine the airfield for additional evidence.

The next day I eagerly arrived at work expecting to continue the hunt and finish up my analysis only to discover that my file was missing. When I asked a duty manager about this he responded, "What file!" It was more a statement rather than a question. Without saying a further word, he strongly urged that I drop my analysis.

This was the last straw for me. Although I loved the work and was very good at it, I realized that the drug war was a joke. We couldn't even identify who or what the *enemy* was. The whole effort was akin to running around outside with a bucket trying to catch rain drops to prevent a flood.

While I didn't have any evidence at the time – I believed that there was so much money involved in this racket, that the drug money seeped its way into legitimate business and politics to become part of the American mainstream. In the recent past there have been more than a few news stories about drug money that was laundered by major national and international banks (just look up *banks money laundering* on the internet, and even CIA involvement in smuggling drugs into the US. Not to mention tragic fiascos like the recent *Fast and Furious* operation which sent guns to Mexico and resulted in some of our own casualties, much of this uncovered by dedicated whistleblowers. While I couldn't prove it, there was no doubt in my mind that laundered drug money finds itself within the coffers of politicians. How else could such a lame *war* be allowed to continue like this for at least fifty years. And things are worse now than they have ever been.

We would have been better off at the end of each marijuana growing cycle if we would just send an aircraft carrier to Columbia and buy the marijuana and other drugs directly from the suppliers rather than dance to their tune in a never ending war which is only making the situation worse. Load it up on the ship, go to the middle of the ocean and feed it to the whales, or make bio fuel out of it – might even cut down on road rage.

I decided that employment in a corrupted and inept government wasn't my bag – and yet conflicted because I did love the work. Years later, after observing the drug war being an increasingly abysmal failure that I appreciated the Constitutional issues involved concerning limited federal powers. The wisdom of our Founding Fathers shining through. Federal involvement in the drug war has probably just exacerbated the situation. We should either fight the war head on as a direct threat to national security using a more creative approach (a lot more Americans die from illegal drug use than terrorists could ever hope to kill, but because we die only one at a time it doesn't receive the sensational 24 hour press attention that only amplifies terrorist attacks) or stop fighting it altogether, rather than continue this nonsense ad infinitum.

But I did learn from *masters*.

Fortress of Deceit

CHAPTER FOUR
A Hint of Warfare
+

Cowards die many times before their deaths; the valiant never taste of death but once.
Julius Caesar
+
+

While working for the military, I saved as much money as possible so I could go back to school. Having made the decision to leave the government I was still at a loss as to what to do. I developed a taste for the operational side of a career rather than just sitting behind a desk in an office and I had previously lost interest in going back to law school. Instead, I stumbled across a field of study that was right up my alley. Northeastern University in Boston offered an MS in Security Administration which seemed to apply some science to Ben Franklins's old adage of, "an ounce of prevention is worth a pound of cure." It also supported my notion of applying Holmes' methodology in the real world.

While I was working on my MS degree an opportunity came up to go back into the Coast Guard as an active duty reservist. I needed the money. I worked in the Coast Guard's Boston Office of Intelligence and Law Enforcement (OIL) for about a year, on a part time basis. The vast majority of this work was a continuation of my previous work in narcotics interdiction but focused on the local or regional level. We had a few minor victories and one big one during this time frame. The big one involved another multi-agency effort to track down yet another mothership laden with marijuana. While the tactics of the smugglers would change based on the effectiveness of the interdiction efforts, at this point in history what the mothership smugglers would do was to travel north through the Caribbean then continue going up the eastern coast but staying well outside the 200 mile internationally accepted exclusive economic zone from the coast. This standard minimized the probability of being boarded by a US maritime law enforcement entity. The motherships would travel as far north as Canada, turn around and start heading south but much closer to shore, then at predetermined points they would start off-loading its cargo to smaller boats as they made their way back down south. Their rationale, which was correct, was that a ship heading southbound just a few miles off the coast was much less suspicious than a northbound ship. This tactic worked for who knows how long before we caught on to it.

The operational and organizational skill of these guys was absolutely brilliant and simple. I, of course, didn't condone what they were doing but I admired their tactics. By this time we had already slammed the bad guys a few times after we caught onto their tactics. So their tactics naturally evolved.

In this case, what they did was load up a nearly 300 foot bulk freighter with tons of marijuana hidden on the inside and then tons of salt on top of that, which they picked up at some Caribbean island. This salt is a legitimate commercial cargo and is used as road salt in the winter months in the northern states.

A bulk freighter is the ocean equivalent of a huge dump truck. Basically any bulk cargo like gravel, salt, scrape mental etc is loaded into the open top load. Pretty much the same as a dump truck. However, these ships typically have a double hull. The inside hull is the cargo hull which contains the bulk cargo and which is typically open to the air except occasionally for a weather covering. The outside hull is what you see and is what floats the ship. The space between the two hulls varies from a few inches on the side of

Fortress of Deceit

the ship to about 2 ½ feet on the bottom near the keel. Between the two hulls are a series of reinforced steel beams that connect the two hulls. At the bottom of the cargo hold were a few hatches, smaller than a street manhole cover, just barely large enough for a thin person to squeeze through.

What the smugglers did was load up what turned out to be thirty-three tons of marijuana into the area between the cargo hull and outer hull at their initial disembarkation point. Then traveled to some Caribbean island to pick up a legitimate load of cargo and head towards the New England coastal area.

It would have been completely impracticable for the ship to off load marijuana to smaller boats on the high seas so their intention was to sail into a New England port, offload its legitimate cargo at a commercial facility, and then when no one was looking – offload the illegal cargo.

There were scores of law enforcement personnel involved in this seizure from numerous local, state, and federal agencies. Involved in everything from developing the intelligence which identified the target, surveillance of suspects, those involved in the actual take-down of the ship and those providing security. When it came to actually offloading the marijuana there were few volunteers. Not too many folks wanted to crawl between the bulkheads and offload this stuff. Aside from the claustrophobia the potential of snakes, rats, booby traps, and exotic bugs was a big deterrent.

So the responsibility fell primarily on the Coast Guard (since we're supposed to be the experts in these things; ships, not bugs), and I readily volunteered to assist in this effort. There weren't any more than three or four coasties working at a time. The short of it was that it took us nearly a week of crawling around the guts of the ship with flashlights and knives and haul out the marijuana one bale at a time.

The bales themselves were pressure wrapped in rip stop nylon sheets and seemed to have been customized to fit in the various contours of the hull. This was quite the exercise in not only wrapping the marijuana but in packing the bales into the hold.

Turned out that there weren't any snakes or rats in the hold; there wasn't any room for them as every square inch of space was packed. No booby-traps either – setting booby-traps would have been a sign of fatality on the part of the smugglers, these people were confident.

Once we dragged the marijuana to the outside hatch other cops would pick it up and deliver the marijuana to waiting semi-tractor truck trailers for evidentiary and later disposal purposes.

During this tour of duty I happened to meet an individual that in my opinion was a pure bred sociopath. I'm sure he could have killed someone with as much ease and remorse as most people would swat a fly from buzzing around one's face.

Turned out he was on the pay-roll of the DEA as one of their snitches. The DEA screwed him however by not paying him his just dues. Apparently, at the time, there was an arrangement in which the government would pay snitches a certain percentage of the value of the contraband that was seized due to their information. Apparently the DEA owed him a sizeable sum but refused to pay him. So the snitch started offering his services to other agencies.

Fortress of Deceit

In the Coast Guard we didn't have any money budgeted to pay off snitches but he came to us primarily to screw with the other agencies. In his first days in our office we (myself and other Coast Guard agents) talked for hours and he provided an extra-ordinary knowledge of mothership activities and off-loading tricks.

Probably the most dangerous job in law enforcement is working undercover infiltrating a violent prone organization – of which drug gangs were particularly notorious. It takes a special breed of individual to do this. The snitch we had in the office was a certifiable nut job – in a league by himself. For some reason he had a personal grudge against drug smugglers, not against any one of them in particular but against the breed in general. He once stated that he'd sleep with the devil if it would accomplish something against the smugglers.

He was scary to be around, and he was smart, which made him potentially dangerous; hence most cops he dealt with used the good cop/bad cop routine (minimizing the good cop part) in any dealings with him. This was more a mental defense rather than some intuitive insight to handle him appropriately…prove that we're tougher than he is. Which was far from the truth.

I used a different approach with him, however. I can't say it was a deliberate conscience decision but I just treated him like I would anyone else. Maybe it was because of my background in psychology, but I couldn't help wonder what demons he must have had to contend with to find himself in these circumstances. This wasn't just a job for him, it was a way of life.

One day when we were taking a lunch break I asked him what he wanted to eat and picked up his favorite sandwich at a local deli, something he really appreciated.

A few months later I happened to bump into him on a sidewalk in downtown Boston. Immediately I jumped into the fight or flight syndrome, whatever the situation required. But we talked for a while and he told me that he actually respected and liked me (at least compared to the other government assholes he dealt with), and if I ever needed anyone killed to be sure and let him know. All because I treated him decently and bought him a sandwich. This was another one of those memorable incidents that I stored for later use.

My temporary reserve detail ended shortly there-after.

While all of this was going on I was enmeshed in graduate school fulltime. I was, however, becoming increasingly despondent over my academic and career potential using my newly earned graduate degree. I found graduate school to be a big disappointment at the time – most of the knowledge gleaned from the required research seemed to be mostly common sense security stuff. It wasn't until years later working for FAA and especially TSA that I realized that the billions of tax dollars spent on the bureaucrats and at the hands of these bureaucrats is questionable at best. They didn't and still don't have a clue as to the basic fundamentals that I had taken for granted in graduate school.

Looking back on it now though, an academic degree concentrating in the basic fundamental physical, technical, and psychological components of security should be required before one can become a staff member or manager

Fortress of Deceit

in TSA – but these clowns don't require a degree in anything for these positions – but more on this later.

Job hunting while nearing the end of my academic program proved to be enormously depressing. To most businesses, security work was pretty much limited to running the company's ID card office, putting a fence around the facility, lock and key control and turning the lights on at night or managing a guard force. Cyber security was still in its infancy and I didn't have the technical background or interest for it anyway; but like other areas of security, has still proven to be well behind the capabilities of the bad guys.

So after I obtained my degree, while I was still trying to figure out what to do with my career, I took advantage of another temporary reserve detail with the Coast Guard. This was in their port safety office.

In the mid-80's the United States and the Union of Soviet Socialist Republics were still locking horns and threatening each other with nuclear annihilation. President Reagan referred to the Soviet Union as the "Evil Empire" and ratcheted up the cold war to new heights – eventually the commies crushed themselves under their own weight. These cosmic events were way out of the purview in the Coast Guard but some genius (and I mean this without any sarcasm) decided it would be a good idea to develop maritime defense plans extending from a few miles inland to a few miles out to sea, just so we could do our small part in this adventure. I was assigned the task of writing a specific portion of this plan – in effect, I was now writing one of those manuals that I previously despised; destroying my own illusion of the military atmosphere being mentally stifling. One learns lessons throughout life.

Naturally the Navy would be responsible for warfare on the high seas and the army for warfare inland. Of course, in the event of invasion all the services would engage the enemy as needed and as their resources and capabilities permitted. But under these proposed plans the threat was correctly not seen as a full scale invasion by conventional military but rather the concern was of small unit or single individuals wrecking havoc in port and harbor environments and nearby facilities. This could include disrupting nuclear power plants near the coast, lighting off the enormous fuel farms where ocean going tankers offload oil and natural gas, destroying key bridges or blocking off ship channels or destroying key communication centers. The list of potential targets in heavily urbanized coastal areas is virtually endless, all viewed as a prelude to conventional war with the purpose of disrupting our own force's capability to retaliate as effectively as they should.

Even by this period of the cold war, there were a whole a string of soviet defectors who enthusiastically opened the doors of the KGB (Committee for State Security), a remarkably similar bureaucratic mentality as our current Department of Homeland Security; as well as the GRU (the military version of their KGB).

My concern was of a smaller organization nominally within the GRU organization called SPETZNAZ. These were the Soviet equivalent, more or less, of our own special forces. Their general method of operation was to parachute, swim, ride, or walk behind enemy lines and assassinate, destroy or otherwise disrupt their enemy's lines of communications. I had the unique and fascinating time of researching and learning much of what we knew at the time of the SPETZNAZ forces. Most of this information came from their own defectors from popular books at the time as well as debriefing reports.

Fortress of Deceit

My effort was to try to get into their mindset so as to figure out how they would operate in the coastal area and what or who they would most likely target. I was struck by a number of the stories I read about them. One of the popular books on the subject at the time reported that when they engage in military training exercises it's a life and death event. Should a trooper break his leg parachuting into a *hostile zone* he wouldn't be medevac'd out until the exercise was over, potentially weeks later. Forced to survive on his own.

In another segment of the book the defector reported that in another military exercise SPETZNAZ troops captured two members of the opposing forces. They threw one on the ground, holding him down and quickly filed down his teeth with a metal rasp. They then asked the second captive questions concerning whatever their objectives were and he rapidly told them what they wanted to know. And this was just an exercise.

Aside from these little nuisances SPETZNAZ troops were typical of special operations forces the world over. Once you understand the military capability of an opposing force it's a relatively easy matter to make plans to try to thwart their objectives. Of course, planning doesn't necessarily equate to successful execution. That hinges on the capability, resources, and leadership of the defending forces, as well as some luck.

A feature of SPETZNAZ that actually caused me the greatest concern was that, according to defectors, a subunit within SPETZNAZ concerned a relatively small group of operatives whose methodology was to enter the US through legal channels as businessmen, government officials, professional athletes, or tourists, carrying no contraband or weapons of any kind. Nothing to give any hint of suspicion.

Fortress of Deceit

In anticipation of hostilities the operative would acquire appropriate weapons and whatever other resources he would need to achieve his objectives from whatever local source he could steal, bribe, legitimately purchase, or make on his own. It is easy enough to acquire fake IDs, guns, knives, explosives, chemicals, tools or whatever tech gear is available and needed. Thwarting this type of operative became my paramount concern. But how?

What I decided to do was act just like how I'd perceived the operative would act in this environment. Use whatever resources were available to disrupt their own anticipated plans. Under the operating conditions that I was bound by – my instructions were to limit my plans to a few miles inland to a few miles out to sea (I believe the actual mileage was classified). There must be a thousand miles of coast line just along the New England coast, plus countless small harbors and ports, boat docks, piers, islands, rivers and who knows what else. The combined resources of the Coast Guard, local, state and federal law enforcement, nature conservation officers etc., wasn't enough to monitor all this space and activity. So I started thinking about the days when I was engaged in narcotics interdiction via the sea.

Perhaps the biggest unused asset in disrupting the smuggling of narcotics via sea were the countless fishermen, pleasure boat operators, tug boat and other commercial operators. Virtually every port and harbor has its own *harbor master* which is a combination of town mayor, politician, cop, and safety officer all rolled into one.

While we didn't use these folks for narcotics interdiction, they would be perfect for maritime defense purposes. They had their vested interest in maintaining their maritime lifestyle and would have made the perfect eyes and ears for reporting any unusual activities. All they required was a little bit of training, some type of organization, and a point of contact to call when they spotted something unusual.

So I wrote my portion of the maritime defense zone plan to incorporate these good folks into the defense picture. The plan had to be signed off on at numerous levels and eventually received formal approval to proceed. At the time this didn't appear to be any big deal – it was a common sense approach to take. Looking back on it though, this was actually quite extraordinary. In the mid-80's when the cold war was at another peak, the threat of nuclear annihilation of a good part of the human race wasn't that far off – the bureaucrats and probably some politicians actually concurred that just regular citizens (in spite of the occasional bad apple), would be a valuable national security asset. Compare that to today: a handful of terrorists wreck havoc (something of which could and should have been prevented – but we'll get into that later) and suddenly the government views all its own citizens as potential enemies until they prove themselves otherwise. Note TSA's treatment of passengers, the government's surveillance state mentality, the dissolution of the Constitution, lying about the premise for war, torture, giving itself the authority to kill US citizens without due process etc., etc., etc. If these current idiots had been in charge during the cold war, very few of us would be here today.

So back to 1985. Once the MARDEZ plan (Maritime Defense Zone) was approved, the next phase was to test the implementation of the plan. *Ocean Safari 85* was a massive NATO military exercise which simulated a "breakout" of a military convoy from Boston Harbor, traversing a submarine infested North Atlantic waters, off-loading military supplies in Europe and continuing the air and ground war there. The exercise involved a number of NATO countries, scores of combat ships, hundreds of aircraft, thousands of military personnel, the US Military Sea-Lift Command, special operations personnel – you get the picture. Like most things, this exercise is even highlighted on the internet.

My little part of it was that I was in charge of the *terrorist* team in Boston Harbor that was assigned the task of disrupting allied forces before the fleet even left the harbor – a perfect mission for SPETZNAZ. Unlike the reported SPETZNAZ military training exercises, however, my job wasn't to achieve an objective at any cost, but rather to provide a realistic training regime to the Coast Guard, local, state, and federal law enforcement agencies and the military units that participated in the harbor part of the exercise – which lasted two weeks, twenty-four hours per day.

For the boats we used in the harbor we *commandeered* the local Coast Guard Auxiliary (which were basically mom and pop boat owners who assisted the Coast Guard on various maritime safety events). We simulated *stealing* these boats. Their knowledge of the local maritime environment was invaluable and they were ecstatic about being able to play in these war games – something inconceivable in today's government paranoid atmosphere.

My colleagues and I developed a carefully choreographed battle plan that involved increasingly complex problems for the good guys to resolve. We conducted ourselves similar to enemy agents with no sophisticated gear or resources who had to beg, borrow, steal, bribe, or kill to obtain what we wanted – which actually wasn't that far off from what we really had to do (minus the killing part).

The first few days of the two week exercise were fairly mild – just walking along the pier taking photos of the military ships and reacting mildly to the guard's orders to move away, then later we started doing the same thing but from the waterside using various small boats that we were able to *steal*, and tempting the good guys to board us. So far we didn't provide any armed or physical resistance but tried to push the buttons of the boarding officers to try to get them to *shoot* us. In those days they actually had rules of engagement they had to follow and torture wasn't even thought of. I must have been arrested half a dozen times in the first week – under the rules, however, I couldn't be held for any more than an hour.

The funniest event occurred near the beginning of the second week when we started to ratchet up the activities.

We used about a forty foot pleasure boat and had five role players on board, all dressed up with horrendous wounds using mulage kits. The pilot of the boat (the owner) was exempt from the exercise for safety reasons and we also had a judge on board who wore a white jacket and had radio communications with the command post and could terminate any given evolution due to safety concerns.

So at three or four in the morning the pilot navigated the boat into the middle of Boston Harbor and turned all his running lights off. We just sat there for about a half hour before a boarding party arrived. They could clearly see a *dead* person on the deck.

From my vantage point, as one of the dead persons lying on the deck in an internal passageway, I couldn't see anything but could hear the radio traffic between the armed boarders and their command post – clearly the pucker factor was increasing on their part as they could tell the problems they had to face were increasing in complexity. Finding a boat adrift in Boston Harbor with five dead people hacked up on board put them over the top. I could hear over the radio traffic that the command post vectored all the other harbor patrol boats to us to provide support as needed. I also had one of my operatives near-by on shore who observed the reaction from the good guys – something that assisted our subsequent strategy.

Even though our own activities were carefully scripted; the reaction from the good guys were not – it was a learning experience on their part.

To give the good guys an advantage by being able to find out something of our ultimate plot, we used the boat owner's sixteen old daughter on this particular exercise. We gave her some information on the description of the attackers and of the boat they were on when they attacked her yacht, and we hid her in the bathroom with instructions to scream and act hysterically if/when a boarding officer opened the door while searching the boat; as well as to provide them this information under their interrogation.

Turned out that when the boarding officer opened the darkened bathroom he was greeted with a blood curdling scream that literally woke the dead on the boat and she was promptly shot (with blanks) nearly a dozen times by the two or three boarding officers in close proximity. So much for the *intelligence* they would have gained.

The rationale of this scenario wasn't just to provide some pucker power training but was specifically designed to check out the good guys reactions to any given incident. Plus, it fell within the expected modus operandi of SPETZNAZ – kill a totally innocent family just to see how the opposing forces reacted to it. Essentially every time there were one of our incidents to respond too, the guys in the command post would vector in all or most of their resources to handle the situation to make sure they *won* the day. So for the rest of the week we tried breaking them of the habit by engaging in multiple simultaneous incidents to deal with at different hours of the day and night.

On the final night of the exercise (about two in the morning) we attempted a suicide boat bomb attack against the command ship in the harbor. The suicide bomb boat's task was to hug the shore and slowly make their way up the harbor to the command ship, get as close as possible and light themselves off.

I was in charge of the decoy boat. Given the expected reaction by the good guys, my boat went up the middle of the harbor past Logan Airport careening wildly and rapidly in the night while racing at full throttle just to get their attention. They vectored three coast guard boats to us and after a maddening chase thru the harbor eventually cornered us in a little inlet. The old man, the owner/pilot of the boat was having the time of his life, wildly careening through the harbor evading capture by the good guys – it was all I could do to hang on in the stern to keep from getting thrown out of the boat. The official judge on the boat was a paper pushing navy lieutenant with no operational experience of anything, he was crouched next to the pilot hanging on for dear life. I thought for sure he was going to terminate our activities due to safety concerns but he was frozen in place. The coasties were in tiny 2-man speed boats but fearlessly jetted toward us trying to flood our engine with their wakes and careening within feet of the bow using the wake of their boat to turn us toward the shore, and nearly succeeded – in this high speed confined environment with the constant twisting and turning the wakes of all the boats caused a churning inferno of water. At some point I managed to climb my way to the pilot house and get close enough to the pilot so that he could hear me shouting to cut the engine. The coastguardsmen were absolutely fearless and were determined to stop us at some risk to themselves. These guys were great. But their enthusiasm was at some significant risk to life, especially just for an exercise.

While this was going on the suicide boat bomb just quietly moseyed up the opposite side of the harbor, got immediately adjacent to the command ship completely unopposed and lit off their explosives. Which actually meant that the exercise judge on the suicide boat bomb called the judge in the command post and told them they just got wasted.

As far as I was concerned my involvement in the exercise was over. I went home to get some much needed sleep. For the previous two weeks I never slept more than a couple of hours at a time. Sleeping on park benches, on a boat pier, on the deck of a boat or on a beach. The best sleep I had was after one of the handful of times that I was *arrested* – fell asleep with my hands cuffed behind my back and some cop's foot pressed against my neck on the bottom of a boat. The waking time I was operating on pure adrenaline. I was not only responsible for my own activities during the exercise but was responsible for some twenty other guys who were involved in these Red Team activities in various places about the harbor.

So after I got back to the office on the following Monday the first thing I was hit with was that after the command ship was destroyed by the suicide boat bomb boat, the exercise rules required that the command post be moved to a pre-determined inland office building which was the alternate command post.

What happened, however, is that the command duty officer on watch at the time called the admiral who was in overall command of this part of the exercise and he made the decision to nullify the suicide boat bomb attack and it was stricken from the exercise record. Ostensibly because it wouldn't look good to have the command ship destroyed even before the major part of the exercise began.

At the time I just thought that, once again, some frigging bureaucrat who was more concerned about some political agenda than dealing with the real world, basically negated any real learning experience from all the effort that went into this exercise as well as the development of the MARDEZ plans. Basically another total waste of tax dollars. And all this was done without disrupting the normal routine of harbor life, was hardly even noticed.

Years later, the suicide boat bomb attack on the USS Cole effectively demonstrated the poor security of tied up navy ships when a terrorist small boat laden with explosives hit the ship. The Cole attack was even less sophisticated than the one we executed. They didn't even have a decoy boat, they just moseyed up to the Cole and lit themselves off.

About this time I was still torn between a career in the government which at times was fun, and initially fulfilling, but increasingly seemed to be totally superfluous and futile; and doing something else. It was also my first exposure to the utility of Red Teaming work, as well as the bureaucracy's instinctive revulsion to Red Teams. Although at the time I ignorantly assumed that this revilement was localized, not a universal condition within government bureaucracies.

CHAPTER FIVE
A Hint of Crime Fighting
+

Mediocrity knows nothing higher than itself, but talent instantly recognizes genius.
Sir Arthur Conan Doyle
+
+

While I was in graduate school and working as a Coast Guard reservist (as a Lieutenant O-3, by this time) I had intermittent contact with a couple of civilian Special Agents for a particular US military service (prefer to keep it nameless) who convinced me that I'd be a natural working in their counter-espionage section. During the 80's, as part of the cold war, the Soviets spent a lot of effort stealing military secrets from the U.S. To the Special Agents, with my recently acquired MS degree in security coupled with my other work history I was a perfect candidate, not to mention my ethnic Slavic background and name. I applied for and was accepted as a Special Agent with this service in 1986.

I went through the ten week Special Agent curriculum at the Federal Law Enforcement Training Center (FLETC) at Glencoe, GA. Much to my delight, FLETC was actually a very good training experience. What I discovered in most typical law enforcement type training is that there is very little focus on history or theory but rather on real world mechanics that will help you do your job and hopefully keep you alive. Whether it was basic firearms training, unarmed combat, or an overview of the laws which mandated exactly what one can or can't legally do while on the street. My most note-worthy memory of the training was a comment one of my instructors made concerning my interrogation techniques; she compared me to the main character in the TV show *Colombo*. Apparently, once I latched onto a particular path with a suspect, I'd just continually irritate the poor chap till he confessed. I took it as a compliment.

Graduation at FLETC was very solemn but without all the pomp of newly commissioned officers in the military. And for the second time in my life I was required to take the oath of office which included the clause, "...to support and defend the Constitution of the U.S..., and to defend this country from all enemies both foreign and domestic." As one might guess, there wasn't a single minute of class time spent on reading the Constitution much less understanding it – other than certain sections as it applied to law enforcement officers but even this was only taken primarily from the point of view of agency policy. Nothing about our obligation to fulfill this oath.

I was getting the impression that, within government circles anyway, the Constitution was some sort of secret document that only certain cleared and wizened men were allowed to read. In fact, it seemed like if the Constitution actually was some closely guarded secret document that spelled out exactly how the government is required to function then people would be clamoring to read it. Someone would have eventually leaked it to Wikileaks and it would be a sensation for a while. I think average Americans would have started making a list of all the politicians and bureaucrats that clearly violated the mandates of the Constitution and demand they be indicted for treason. The fundamental premise of the Constitution is that it puts specific limitations on the powers of the federal government and that it's the legislative branch that is supposed to be the dominant institution within that government.

Unfortunately, in this day and age, watching a politician or bureaucrat recite his oath of office is about as meaningful as listening to them spout off their favorite recipe for pizza sauce. I'd wager that with all the popular food shows on TV that politicians would get a bigger TV audience if they did spout off their favorite food recipes rather than just an oath of office – boring!

In World War II, in NAZI Germany, the newly commissioned soldiers had to swear a personal oath to Adolph Hitler. I'm sure this simple act helped prolong the war and resulted in their fanatical fighting to the bitter end. But this was a time when an oath actually meant something to the individual. Same thing applied to Japanese soldiers swearing an oath to their Emperor.

Unlike when I went through Officer Candidate School, where I barely survived, at FLETC I excelled in the entire curriculum and graduated somewhere in the upper part of the class. But this was much more in the right current of life that I felt I was meant for.

Upon earning my Special Agent credentials, my first duty station was in the mid-west territory based near Chicago. This was a major training base, especially for enlisted personnel. In typical bureaucratic fashion, however, instead of being assigned working counter-espionage cases I was instead assigned the job of working felony level crime investigations. I was later told by one of my colleagues that while certain elements of the agency were glad to have me on board and were eager to have me working counter-espionage, the dominant bureaucrats were leery of having someone with a "Soviet" sounding name working in their counter-espionage section. I thought this was funny and ignorant at the time given that almost all the spies that were being caught in the 80's had Anglo-Saxon or even American Indian names.

Fortress of Deceit

Well, I thought to myself at the time, if I do a good job at solving felony crimes, then in a couple of years when I'm eligible for a transfer I'll put in for one of these counter-espionage positions. So I enthusiastically jumped into my new role of combatting felony crime.

The agency office I was assigned to had twelve Special Agents whose task was to investigate a whole assortment of crimes. Everything from shop-lifting from the base department store, vandalism, theft from or involving military personnel, illegal drug use or sales of, burglary, muggings, murder, rape, child abuse, destruction of government property, white collar crimes and stuff that I didn't even know was a crime. In those days you could be booted out of the military for being a homosexual, and it was up to this agency to investigate these crimes. I learned a lot about certain aspects of human nature that I wish I could forget. Contrary to the spit and polish illusion of military bases, crime was as rampant as in any small city.

During my first week on the job I already starting picking up negative waves that this occupation wasn't meant for me or the current of life my gut instinct told me I was destined for. Later that week a couple of fellow agents took me to the base's police department where I'd be spending a lot of my time, and introduced me to the local cops I'd be dealing with. In the course of touring their facility I happened to notice their bulletin board which contained photos and descriptions of wanted felons and other miscreants. Contained there-in were a couple of mug shots of a big dog, front and side views, just like the human mug shots. The front mug shot obviously showed a very happy dog with his tongue dangling out, in sharp contrast to the human mug shots. Well, I had to ask.

Turned out, just a week or so prior to that day, the police received a phone call from a neighbor of a house in the enlisted base housing area. They heard a dog howling inside the house. So the cops arrived, the howling was still going on, and the cops eventually smashed through the front door. On the floor of the living room they found the wife naked on the floor engaged in sex with the male dog. Apparently the dog got stuck and started howling, the lady's face and chest were ripped up from the front paws of the dog. Lots of laughs at the police station. Later that evening in my brand new studio apartment, I sat at the kitchen table, put my head in my hands and wondered what the hell I got myself into.

But life and work went on.

Typically the way things worked at the office was that each agent was assigned rotating duty for a few days in a row, any crime that was reported during this time frame usually was assigned to the agent that was on duty – day or night. On some bizarre level, as I recall, about 90% of the violent crime cases seemed to occur on the shifts that I and another agent had. These crimes included rape, murder, physical assaults, etc. As a consequence the two of us developed a quick bond and would frequently help each other out on our respective cases.

Today the various talking heads in the media are making a big deal about the sex crimes in the U.S. military in general and specifically in the various military academies; where, one would think, a higher level of behavior would be demanded. These situations are indeed terrible, but even in the mid-late 80's sex crimes on military bases (at least on the base I was assigned and from reports of some of my colleagues around the country) were a virtual epidemic, and ignored except for the routine criminal processing (this doesn't even include the officially unreported incidents I was made aware of).

Things were so bad on the base I was assigned too, that when I had the duty on certain nights I wouldn't even bother going to bed. I'd just stay up all night drinking coffee, watching movies or reading and just wait for the inevitable call from the base police or one of the other local police departments reporting the latest rape involving a military service member victim and/or perpetrator. I'd then put my shoes on, holster my service revolver and head either to the local hospital to interview the victim or to the local police lock-up to interview the suspect (assuming, of course, that he or she was already in police custody).

A particularly noteworthy case of mine involved a service member who was the victim of an attempted rape. She was alone walking back from the base enlisted bar in the wee hours of the morning going back to her barracks. Apparently her would-be rapist followed her from the bar and at one point grabbed her and carried her behind the post office, threw her under a mail truck and proceeded to take her clothes off. She was fighting and screaming the whole time which attracted the attention of a roving base police officer, who effected an arrest and the girl was sent to the base emergency room.

Around 3ish in the morning I received the expected phone call from the police department and following long practiced procedure went to the hospital to interview the victim. This was a pretty much standard rape case (some were quite on the weird side) except that the police broke up the party before the act was consummated and the girl was beaten up a lot more than most victims. Small bruises and minor cuts all over; but the most distinguishing feature was that she clearly had finger marks on her neck where the guy tried to strangle her. After I got her signed statement I went to the police lock-up to interview the suspect.

In large part, I believe, when I first started interviewing (we didn't call it interrogation) suspects I developed the habit of avoiding any good cop bad cop baloney. Following all established police/legal procedures (Miranda Rights etc); I would get the suspect (whether male or female) as comfortable as possible, given the sparse accommodations of police interrogation rooms. Then, if the person wanted it, I'd get them something to eat or drink. Sometimes I'd even get the same food/drink as the prisoner and have him pick which ever sandwich/drink he wanted and I'd take the other – just to get him to trust me. Then I'd get him to start talking about himself; where he grew up, what kind of classes he liked in school etc. Being careful not to lead the subject but just nudge him to talk about himself in the direction we had to go.

Then eventually we'd get to the here and now and start talking about how and why he wound up in police custody. What I discovered is that most people, even in these high stress situations (being under arrest) actually liked talking about themselves. Probably for most of these people I was the first one in their lives to actually listen to them. And they opened up to me. I couldn't help but wonder years later when there was a big debate going on after 9/11, about our government's use of torture (something I never thought I'd live to see); that we could have acquired much more valuable information from our prisoners by sitting around a campfire eating falafel and smoking hashish rather than waterboarding and other tortures – torture being one of the bigger smears against what used to be a country that was a beacon of light for humanity.

Fortress of Deceit

When it came to the sex crimes we'd get into whatever kinky stuff turned the suspect on and what it was about the victim that attracted him to her (in most cases). In obtaining a statement from a suspect that could be used in a criminal prosecution the investigator had to obtain as much information as was feasible and relevant to the case, and the sleazier and grosser the better.

When I first started interviewing this suspect I had flashbacks to the sociopath that I had met back when I was in the Guard. When I dealt with him it wasn't so much a deliberate approach but rather an unconscious method to communicate with him, just as I would do with anyone. As a criminal investigator, however, I had to make a deliberate effort to talk to suspects in the manner I previously described. Some of these people had a cloud of sleaze that enveloped them. Others just engaged in a spontaneous act and happened to get caught at it. After I'd spend hours with these people my first instinct was to go home and take a shower just to get the grime off me. But the thing I discovered was that very few of my cases ever went to trial. The signed statements I obtained from most of the suspects left little room to bother with a trial and most of these people just plea bargained their way out without wasting time in any legal proceeding. I was even starting to think I was a bit of the stud when it came to doing criminal investigations since few of my cases ever went to trial, even the defense lawyers weren't going to waste their efforts.

Back to the rape suspect; when I arrived at the police station the cops told me I had an easy one – this guy already blabbed about trying to the rape the girl.

When I started to interview the suspect it didn't take any *softening* to break him down. He readily went into great detail of how and why and what he intended on doing and stated he was trying to strangle the girl to get her to stop screaming. He admitted that he probably would have killed her if the cops hadn't intervened. This was the shortest interview I ever conducted. We could have been talking about the last time he stepped on a bug and it would have elicited the same kind of emotional response from him. The guy was a certifiable nut job – another sociopath. But, I got my signed confession and didn't give the situation a second thought. It was just one of countless crimes one processed.

A couple days later, however, I was driving on the military base and happened to see the nut job walking down the street. I pulled a U-turn with my car and followed him at a discreet distance. He was dressed in the base uniform of the day carrying some books. A few minutes later he entered one of the classroom buildings.

So I went to his Command to find out if he escaped or if there is something weird going on here. Upon talking to the OOD (Officer of the Day), I discovered that he was confined to barracks for one night and then released so he could continue going to school. It was then that I discovered one of the unique schisms between the civilian court system and military justice system. Unlike in a civilian court where the suspect is brought before a magistrate and bail or not is established; in the military a suspect is turned over to his command who can send the suspect to the brig, engage in non-judicial punishment (minor administrative punishment), or let the guy go, or even give the guy a medal. So while this guy gets to go to class, his victim couldn't go to her classes because she wasn't released from the hospital yet.

Kind of made me wonder what the point of all this hard work was. Shortly after this I had to investigate another predictable rape case. This one concerned an eighteen year old petite girl from some small town in West Virginia. She joined the military to escape the dead end poverty she lived in. Her assailant was male and about the same age as the victim. It was another pretty much cut and dry rape case.

A couple of weeks later she was raped by the same guy. This was the last straw for me. I went into my boss's office to convince him that I could eliminate at least 90% of the rape cases involving personnel on this base, IF he'd arrange for me to give a one hour briefing to these personnel during the first week of their base indoctrination training. I could convince the female sailors to take appropriate steps such as not walking alone at night (even on a military base, which gave one a false sense of security); and make a convincing enough argument to the males that you don't want to be sitting across from me at three in the morning in the police lock-up – I'm always in a bad mood then, and increasingly so.

This would save, I argued, tens of thousands of tax dollars in processing these cases in the military criminal justice system. Thousands more in incarcerating these individuals (if it ever actually happened); not to mention the thousands of dollars already spent in the service members training in the event they were eventually booted out of the military, plus medical costs and of course the physical and mental trauma of those involved – which didn't really concern the bureaucracy.

I already knew that my boss was a goof and a dangerous bastard but even his response surprised me. He immediately wafted into a loud screaming tirade challenging my competency as an investigator, chastising me for not knowing what my job is – "your job is to investigate felony crime, not prevent it", he ranted. I had to sit there for at least fifteen minutes being screamed at by a lunatic. I just sat there with my mouth gapping open totally incredulous that he was behaving like this. I had just passed my one year probationary period, meaning that in order to fire me he'd have to document cause and couldn't just fire me because he wanted too.

Even by this time I made a habit of pushing this banshee's buttons though. In this latest screaming session I was actually hoping he'd give himself a heart attack or a brain aneurism – although the latter was unlikely given that a brain was required to start off with. After he gulped his last gasp of air I would have just quietly left his office and shut the door behind me. I didn't know anyone in the office that actually respected or even liked the guy, only tolerated him because there wasn't any choice. It would have been an interesting headline in the news: "criminal investigator manager dead in office for a week before anyone noticed."

It also hit me kind of hard, far from being the stud criminal investigator I thought I was, it was the military judicial system that didn't waste much time with the criminals we served them on a silver platter. From my observations, the persons guilty of relatively minor crimes just received a slap on the hands so they could get back to their costly training. The ones guilty of more serious crimes were discharged and sent back to the civilian world for them to deal with the problem. Some of the more prominent criminals did do time in the military prison system, but I'm not aware of any of my *clients* doing time. I think a big part of this had to do with the over-riding military atmosphere - after all, these people were part of an organization charged with killing and destroying things upon command and putting their lives on the line. A little bit of crime, nothing to fret about. Upon reflection, this is what happens when you mix a required military (ie: warrior) ethos for legitimate national defense purposes with the latest political fad.

Fortress of Deceit

But, life continued:

Life as a civilian military criminal investigator was jam packed. One might work on half a dozen different investigations every day, not to mention other types of work. While all this stuff I presented about rape and other violent crime was going on, there were other significant happenings.

One of the mismanagement trends that commenced a few months after I started working for this outfit was a major bean counting effort initiated by it's headquarters in Washington, DC. The purpose of which was to document how much time each office spent investigating each of the assorted crimes and other duties we engaged in. As it turned out, even before I arrived on scene the agency had already completed major man-power studies – such things as how many hours, on average, it takes to investigate homicides, burglary, grand theft, larceny etc.

It's very difficult for a federal law enforcement bureaucracy to justify its existence when examined under an unbiased microscope. But one way bureaucrats have learned to fog the eyes of Congress is by quantifying everything. For example (and I'm just making up these numbers): two years ago the agency initiated 420 homicide investigations, this past year we initiated 557 of these investigations. "Hmn?" A rational mind might surmise, homicides seem to be going up, we need more money and resources to investigate these crimes. Of course, they don't include the fact that only 23 of these were actual homicides, the rest were deaths due to natural causes or accidents. Furthermore, we knew it was most likely accidents that killed the individuals even before we started the investigations; but it sounds a lot sexier to talk about homicides rather than heart attacks, or work place accidents or choking on food.

Next might be some other numerical indicators such as: it takes fourteen hours to complete a certain type of investigation and we spent 129,426 man hours doing this work. Hmn? 129,426 divided by 14 equals 9244.7 is the number of investigations of this type we conducted. Add this to the number of hours spent, cases opened, divided by the number of agents on the payroll and you can demonstrate that we need more agents to adequately do the job. More agents mean bigger offices, more support staff, higher salaries for managers to manage, more regional and headquarters staff to count all the beans. The bigger you are the higher your status. The more tax-payer resources it costs and on and on and on.

And the Congress loves this stuff.

But that doesn't tell the whole story. In order to count all those beans, somebody has to first plant the bean seed. Us field agents had to document how we spent every ten minute increment of the work day. We received a small booklet, written in very tiny print which contained codes for all the various tasks that we could possibly spend our time on. It was quite the elaborate, if not sophisticated method of generating, collecting, collating, analyzing, computing, and documenting data on work force management that was presented up the chain and had a direct bearing on the tax payer money that the agency was given. The process was so detailed that it didn't just have a category for burglary; it was broken down into sections of driving to and from a burglary, interviewing burglary witnesses/victims and suspects, burglary crime scene processing, burglary administrative work (which included things like packing up evidence and sending it to the lab).

It was quite the detailed process. The problem was that if one was diligent in filling out the form it would normally take between one and two hours every day just to fill it out. In fact, there was a category in the booklet for "form; filling out of."

As the program evolved, it became apparent that thousands of man hours agency wide were being spent just filling out the form. But this, of course, didn't particularly look good in the final data compilation so at some point headquarters issued an instruction to the field agents to stop using the category to document how much time was spent doing this nonsense. Instead, it was implied that we were to incorporate it into the other more legitimate ways to spend one's time. If you spent the latter part of the day, as an example, conducting an arson investigation, at the end of the day when you're filing out the form you'd just put the time in as a subcategory of "arson" rather than the catch-all admin category.

This was the beginning of the souring of this entire program. Whatever real benefit there was in collecting all this data in terms of human resource management or federal work force management or whatever the catch phrase was at the time soon deteriorated into a frivolous exercise in futility. Garbage in garbage out, as they say. Agents were now unofficially forced to start fudging an official report.

The very notion of fudging anything for a Special Agent was repugnant. We went to great lengths to ensure that the slightest details of a criminal investigation were appropriately documented. If an agent made a minor mistake in a statement in which he misquoted a suspect using the word "the" instead of "thee" he'd spend hours, if necessary, making sure the mistake was corrected. Now we were compelled to start lying in official reports. It caused a certain bit of discombobulation and, in turn, resulted in a further deterioration of our professionalism and integrity. Soon I, as well as a number of other agents just started printing in random codes in the form as rapidly as possible and finish the stupid thing in five minutes. If headquarters wasn't going to take this stuff seriously there was little point in wasting any more time than was necessary on this. Particularly when we were already so over-worked.

But we continued to drift into the dark side.

Apparently in this bean counting scheme, a weighted scale also played an important role. A murder was a more serious crime than a rape and hence counted more in beans than a rape. A rape, in turn, was more than a simple battery, which was more than an assault etc etc etc.

I don't know how many times, when I was given another case by my boss, in which I was ordered to open the investigation as a much more serious crime than it actually was. As an example, some service member was in the study area of a barracks, she took her jewelry off while she was studying, went to the restroom and upon her return discovered someone stole her jewels. I was ordered to open the investigation as a burglary even though it was a simple theft, and subsequently proved the point.

The significance of this is that when the case is *opened*, the situation is given a case number and logged into the computer where it remains as entered. If the incident later warrants charges less than how the case was originally opened it did not change how the case was originally classified. So a "theft" in which the bureaucrats allocated three hours for an agent to complete was considerably less complicated than a burglary which was allocated twenty hours to complete. The net effect of all this was that the agency itself was guilty of theft from the American people by falsifying data which would be used to make a bigger bureaucracy at tax payer expense. It was my understanding at the time, that the agency copied this work-force management hooey from the FBI.

But we didn't take this garbage sitting down. A number of agents in my office complained to the same managers about this nonsense but the managers responded in the typical bureaucratic manner: Instead of addressing the problem and fixing it as necessary, the managers would make veiled threats about an agent being insubordinate, not a team player, or our annual performance review could be adversely effected. Since about 90% of the non-supervising agents in the office had less than five years on the job it quickly resulted in the silencing (for the most part) of overt discontent of these policies. This was, in fact, a very effective means of acculturation; of breeding a mindset on the part of employees to not question stupid policies and to blindly accept the management culture if one wanted anything resembling a successful career within the agency.

Several of us, however, still weren't intimidated and continued to protest this nonsense. In my case, this in turn resulted in a further backlash from management. Since I had passed my probationary year I couldn't be fired just cause they didn't like me; they either had to justify a legitimate reason (which I never gave them any ammunition to use against me, as much as I protested doing this nonsense I nevertheless did it the way they wanted so they couldn't tag me for being insubordinate) or they could make my work life so miserable that I'd just quit. I became convinced that my boss was intentionally assigning me unnecessarily hazardous work.

Fortress of Deceit

The first big case of this nature concerned a male of Native American ethnic background. A couple of days before he was discharged he passed a desk where some woman was counting her money or some such. At one point she turned her head and when she re-focused her attention on her money she discovered that $20.00 was missing. The only person in the immediate vicinity was an American "Indian" looking fellow. By the time the local cops figured out who the most likely candidate was, two more weeks lapsed.

When my boss assigned me this case I first argued that this doesn't even come close to being a felony and that no JAG (Judge Advocate General, the military equivalent of a civilian District Attorney) in his right mind would waste time with this case. But trying to use logic and common sense in attempting to reason with this nut case was a pointless exercise. So I then suggested that we just take $20.00 out of petty cash and just reimburse the lady for her loss. She'd get her money back, it would be a lot cheaper for us, the Indian will continue doing whatever he's up to whether we find him or not, and I can go on to doing more important things.

Well, whatever synapses were still firing in his lower brain functioning were beginning to overload and I knew I was moments away from being written up for insubordination. So I said, "Yes Siirrrrr", and soon found myself on a jet plane to Souix Falls, South Dakota in the middle of the frigging winter, heading towards the Pine Ridge Indian Reservation.

Upon arrival there, I picked up a rental car and after a couple of stops I tracked the individual to his most likely current residence (an uncle) which was located near a small town about fifteen miles from Wounded Knee.

Fortress of Deceit

In the early evening of the second day I was driving towards the town, still about an hours driving time away and passed a Native American radio station situated on a small hill. So I started fiddling with the radio dial in the car and eventually found the station.

I got in the habit early on, whenever I traveled, to absorb as much information on the local culture as I could. Things like reading the local newspaper, watching local TV, and listening to the radio. In this case it was a local tribal radio station. In between the music the announcer went through the same type of stuff I've heard all over; things like the cattle situation, weather, the school and some local politics.

What was interesting though were the local songs. Over the course of a half hour or so, every single local song (sung in English) dealt with the subject of the evil white man and the lone brave warrior fighting until his last breath against overwhelming odds. And I couldn't argue the point.

The native American peoples certainly had a rough ride interacting with the European conquest. Apparently the hostility about these times hasn't dissipated much. This wasn't the first time I was in this part of the country but the atmosphere was no different than the southwest when I lived there. I came to admire and enjoyed the local tribal cultures I occasionally stumbled upon. But I certainly didn't expect anyone here to appreciate the fact that I was very sympathetic not only to their history but also to their current plight.

Under the circumstances, I half expected the radio announcer to provide a description of my car and its current location. The irony of the situation didn't go un-noticed either. The town I was going to was about fifteen miles from Wounded Knee, which is a place of great symbolism for some elements of the Indian movement.

According to the popular history: On December 29, 1890 US Army troops killed about 150 men, women and children of the Lakota Tribe. It is recognized as the end of the war between the white Europeans and the native Americans. Then: on February 27, 1973 a group of Indians staged a protest at the site of the Wounded Knee massacre. Russell Means, who appeared in the recent movie, *The Last of the Mohicans*, was the leader of the American Indian Movement (AIM) engaged in this (I bumped into him years later on the metro in DC, when they opened the Native American Museum there, something of a hero of mine). I don't think most people could find South Dakota on a map much less Wounded Knee; but the nerve of some Indians occupying some space and staging a protest resulting in a federal siege which lasted over two months and involved the deaths of two US Marshals. There are conflicting voices over the circumstances of the unfortunate deaths of the two Marshals, the Indian's and the government's. I have no idea which is closest to the truth.

It was clear, just based on the radio, that both sides had yet to kiss and make up. So I was picking up a lot of negative waves. I spent the night at a little flea-bag motel and first thing in the morning left to go to the town.

I was driving in the middle of no-where, just some rolling hills of high desert plain with traces of snow scattered around and found the town after rounding a bend in the road. The town itself was in nowhere's ville. No residences anywhere and nobody on the street. I don't know if the place even had a name. It was like something out of the *Twilight Zone*. Normally in a situation like this, I'd go to

Fortress of Deceit

the local tribal police headquarters and let them know I was in their territory, show some brotherly law enforcement officer respect, and check if they could help out. But in this case I was too embarrassed to tell them what I was doing here, and hoped that I'd be able to sneak in and out before they knew I was here.

As I recall, the town itself consisted of four or five buildings. While the road I came in on was paved, the one crossroad was a dirt road. I passed a post office which was flying the stars and stripes flag, the state flag of South Dakota and what I assumed was a local tribal banner. The post office was by far the best maintained building in town. I'd get back to the post office later to see if they could help me out in trying to find my perpetrator. So I parked my car in front of the largest building in town, about the size of a modest one family home. It was obvious that it was a general store of some type and I hoped to get some coffee and maybe something to eat. Upon entering the store I observed that I had nearly as much food in my refrigerator and cupboards back home as was contained in the entire store. So I settled on some fermented bottled juice and a packaged stale donut.

Not too many strangers stopped in this town much less bought anything at the general store. So it was easy starting a conversation with the proprietor. We started off with just some miscellaneous talking and I ended up spending four hours talking to him, getting a valuable and extremely interesting rendition of the history and present situation on the reservation.

Turns out the proprietor was a half-breed Indian (indian/white) (he used the term "Indian", not "Native American", as well as "half-breed"), and was one of the lawyers representing some of the Indians from the 1973 incident. It was a fascinating story, and he even helped me out in tracking down the person I was looking for. I left him a business card which he stuck on the counter wall behind him, adjacent to a handful of other business cards. But after four hours I had to get back to the hunt.

I spoke to a few more people and soon found myself driving up a dirt road toward the mountains, across dry creek beds and over rickety bridges. There weren't any road signs or addresses to look for. The directions I received were things like: turn into the mountains just before the third creek then follow the road till you come to a "Y" and turn left, drive for about ten to fifteen miles till you see a broken tree and turn toward the open desert.

I missed some of the turns and had to backtrack a number of times. Driving over a creek bed without realizing it was a creek or missing a turn as the dirt road at times was nearly indistinguishable from the surrounding countryside. Being mid-winter, the sun set early, combined with rolling dark clouds it was pitch black by about five or six in the afternoon.

Several times I had to get out of my car, flashlight in hand and make sure a bridge was sturdy enough and wide enough to accommodate my car. During the day in this type of environment the ground would frequently thaw out and with the aid of the melting snow would turn the road to mush, but at night the freezing temperatures would re-freeze the road, so I wasn't particularly concerned about getting stuck unless I ran into a ditch or a small bridge collapsed beneath me.

After a couple of hours of driving through the hills I finally found what I was looking for; a makeshift shack, about the size of a one car garage, situated in the middle of nowhere. I turned my headlights off as I drove the car into what passed for a driveway and stared at the curtained window for a few moments to see if anyone noticed my arrival and looked out the window. They hadn't. This would be an advantage.

I sat in my car for about a minute just assessing the situation. It was a bitterly cold evening, no light anywhere except for the glow from the curtained window and cracks in the house itself. I couldn't tell if it was snowing or just the wind blowing the ground snow almost horizontally across the landscape. No other houses were visible, no telephone poles, no car, no nothing.

The only other characters in the scene were two dogs who didn't seem to be the most welcoming of creatures. One was a tiny ankle biter dog that was barking as ferociously as it's nature permitted. I could barely hear it barking around different positions about the car, above the howl of the wind. How it survived outside in these conditions was beyond me. The other dog was a massive hound, standing on all four feet it was looking directly at me through the driver's side window, eye to eye. It just growled and bared its teeth at me. The Hound of the Baskerville's resurrected, was the first thought I had as we just starred at each other for a few moments.

The dogs didn't really have me too concerned about my personal safety. I most always got along well with animals; more so than with a lot of people. In the worst case scenario I could shoot the dogs if my life depended on it. But this was such a ridiculously stupid reason for me being here in the first place that my first priority was to make sure I left here without harming the animals, or having the situation deteriorate to the point where I might have to defend myself from whomever was in the house.

Fortress of Deceit

As I assessed the situation, I couldn't determine which was the most pathetic; the extreme poverty of this place or the agency actually sending me out here to do this nonsense. I knew no indian in his right mind around here would open the door to some pale face government agent and invite me inside, particularly on a night like this.

Now that I found the place I seriously considered turning around and going back to the motel. It took me some two hours to find this place once I left the main road; and it wasn't worth coming back to in the morning, plus I had to leave tomorrow for my return flight home.

In keeping within the finest traditions of the agency (and I mean this seriously), I wasn't about to falsify my report by stating that I actually talked to the residents here if I didn't actually make the attempt. Nor was I prepared to document in my report that I made it this far, got cold feet, and left without completing the investigation. So my only real option was to bang on the guy's door and see what happens.

So I unclasped the buttons on my overcoat except for the bottom one. I carried my firearm in a shoulder holster and wanted to make sure I could easily get to it should the need arise. I kept the bottom button clasped to keep the coat from flapping around and provide some protection from the wind and the cold.

I also took my gloves off. I didn't want to have to fumble with my gloves should I have to draw my weapon or fiddle with my car keys should I need to leave in a hurry. If everything worked as planned my hands would be exposed to the cold only for a few minutes and I could take that with little concern.

Fortress of Deceit

So I opened the car door a few inches and the big dog lunged inside after me. But his shoulders couldn't make it past the opening. I held the door tight and effectively had the dog's head wedged between the door frame and the door. I kept squeezing the door tighter until the dog stopped growling at me. He couldn't come in and couldn't escape, neither could I at that point. When the dog relaxed a bit I petted his head, scratched him under the chin and let him sniff my hand.

I then opened the car door and pushed my way out. I decided to roll down the driver's window and leave the car running – in the event I had to make a tactical retreat. At this point the hound was very friendly, a bit too friendly. He kept standing on his hind legs trying to either lick my face or maybe even take a bite out of it. On his hind legs, the dog was a little taller than I am, at a bit over 5'10". As I was walking toward the house it was a simple matter to sidestep a little so the dog couldn't rest his front legs on me and kept falling down to all four feet on the ground. This just kept him jumping up and down around me as I walked the thirty feet or so from the car to the house.

As I approached the house I observed that the entire front of the house consisted of several wooden doors, miscellaneous pieces of wood and sheets of metal, all fastened together somehow to form a wall. I wasn't even sure which of the doors actually functioned as a door and which made up the wall.

When I stopped walking, the big dog was now able to plant his front feet on my torso without falling down and would bring his teeth toward my face. Every time he jumped up on me I'd put my left forearm into his neck to keep his teeth away from my head. This caused the dog to fall back on all fours and lunge at me from a different direction.

I found myself in a wrestling match in which I'd eventually lose. While this dance was going on the little ankle biter dog was acting according its nature and was gnawing on my right ankle. Under the circumstances, what with wrestling with the big dog, the bitter cold, the adrenaline, and trying to do my job, I just ignored the little mutt.

At one point when the big dog fell to all four feet I grabbed the skin around his neck and with all the strength of my left arm I was able to keep his head down against my left knee. This allowed me a moment to peak through a crack between the doors/wall and I could see that the sole sources of light in the place came from a fireplace and an incandescent light bulb dangling from a wire several feet from the ceiling. Must have a generator going here, but I couldn't hear it what with the roaring of the wind. Clear plastic sheeting covered the interior walls to cut down on the wind inside. Otherwise things were quiet. Apparently, with the howling of the wind, and the *security* their dogs provided, they didn't hear or maybe just ignored the drama going on in their front yard.

So I knocked on what I thought was the door and could barely see through a crack in the wall that two people, at least, were inside. An old man answered me through the wall but wouldn't open the door. For two or three minutes the two of us engaged, in English, in some futile conversation with each other with me trying to squeeze out of him the current location of his nephew, and he insisting he hasn't seen him for several years. At one point he said something in his native language, as if he was ordering his dogs to eat the pale face forked tongue devil on his doorstep.

Fortress of Deceit

I assumed the individual I was looking for was in the house – but so what.

This was as pointless as I figured it would be so I decided to leave. Satisfied that I could document that I wasted enough tax-payer's money on this nonsense in the best of government work. It was an easy matter navigating back to the motel. Just keep heading downhill.

After I arrived back at the motel I discovered that my over-coat was ripped to shreds from the paws of the big dog and the little one tore up my trousers and broke the skin when he was chewing on my ankle – the full length thermal underwear I wore provided protection for more than the cold. A little first aid and I was fine. Including travel time and paper work, I spent about five days on this case. While I treated my ankle I figured that little dog survived these brutal elements out of sheer meanness.

Unfortunately, this nonsense didn't end here. Within two or three weeks of my adventures at Wounded Knee, my partner was given the task of tracking down another recently discharged service member with an African American ethnic background – and asked me to assist; which, of course, I did. As with my Native American friend, this individual committed a minor crime before his discharge, something that barely qualified as a misdemeanor and we knew that no JAG Officer or DA would waste any time with it. Our mission, which we had no choice but to accept, wasn't to apprehend the perpetrator but to find him and try to get a statement from him describing his side of the story. We couldn't legally arrest him for this misdemeanor.

The man's last known family address was in the middle of Chicago. Hopefully things have changed for the better; but in the mid to late 80's, Chicago had a series of mountain ranges of high rise tenement buildings inhabited entirely by poor folks with an African ethnic background. Just based on local news stories the place was rife with crime: drugs, prostitution, muggings, thefts, murders, violent gangs, the whole gamut. The place we were going was right near the middle of it. So I packed some extra ammunition, suited up in my body armor and off we went.

The first thing we did was go to the local police precinct as a professional courtesy to let the local cops know that we were encroaching on their territory for a brief time. Unless one was working on something really sensitive or required a bit of covert or surreptitious activity, a little bit of notification to another law enforcement agency with adjacent or overlapping jurisdiction could go a long way towards smoothing out any potential difficulties. In this case, there wasn't anything secretive about what we were going to do, it was just plain dumb.

We also had the additional motivation that if the guano hit the fan our lives might depend on them to extract us. If they knew ahead of time that some fellow law enforcement officers were in the area and needed assistance they might expedite their response.

So we spent about a half hour with a police lieutenant who gave us a brief rundown of the recent history of the place. He also explained that the police don't even patrol these neighborhoods so as to avoid sparking off a major incident. He was very helpful and at one point he asked for our office phone number, in the event, he explained, that he might need to call our office in case anything untoward happened. A few minutes later he excused himself and invited us to look at a map of the area. He came back to us a few minutes after that with something of a smirk on his face. I suspect that he called our office up to confirm that we really did work for the feds and to see if we were really as dumb as we appeared to be.

But he gave us his personal office phone number and told us to call him directly if we needed any help and he'd send their equivalent of a SWAT team to fish us out of there. It was a nice gesture, but these were the days before cell phones and the only way we'd be able to call him is by smashing into someone's apartment and hope they had a working telephone. We did have a radio in the car but it had very limited range and probably wouldn't work in the valleys of these man-made mountain ranges, plus we had our own frequency (which wouldn't even reach our own dispatch office from this distance).

So with a renewed buoyancy and adrenaline starting to rise we headed for this war zone. I wished I had brought more ammo but was grateful for wearing my body armor. Something I rarely did except on raids and such.

It was another bitterly cold Chicago day. I was wearing my firearm in a shoulder rig beneath my brand new overcoat. Once we arrived at the towers it took another thirty minutes or so to find the right building. We then drove around the building once and scoped out the quickest route to escape should the need arise. Nobody was out on the street, it was too cold. Nobody was driving a car either, although there were a number of parked cars. We parked our car directly in front of the building and stepped out.

As I recall, the apartment building was some ten to twelve stories high. Each apartment opened up to the outside onto a walkway. The whole front face of the building was covered with a wire mesh fence that prevented anyone from falling or being thrown off the walkway. The wire mesh itself consisted of holes a little smaller than the size of a tennis ball, a standard chain-link fence, but was transparent enough to clearly see the doors and windows beyond. There were only two ways to get to the upper floors. A stairwell and elevator construction was attached to either end of the building.

Every building around here looked exactly the same. The building on the opposite side of the road opened up just like this one, facing the road. The apartment we were after was on the fifth floor, so we entered one of the stairwells and prepared to hoof it up. The stairwell/elevator combination was unheated, enclosed in a brick wall except for little glassless windows on each landing covered with the same iron mesh netting. There weren't any artificial lights in the stairwells either so it took a moment for our eyes to adjust. I pulled out my flashlight (which I carried everywhere, got in that habit from my survival camping days) and looked inside the unlit elevator. I wasn't going to ride the elevator but was checking to make sure no one was hiding inside. Instead I found piles of feces and a pool of as yet un-frozen urine.

So we walked a few feet to the stairwell and my flashlight revealed that more of the same was on the stairs. The extreme cold numbed the smell. We backed out of the stairwell and decided to try the stairs on the opposite side of the building. So we just casually walked down the sidewalk in the front of the building as if we were just out for a Sunday stroll. About half way down the sidewalk I noticed that some very big and well-dressed black guy was staring at us through the wire mesh on the third floor of the opposite building. This just encouraged us to walk slower and act *cooler*.

As we neared the stairwell I already had my flashlight out, then entered the cavern, checked out the elevator and stairs and found the same toilet situation. We resolved that the only way to get this job done and get out of here as quickly as possible was to walk through this mess, do our stuff and get out of here.

With the aid of my flashlight we avoided stepping in the piles of feces, but with the herd of people walking these stairs the stuff was tracked all over the place and you couldn't help stepping in it. We side stepped most of the pools of unfrozen urine and crunched through the frozen part. When we reached the third floor I stepped into the walkway to check on our car. It was still there and no one was near it. The street was still vacant, but two more gentlemen joined the first one we noticed on the third floor of the adjacent building.

Finally we landed on the fifth floor and counted our way down the apartments until we arrived at our target apartment about half way down the walkway. I was behind my partner and he whispered to me that one of the local muscle was standing at the far stairwell, just staring at us. As we neared the final steps to the apartment I took off my right glove and was about to open my coat in order to have quicker access to my firearm and simultaneously turned to check our rear, just in time to see another muscle-head stop at the end of the landing behind us.

Long before the days of the cell phone these guys had a pretty good surveillance and response system set up. But I didn't want to appear like a buffoon fumbling with my coat, nor did I want to provoke a violent response from the watch dogs, so I just slipped my right hand inside my coat pocket hoping the goons would think I was holding onto my hand gun.

Fortress of Deceit

I backed up to the brick wall and just kept alternating looking from one goon to the next, trying to appear as cool and casual as I could muster. Loud music was playing in the apartment and my partner had to bang on the door several times to get somebody's attention.

Finally, what sounded like a teenage girl's voice, somebody finally answered his summons to open the door. She complained that she couldn't understand him on account of the loud music [inside her own apartment]. My partner was yelling back that she might want to turn down the music but this suggestion was useless. I'm sure this screaming match went over well with the two goons.

Eventually he was able to get out of her that our subject wasn't home and she didn't know where he was. This was turning out to be as pointless an exercise as we both knew it would be. We didn't have a warrant for his arrest and no search warrant. If she didn't want to open the door for us she was perfectly within her rights not to do so.

After a few minutes my partner and I just glanced at each other and we agreed that it was time to get out of here. With my right hand still in my coat pocket grasping a non-existent gun, we walked toward one of the stairwells. As we approached the guard dog, he said, "What chew doin here man?" And in a pained effort to maintain my cool exterior I responded with, "Well, we're not selling cookies." And just kept walking with a very forced slow gait.

As we entered the stairwell, we passed another muscle-head just standing there. I guessed, based on his slightly heavy breathing that he probably just ran up the stairs and stopped when he heard us coming around the corner.

Fortress of Deceit

When we were out of earshot of the goons we just started jibbing each other about running down the stairs as fast as we could and beating feet out of this neighborhood; but we decided that if we ran we'd probably slip on the stairs and wind up covered with all this slop. So we just ambled on as if we owned the place. As we were walking I also removed my revolver from its holster and held onto it hidden within my coat pocket, just in case. And for real this time.

At the second floor landing I strolled onto the walkway and glanced at our car to see if we'd have any unwanted company. Nobody was on the street, the intense cold gave a warming and welcoming embrace in this environment and probably prevented this nonsense from escalating.

Once we reached the ground level and outside we just started laughing. My partner had the car keys and I reminded him to make sure he opened the passenger side door before he ripped out of here, or else six rounds of my revolver would be in hot pursuit of his back. Before I even had my seat belt buckled he floored the gas pedal and we careened out of the projects ignoring the traffic signals and stop signs.

About fifteen minutes later, when we were safely ensconced on the open road we pulled over next to a phone booth, too embarrassed to re-appear in front of the police lieutenant again, and I just gave him a quick call to inform him that we concluded our business and that if anything happens there now, it's not our doing. He just chuckled, thanked us for letting him know, and hung up. I cleaned my shoes as best I could by shuffling my feet through several piles of snow. Instead of going straight back to the office we detoured to our respective homes, I ended up throwing my shoes away. It was pointless trying to clean them. A quick change of clothes and back to the office to fill out the time sheets, after another complete waste of a day.

Well, about this time several agents in my office (myself included) pretty much had had it with the management team in our office. Each of us, quite independently from each other, submitted formal grievances to Headquarters complaining of our managers.

Headquarters, in turn, sent a couple of their trusted managers to our office and conducted something of an investigation. In my interview with the headquarters managers I informed them our bosses were dangerously incompetent and were either going to get one or more of us killed or they were going to place us in an unnecessarily hazardous situation in which we might have to kill someone else in self-defense, and for no good reason. There were also some lesser allegations such as management engaging in reprisal toward those of us who resisted doing the frivolous work we were assigned instead of concentrating on our primary mission.

It took several months for headquarters to finish their investigation, which for the federal government was actually pretty quick. In my naiveté of the time I fully expected that headquarters would want to know about its incompetent managers and deal with them appropriately. But I was grievously disappointed to learn that headquarters sided with the managers.

In their final report, headquarters made two very salient points: The first was that they admitted that our managers "may" have a problem with judgment but that they nevertheless acted fully within the scope of their duties as managers. The second point provided a listing of the many and varied duties of a Special Agent. This list included things like: investigate felony crime, conduct crime scene processing, interview witnesses and suspects, process evidence, observe autopsies, conduct security assessments of certain military installations, engage in protective service details and a host of other duties. Last on the list, and which received special emphasis in their report, was "and other duties as assigned." Essentially, headquarters told us that we were screwed. In a subsequent conversation with one of the managers involved in this charade of a process, I asked him at what point would headquarters like to know when these managers go totally off the deep end. He asked me to explain. So I said words to the effect, "For instance, if these clowns assign me a long term project to do nothing but count how many times the sun sets every day, would you want to know about that"? He just glared at me. I figured my career was pretty much over and first started to consider a different line of work. But the situation which clinched my decision to leave the agency was when I was assigned another ridiculous waste of time of a case.

This was the notorious case of the missing base fiddle. Right after I came into work one morning my boss told me to drop what I was doing and go over to the storage facility of the military Band to investigate a burglary. So being the dutiful Special Agent I went immediately to the base band and discovered that someone walked off with their base fiddle.

In the U.S. military, there is a very good system of inventory controls which is designed to keep track of absolutely all military hardware and property. This includes everything from missiles to small arms ammunition to stationary. You can't use so much as a military shoe lace without ensuring that all the forms are appropriately filled out. Of course, sometimes the system breaks under its own weight and things go asunder. Which is what we had here.

When I arrived at the base's band building I interviewed the sailor who reported the crime. Turns out he had just assumed the duties of OIC (Officer in Command) of the base band about two weeks prior. In the course of doing the change of command inventory of the property he was responsible for, he discovered that a base fiddle was missing. So he did what he was supposed to do; reported the missing property through official channels and it eventually made it to my office.

Initiating my examination of the crime scene, there were no signs of forced entry into the storage room so I proceeded to interview and obtain statements from a number of the current band members. Turns out the fiddle was a piece of junk. It had no strings, a broken neck, cracked body, and was piled up into a corner waiting to get thrown away anyway. The former OIC never bothered to have the fiddle "surveyed" or properly documented, certified, and verified that it was junk so it could be thrown away.

So I made the investigative conclusion of one of two possibilities: first, some young band member, not familiar with the military bureaucracy, figured he was doing everyone a favor and just threw the fiddle away; or two, the same type of bureaucratically naïve sailor pilfered the fiddle for his/her own nefarious reasons. In either case, who cares, he did the band a favor, my report documented these possibilities, case closed. I had already wasted enough time on this bogus burglary.

But NOOOO! My boss wasn't satisfied. This was US military property and it must be found, regardless of the cost. By this time I already knew my boss was insane, and the brass in Washington loved insanity, but I figured I might be able to turn the table on this nonsense and use the system against itself to put an end to this crap.

I decided to do an extremely thorough job on this case, more so that what would normally be required even if it was a legitimate case. My intention was to make this case such a ridiculous monstrosity of a waste of time and man power that in the inevitable bureaucratic review of on-going investigations it would raise a red flag with somebody in authority.

So I interviewed every member of the base band I could find. I interviewed friends of the band members. I interviewed people who ever saw the band play (to determine if they remembered seeing the base fiddle).

Conducting an interview in a criminal investigation wasn't just a matter of talking to someone for two minutes while we're walking down the street. The suspect or witness either had to come to my office or I'd have to track them down at their duty station. Then they'd have to write out a statement, I'd review it for accuracy and completeness, and they'd have to swear to its truthfulness under oath. Even if they had nothing relevant to say, this process could take an hour or more, not counting travel time or other paper work I'd have to do on this in order to appropriately document that the interview took place.

At this point in the investigation the information I obtained was that most of these people remembered that the fiddle disappeared several months prior to this incident being reported and that one person in particular seemed to have become particularly friendly with the fiddle. Occasionally seen in close proximity to the fiddle and even touching it. The suspect was also transferred to an overseas duty station at the approximate time frame in which the fiddle disappeared.

Several other former band members had also been transferred about the time the fiddle disappeared. The possible international implications of this case only egged me on further. I sent investigative "leads" (requests for assistance) to agency offices around the world asking them to track down the suspects I identified to them and conduct an appropriate investigation.

I was convinced that at least one of these agency offices would refuse to waste the manpower on such a frivolous case. But I was wrong, over the following couple of weeks, reports of their investigations gradually filtered back to me. These reports documented not only the statements of the suspects that were interviewed but also the results of the searches of their private living quarters and personal property. All of which resulted in negative findings, no base fiddle was found.

The one hold out was the suspect whom others testified that he seemed to have developed a special fondness for the fiddle. Turns out he was assigned to a unit that was currently on deployment and which was based in Italy, and the unit wasn't due back for another month. So I went about my other business in the meantime.

When the month passed I received correspondence from the Italy based agency agents stating they had found the base fiddle. As it happened, two agents met the unit as it returned to its base. They immediately detained the suspect in question, who readily admitted he had the fiddle. Turns out the suspect was fairly new in the military and wasn't familiar with the paper work bureaucracy. He assumed he was doing the military a favor by getting rid of the junk of a fiddle. He put lots of his own money into repairing the fiddle, getting it into fully operating condition. But that wasn't the end of the mystery.

    The perpetrator was subject to what is called a "Captain's Mast" or non-judicial punishment. This type of proceeding is for relatively minor disciplinary actions that the Commanding Officer of any unit has the legal authority to conduct as a means of maintaining discipline. Sanctions are limited to such things as restricting the person to the base, assigning additional duties, or docking the pay of the suspect in limited amounts and for a limited duration. Whatever the penalty, none of it justified agency involvement. I don't recall the specific penalties the person was subjected too.

    Meanwhile, the agents in Italy had this big base fiddle taking up all the room in their evidence locker and I drafted a message back to them that they should just let the sailor have it, dock his pay for the assessed value of the fiddle (which was negligible, since they were going to throw it away anyway), slap the sailor on the hand and end this nonsense. It was clear that my attempt to use the system against itself for the purpose of achieving something positive, had failed. It was time to stop wasting time on this case. But when my boss reviewed my note I was chewed out again. "This is United States Military property and must be returned to its assigned post of duty", he raged. So off went a message to Italy stating that the base fiddle had to be shipped back to us.

    Several more weeks went by when I received a phone call from the base's shipping and receiving warehouse. They told me they had a great big wooden box on their floor with my name on it and I needed to take it off their hands.

Yes, indeed, it was a big wooden box I discovered when I arrived at the warehouse. It was a custom made wooden crate, about the size of two coffins laying adjacent to each other. The fiddle couldn't just be shipped the cheapest way, it had to be properly handled as "evidence" just as if it was crucial evidence of a murder case. It was in a plastic wrapped, sealed, custom designed interior to keep the fiddle secure, a ton of insulation and an extremely sturdy crate. The crate itself was craftsman quality. It was a real shame to break it open.

I called the base band up and had them meet me at the receiving warehouse. When I saw the crate I immediately started laughing and kept giggling for nearly the whole hour that it took to break open the crate and unwrap the fiddle. The crate was so heavy that a crane was needed to move it but none was available, so we had to unwrap it where it lay, much to the concern of the shipping and receiving people. They literally thought they had a human being on ice in the crate, that combined with my constant giggling, they were really concerned.

As soon as I found the paperwork I signed the shipment over to the band, and finished writing up the case when I returned to the office. Case closed.

I lamented the whole situation. I estimated this cost the tax payer about $10,000 in those days. Not only in terms of the scores of man-hours expended, including not only mine but that of the agents overseas, but it cost a small fortune just to pack up the fiddle and ship it. It may also have ruined the career of an otherwise highly motivated and spirited service member and most certainly soured his attitude about the military. I even received something passing for a "pat on the back" for a job well done from the boss man.

Fortress of Deceit

It was time for me to leave. In the waning months of my career with the agency I did a lot of soul searching, trying to figure out what I wanted to do with my career. On the one hand I was so disenchanted about working for the federal government that I wanted nothing to do with it anymore. On the other hand, working for a civilian company, selling shoes or sitting in an office all day would drive me nuts. I also realized that not all of my experience working as criminal investigator for the agency was as negative as I have portrayed. Some of it was quite fulfilling work and something of the challenge I was looking for. These Special Agents certainly knew how to conduct an investigation; something I took for granted at the time, but later realized was quite astonishing. I also realized that these Special Agents do more work in a year than most people do in five.

One of the more interesting criminal cases I worked on was assisting in a suspected serial murderer investigation. I spent nearly a month going to all the police departments in Illinois and Wisconsin going through all their unsolved murder files that occurred within the two year time frame I was looking through – a time frame in which the suspect was known to have lived in the area. The purpose was to find any commonalities between these unsolved murders and the victims of the suspected serial murderer that was recently arrested in a different part of the country. Went through over 700 files. Found a few that were similar and reported the details up the chain. I found it incomprehensible what some humans do, not to mention the scale of these crimes. Not related to the serial case, but one of the more grotesque files I looked through was the murder of some old lady, the murderer tried getting rid of the evidence by flushing her down the toilet in pieces, at least until it clogged up.

Fortress of Deceit

The training provided by the agency was top notch. Including everything from processing homicide scenes to interview/interrogation techniques to advanced weapons training. Even some of the other work we did was interesting: conducting security surveys of sensitive military facilities, protecting visiting foreign military dignitaries, and even "other duties as assigned"; but this wasn't enough to keep me in this outfit. It was the agency's job to clean the house of the military, but if the agency couldn't clean its own house I didn't want anything to do with it. It also hit me kind of hard, the seed was planted when I was working in narcotics interdiction and later confirmed with this outfit: There was a symbiotic relationship between crime and federal law enforcement. Federal law enforcement depended on the criminals to keep up their fine work (otherwise we'd all be out of a job), and the criminals depended on the lame law enforcement efforts so they could continue their nefarious activities. The more crime the better, made all the parties happy in this expensive dance. I can't say that the federal government actually propagated crime, but the government certainly didn't have the heart to eliminate or even attempt to minimize crime (with some exceptions). The law enforcement bureaucracies depended on the continued viability and growth of crime for their own sustenance. From my experience, on the street level the front line cops dutifully and bravely did what they could to fight crime, but on the senior administrative levels it was clear that the maintenance and growth of the bureaucracy was paramount, not the elimination of, or even minimizing of crime. It was also the first taste of enforced mediocrity in government that I observed.

Being thick headed, it also finally dawned on me that working all these violent crime cases was taking its emotional toll on me too. My partner and I developed a *gallows humor* that enveloped us like a cloud, but preceded us everywhere. Even at lunch or the occasional dinner out we'd try making each other sick by comparing each other's food to the latest autopsy we just sat through, or the latest victim we had to interview in the hospital, or the latest crime scene. Talking about this stuff was nothing compared to sticking your fingers in it, breathing in the fumes, and being around it all the time. So we made a big joke about it – just to relieve the stress. The clincher though occurred when about eight or nine of us from the office went out to lunch one day – I think it was for someone's birthday. After we all received our food, my partner and I just naturally drifted into a malodorous discussion of our respective lunches, oblivious of everyone else around. At one point in a sudden fright he grabbed my hand as I was about to stab for more spaghetti and in a loud voice said, "Don't eat that!", and slowly pulled a strand of spaghetti off my plate wiggling it around exclaiming, "that looks like a vein." I carefully grabbed the red sauced covered spaghetti out of his hand, intensely examined it, gently wiggled it as if it were alive, put it my mouth, and with exaggerated chewing motion I said, "ya know, I think you're right, it is a vein." And suddenly everyone else just got up and moved to another table.

My partner and I just starred at each other for a few moments wondering what's going on. We had a brief discussion about maybe we should tone down our rhetoric a bit, but then decided to hell with it, any time anyone else wanted to help out on our cases they'd be welcome to it. No volunteers.

And, to top it all off, I never even came close to engaging in counter-espionage work, which is why I joined the agency in the first place. I discovered that this wasn't much of a priority despite the fact that the Soviets were heavily targeting this component of the military. Part of this was entirely bureaucratic. It could take months of an agent's time to engage in just one effective counter-espionage situation (trying to hunt down and thwart a would-be spy), but that still only counted as one bean. During that same time frame an agent could plant scores of beans working traditional crime cases; so it was more productive in this bean counting bureaucratic culture to have agents working crime (even petty crime) cases than it was to engage in even one counter-espionage case – which would have had a much greater positive impact on the security of this country.

This bean counting culture also manifested itself in another area: Once an agency saturated itself with beans and couldn't figure out how to generate and count more beans, they'd engage in mission creep. That's why the FBI (in my opinion) when I was still involved in the drug war slowly started getting more involved in interdiction activities even though there was already a whole agency set up whose sole responsibility was executing that drug war – namely the Drug Enforcement Administration.

I also believed that there was an even higher level interest in not engaging in more effective counter-espionage efforts: If an enemy stole sensitive military secrets from us, that was used as an argument to spend even more money to further advance the military/industrial complex, to continue staying at least one step ahead of what we allowed the bad guys to steal from us, rather than prevent the theft in the first place. This expensive dance continues, all thanks to the ignorant and compliant taxpayer/voter and total lack of interest on Congress's part. This experience also exposed me to bureaucratic bigotry and stupidity: Some of my comrades told me that my name was too *soviet* looking to risk having me serve in that section.

Fortress of Deceit

I stopped watching cop shows/movies because of this experience. They're too nauseating to sit through, and not because of the gore. But I did develop a healthy respect and admiration of those cops on the front line that deal with these monsters on a daily basis, not to mention my fellow agency colleagues. But this was not my path in the river of life.

CHAPTER SIX
The Tombstone Agency

+

There is nothing so important as trifles.
Sherlock Holmes

+

+

As the river of life would have it (around 1987-8); I found myself in a violent eddy of a current, swirling round and round, desperately trying to escape and continue my journey downstream. But I couldn't find my way out of this trap and felt like all I was doing was keeping my head above water. I happened to meet another individual who eventually recruited me to work for the Security Division of the Federal Aviation Administration. Sam (not his real name) was a former agency Special Agent that previously worked in the same office I did, but quit just a short while before I started there. Every few months he'd drop in on the office just to visit with his old buds there.

Sam was another one of those unique and memorable individuals that one occasionally stumbles across in life. He was a charismatic Italian, spent some ten years as a Chicago police officer and got a job doing the same BS I was doing with the same agency. He lasted about a year though before he was able to get an in-house (federal) transfer to FAA Security. I had the feeling that Sam knew all the important people in Chicago and everyone else knew Sam. We both felt pretty much the same about the agency. Many special agents in the federal government really get off being able to carry a gun around and having federal *police* credentials. This stuff didn't do anything for me. I didn't look at a gun any differently than I did an ink pen and pad of paper. It was just a tool to get a certain type of work accomplished. Although I did strive to become proficient with its use. So

Fortress of Deceit

Sam comes along and explains that FAA Security is looking for a few good men – that can shoot.

In the mid-late 80s the world was hit with a wave of relatively small scale terrorist attacks. Most of these were centered in Europe and the Mediterranean theater and most were perpetrated by muslim radicals. Although there were some indigenous anarchist types about, most of these latter types were spawned as a result of the anti-Vietnam war protests or the old European colonial era around the world; but these were gradually petering out due to lack of interest. Most of these terrorist attacks consisted of small bombings as well as airplane, cruise ship and train hijackings including targeting the US which had some of its own commercial air carriers hijacked during this time frame.

Perhaps the most notorious incident involved the hijacking of TWA-847 in which the US Navy sailor Robert Stethem was killed and his body dumped on the tarmac of Beirut airport. As a result of all of these, but particularly the 847 hijacking, the Security Division of the Federal Aviation Administration was ordered to ramp up its Federal Air Marshal (FAM) service. So they started hiring a lot of former cops and ex-military types to fill the bill. So at Sam's urging I applied for and was accepted as a FAM.

In my initial application process I was interviewed by three managers who made it very clear that they have neither the expertise nor the experience to engage in anti-terrorist activity and they were looking for the next generation of employees to come in with that expertise. They assured me that with my background as an officer in the military, as a federal special agent, and with my graduate education in security that I would have a meteoric career. I assumed at the time, but you know what happens when one assumes, that they meant that I'd be a rising star as opposed to crashing and burning as meteors tend to do. The latter turned out to be the prophetic statement on their part.

But there were some problems in bringing me on board. Due to the over-riding diversity issues involved they had to hire a black male, in his mid-40s, with a high school equivalency degree whose career highlight was working as a bank security guard. For some construed reasoning he was rated as more qualified for the job than I was. Since he only qualified at the lowest pay grade, I had to come in at the lowest pay grade too.

Well, it still didn't take me long to decide to transfer to FAA anyway. I'd gut out the pay cut and reduced pay grade and chalk it up to my contribution to diversity. I had to leave my current agency as that environment was slowly killing me; but more importantly, applying my skills and interests to the *war on terrorism* was the dream occupation I was looking for.

I was based at O'Hare Airport in Chicago. A few weeks after I showed up at the office I was sent away to FAM basic school which was located at an obscure government air base in Arizona. The base was actually part of the same FLETC organization that I had previously gone through in Georgia and was known as FLETC West.

In any type of basic federal law enforcement or military training the stress level is only natural to increase on the part of the new students. On the first day I observed a lot of the students in my class had trepidations about the course, not least of which was being located in the middle of a desert, miles from civilization. The class consisted of about thirty individuals. Roughly half had prior military or law enforcement backgrounds including from military elite units, several federal law enforcement agencies including the FBI, as well as various state and local law enforcement agencies. The other half didn't have any relevant backgrounds. Most of these were secretaries or admin types from the FAA, which didn't seem right given the potential volatile environment that we were expected to operate under. But mine's not to reason why.

In my case, however, I was in paradise. I was back in the desert, which I had come to love from my previous tours of duty in the desert, plus, for the first time in my career I felt like I was in the proper current in the river of life. And just being away from the agency was a vacation in itself. I ended up excelling in all the various disciplines we were trained in; everything from academics, physical fitness, unarmed combat, shooting skills, and explosives. Even my previous unhealed broken bones popped back into place.

On graduation day, it was another typical government ceremony, not unlike when I graduated from the Special Agent course for the agency. They made a point of honoring folks in three categories: academics, physical fitness and shooting skills. I missed getting the academic award by a percentage point. Five of us received the physical fitness award including myself; and I was tied with two other guys for the tactical shooting skills with near perfect scores on the final shooting exercise. For the first time in my career I felt I was on the right path and everything just fell into place.

As one might have guessed, at one point in the ceremony we had to stand up, raise our right hand, and take that gawd-forsaken irrelevant oath again. Swearing to abide by the US Constitution when we didn't spend one minute in a two month course even reading the document. This time around I just winced a bit; as I was eager and enthusiastic to get back to my office and fire up my new vocation.

By this time in my career I had a bit more experience and knowledge under my belt. Among other things I had the opportunity to expose myself both operationally and/or academically to some of the internal mechanics of outlaw motorcycle gangs, the mafia, and other criminal fringe organizations. One of the more interesting things I learned about the mafia is that they had a ceremony when a new recruit was accepted into the *family*, he had to swear an oath to the organization. Even in some outlaw motorcycle gangs, when a new member was accepted into the group, they engaged in a ceremony where the recruit had to swear an oath to that gang. In both cases, if a member violated that oath they would be dealt with in the harshest manner – which usually meant being killed. But in the federal government, when one is required to take an oath of loyalty and abide by the rules (ie: the Constitution) you don't even have to know what you're swearing an oath too. On top of that, if you break your oath there's no penalty whatsoever. It wasn't till years later, regarding my attempts to prevent 9/11 that I discovered that one is actually penalized for abiding by this oath.

Upon FAM graduation, I put all these philosophical issues aside and just jumped into the appropriate current of life that I was meant for. As it turned out, working as a Federal Air Marshal made up only half my job. The other half was that I functioned as an FAA Special Agent. In fact, I had to go to another government basic agent course but this was entirely an FAA academic course based at the FAA's big training facility in Oklahoma City, Oklahoma and only lasted about two weeks. This was probably the most difficult training course I've ever been through. Not because it was hard but because it put you to sleep. Any one that actually stayed awake all day in class had to be half brain-dead already. The course didn't teach anything about aviation security, but was merely an exercise in how to do all the paper work that was required of an FAA Special Agent. Upon graduation we were presented with yet another set of credentials but at least we didn't have to swear to anymore irrelevant oaths.

    Within about two weeks on the job in my new office at O'Hare International Airport I realized that FAA's concept of aviation security was a total joke. FAA orchestrated a great façade of security: screening checkpoints at airports, lots of security warning signs, fences around the airport etc. All this window dressing did little more than keep honest people honest and keep dumb people from straying someplace they didn't belong and hurt themselves. Even the credentials we carried looked like impressive police type credentials but we didn't really have any authority to do anything. *We didn't carry no gun* (not when wearing the Special Agent hat). We just ran around the airports with little more than figurative clipboards and every time we saw a violation of the security rules we'd write up a violation against the effected airport authority or the airline. Once the paper work left our hands it went to the FAA legal department and they'd send the violation notice to the airport or airline. Then their legal types would bicker with the FAA lawyers and the fines would eventually be watered down to next to nothing. This circular eddy went around ad infinitum. Essentially all FAA did was document that there was some degree of security, good or bad it didn't make any difference, maintaining the bureaucracy was what counted – nothing has changed since then. The seeds were already planted in a security system that ensured that the 9/11 terrorists would be able to accomplish their deeds so effortlessly. Around 1992 I first heard of an effort by some FAA Special Agents of the need to harden the cockpit doors on commercial airplanes, as they knew nothing we were doing would prevent or deter a hijacking. Of course, this recommendation didn't get anywhere.

In fact, long before the 9/11 attacks, FAA already was given the moniker of "Tombstone Agency" by members of Congress and the news media. Meaning FAA never made any improvements in its air safety and security programs until people got killed first. And I mean this quite literally. Check the term out on the internet and one will be inundated with hits of FAA prior to 9/11. Perhaps the most famous case that dramatized this bureaucratic mentality was the case of Hale Boggs. For years flying enthusiast were pressuring the FAA and Congress to mandate the installation of emergency locator beacons on certain classes of general aviation aircraft. Then Congressman Hale Boggs crashes in Alaska (on 16Oct72), never to be found again, and suddenly the bureaucrats think this is a novel idea and required avionics systems to have the beacons.

So here we were, a small army of FAA inspectors, running around airports all over the country and overseas doing security inspections, not even looking for loopholes in security that terrorists could exploit, write up endless cases that eventually went nowhere. And the next year, just do the same thing all over again. This was the most irrelevant job I had ever experienced or ever heard about. While the agency was an exercise of shoveling manure on the farm, someone had to do it (pick up the pieces after a crime); in FAA, we relished and played in the manure. The only thing that made it bearable was that this was only half the job. The other half of the job was working as a FAM (which I really enjoyed), but I'll get into that later.

Fortress of Deceit

My one memorable experience wearing the FAA inspector hat involved an X-Files (from the TV Show) situation in which I was sent to some remote Pacific Islands to investigate local natives who were using black magic against the one airport on the island. This came under the guise of doing one of our inane airport inspections. Many islanders preferred to minimize the modern incursions into their lives; and I couldn't blame them, these islands were absolutely magical. I asked my local contact what people do on the weekends on this island as there were no movie theaters nor any other entertainment venue that I could see; and found myself suddenly invited to participate in one of their weekend activities. Instead of sitting on their butts watching sports on the boob tube, they'd gather up their hunting dogs and run off into the jungle hunting wild boar with machetes.

On another day in that little adventure, my local contact took me on a tour around the island in his personal small boat, a little bigger than a station wagon. We stopped at an outlying island (not bigger than a city block) about a mile off shore of the mainland to do some fishing for lunch. The water was crystal clear. When I was snorkeling (no scuba tank) about twenty feet beneath the waves I witnessed yet another of those unusual ocean phenomena. I was mesmerized by a current of water that passed between this outlying island and the mainland but it was heading nearly straight down from the surface. It was almost like a tornado in reverse, with the force directed downward, except it wasn't spinning. I could clearly see leaves, sand, and other detritus moving down into a dark void where the sun light even feared to tread. There was even a clear border between the relatively still water where I was, and the swift downward current. I was feet from the current and just slowly drifting toward the event horizon between the two water masses; completed mesmerized by the sight. I put my hand through the border and felt the strong tug of the ice cold downward current and quickly withdrew my hand. "Yeow", it occurred to me, a person could disappear in this environment and nobody would have a clue as to what happened. Even though I could swim like a fish, this was way outside my comfort zone. I immediately swam to the surface and away from that corner of the island. I was reminded of a story I had recently read in the local paper about a Peace Corps worker that recently had disappeared in the ocean, never to be found. Couldn't help but wonder if he was down that same gorge.

I continued exploring the underwater world though and came across a huge piece of bleach white coral growing out the side of the island ten feet below the surface. It was about the size of a small house but perfectly rounded. I moved closer to the coral to get a better look at it when a current suddenly pushed me toward it. I had to use my hands to push against the coral and the coral cut a score of tiny gashes in my hands which started bleeding. I pushed myself about five feet from the coral careful to keep my distance, kicking with my webbed footwear. The bleeding was minor but left streaks of red in the water. Maintaining my distance from the coral I swam beneath it to see what was under it, but it was pitch black from its shadow. Suddenly a huge shark came out of the darkness right at me. When it was within arms-length of me it quickly turned to the side and swam around me.

Remembering my Coast Guard survivor training, I forced myself to at least behave as calmly as possible, barely moving my hands and feet and slowly floating back to the surface. The shark was just milling around about a dozen feet from me, slowly moving closer and then further away. When I broke the surface I took my mask off and yelled at the locals in the small boat, "There's a shark down here!"

Fortress of Deceit

Put my mask back on and went under the water again to keep an eye on the shark, which was still just milling around.

The boat was about a hundred feet from me and I forced myself to swim very slowly toward it, recalling that sharks are attracted to spastic movement. After what seemed minutes, I came back to the surface and yelled again, but they were just standing in the boat holding fishing poles. Either couldn't hear me, or couldn't care less about the hairless white ape in the water making an ass out of himself. I continued slowly moving toward the boat and it occurred to me to grasp my knife, to at least go down fighting. With my head underwater, I could see that I was about ten feet from the boat, I turned around in the water looking for the shark and found it about the same distance behind me, sniffing the dribble of blood flowing from my hands. I figured it was going to grab me and hack my leg off just as I started to climb into the boat. With a surge of adrenaline, I propelled myself out of the water, went airborne and landed on my head in the boat. The martial arts masters I mentioned previously were amateurs compared to this.

I asked the locals if they heard me screaming and they nonchalantly explained that they did, but you needn't worry about a shark attacking until it starts circling around you. This shark was just milling around; curious, but not hungry. If it was a barracuda, on the other hand, it'd come right at me without any warning, giving me a quick lesson on the local wild life. I raised my head above the gunnel of the boat, peering over the side. "Thanks for fucking telling me!" I was way outside my element here.

It was a long time before I would even take a bath again, leery of any sized body of water. Even now I always look and think twice before I enter or even go near any big water.

As to the black magic; their attempts to kill me didn't work. It was a great trip, and great folks on the islands.

There were basically two types of people that worked in FAA Security. The first were the people with prior military and/or law enforcement backgrounds that had a more realistic approach to security, no training mind you, but at least they had the right attitude. The second, and by far the most dominant in terms of sheer numbers and control of the bureaucracy were paper pushing misfits who thrived in this endless paper work eddy. Even the air marshal section was contaminated, which was roughly (based on my own observation) composed of about 60% to 70% of these people. It was a miracle that FAM's, during this time frame, didn't accidentally kill anybody or destroy an airplane due to a negligent discharge of his firearm.

The one good thing the bureaucracy did, at least initially, was give a lot of support to the FAM program. It was primarily because of the FAM program that FAA was gifted with a major increase in employees – which in turn gave the managers higher pay grades because they had more folks to manage. FAMs were given several hours off each week to work out, train in martial arts, etc; and another several hours each week to practice and develop our shooting skills and they provided an ample supply of ammunition.

We had several FAMs in my office who were gung-ho lean, mean, fighting machine types and we milked as much time as we could to do our own training. Unfortunately there wasn't any organized training regime, it was pretty much left to the ingenuity of the individual FAMs. We also had our share of misfits, former admin types, who milked the time off to do whatever personal business they could get away with; doing only the minimal training to get by. Soon the schism between the operational capabilities between the former military/police and the former admin types widened.

When we had to wear the "Special Agent" hat, we did the absolute minimum amount of work possible just to get by. It was a totally discombobulating atmosphere. The bureaucracy of FAA had absolutely no concept of terrorism. To them, aviation security was little more than hassling the airline industry and airports, usually in the form of exchanging nasty letters. Participating in this charade was a complete waste of time.

So as fate would have it, a few months after I became a bona fide FAM, our office hired another former local police officer; this one from some town in Missouri. This guy bore a striking resemblance to Mick Jagger (of Rolling Stones fame), so I'll refer to him as Mick. Mick, just as his namesake, was skinny as a rail, but he knew how to fight dirty. He couldn't shoot the broadside of a barn if he was touching it, but he was the best firearms instructor I ever had. Under his tutelage we quickly ramped up our tactical shooting skills well beyond the agency standards. Not just in individual skills but in training in two or three man groups on ever increasingly complex tactical situations. Things like bursting into a room and *killing* half a dozen targets within seconds.

Mick was a total firearms nut and was in fact a frequent contributing author to various gun and survival type magazines. He also felt the way a lot of us did about the joke of FAA security; and he made it an even bigger joke. While in the office with our 'Special Agent' hats on, we would frequently receive phone calls from airline or airport officials with questions concerning some petty security issue, or to report a violation by one of their employees (they received additional slack by self-reporting violations) or to bring up some other minor related security issue. Most of the gung-ho FAMs would resolve these problems with the least amount of fuss, but the geeks would jump on this stuff and thrive in the paperwork. The bureaucracy favored the folks that opened up the most violation cases against the industry. So most of us weren't particularly well liked by the bureaucrats and the feeling was certainly mutual, if not more-so.

I gave our division manager and his deputy the nicknames of *Yogi* and *Booboo*. The nicknames didn't really catch on though until folks observed the two of them standing together in a meeting or walking down the hall where the resemblance to the cartoon characters was most obvious. In spite of increasing morale problems, they must have thought we had a happy little office whenever they came over to visit, what with everyone smiling at them.

Inevitably they found out about the nicknames and someone ratted me out as the creator. None of the managers had the gonads to confront the gung-ho FAMs directly out of fear of being shot or knifed, instead they would just do so administratively, behind the scenes in terms of denied promotions and job transfers etc.

Mick had the knack of talking very convincingly with the accent of almost any indigenous population group of a country that we visited as FAMs. One day Mick got so frustrated in dealing with management and these idiotic phone calls we routinely received that out of the blue when he answered the phone he used the Sergeant Shultz accent (from the old WWII *Hogan's Heros* sitcom), waited for the caller to speak his piece and said, "I know nuuthing, NUUTHING," and promptly hung up the phone. A short while later he picked up his phone again and shifted to a NAZI Gestapo voice. He engaged in a lengthy hysterical conversation with the sap on the other end of the phone eventually articulating, "Your papers are not in order, your papers must be in order or we will ground your planes," and promptly hung up. This went on all day, shifting from a chinese laundry voice, an inner city black and south Asian, and a red neck Billy Bob. Political correctness was totally lost and no-one was spared. We were all laughing so hard we couldn't get any work done, even if we were inclined too.

The next day Mick and I wandered over to O'Hare and went to the various offices that called us the previous day. We went in under the pretense that we just happened to be in the area and stopped in to say *hi*. The folks that called us would timidly bring up the subject that they called our office yesterday and very delicately complained about the difficulty in understanding and working with the FAA agent that answered the phone. They were very careful with their *complaint* as they were very sensitive to the diversity issues. We just kind of shrugged our shoulders and said it must have been one of the new guys. The issues they all called up about were the typical BS that usually resolved themselves anyway.

Mick continued doing his *international* days about once every few weeks for some six months, when management slowly started to catch on to this, so he abruptly stopped. While these shenanigans were going on, or rather maybe in spite of them, there were some serious efforts to try to improve security.

Fortress of Deceit

As Federal Air Marshals, we flew all over the world and although it wasn't our job to assess security one couldn't help notice how lame aviation security was in thwarting terrorism. We had a vested interest in this status given the fact that we were the last line of defense should terrorist decide to attack a plane we were on. A number of us got together and sent an anonymous letter to the Secretary of Transportation, trying to convince him that he needs to look into the FAA misfit's version of security as it's a big accident waiting to happen. We signed it anonymously as *a group of concerned Federal Air Marshals* since the threat of retaliation for up-setting the bureaucracy was very real. The Secretary did nothing, but our allegations were sadly vindicated on December 21, 1988 when terrorists blew up Pan Am 103 killing 270 people after putting the bomb on the plane in Frankfurt, GE. A place we frequently visited, and I had previously flown on that doomed aircraft.

Well, one would have thought that this would have caused a major investigation into the FAA Tombstone Agency, but all Congress did was dump more money into this failed agency, authorized them to hire more people and basically FAA Security continued operating the same way they always did. In fact, history showed that after every major (involving deaths) aviation incident we effectively got bonuses in pay – in terms of higher pay grades and salaries and a bigger bureaucracy. There-by reinforcing this failure based tombstone mentality.

Nine months after the Pan Am 103 tragedy FAA sent a troop of Tombstone managers and field agents to Frankfurt to fix the problems that allowed the terrorists to get the bomb on the plane there. It took FAA nine months after the bombing to get around to trying to fix the problems that Pan Am had in Frankfurt; which, by the way, weren't any different from any major airline or airport.

Fortress of Deceit

As it happened, the river of life propelled me onto this team as its junior member. After countless hours of wandering around Frankfurt airport at all hours of the day and night, I became even more convinced that all these security systems we had in place do very little more than keep honest people honest and keep dumb people from stumbling into or causing accidents. But they did absolutely nothing to prevent a half-witted terrorist from doing just about anything they wanted to do at virtually any airport. The real deterrent against aviation terrorism was to enhance the human element. All the fences, signs, high tech detection equipment, computers and what not make useful tools buts its human beings actually looking for the terrorist profile that is the only real deterrent. Unfortunately, the bureaucracy, then, as well as now does just the opposite. Spend as much money as possible on all these high tech toys and other programs (TSA refers to them as multiple layers of security); and the people do little more than service the machines and computers. Basically turn the machines on in the morning and turn them off at night. Even the theater at checkpoints have the screeners looking for stuff, rather than looking for terrorists. The computers essentially run continuously with a bit of maintenance. Common sense would seem to have indicated that any half-wit with the motivation to do so can do a tap dance around these security systems. But common sense is a rarity in the government bureaucracy.

So after I returned from Frankfurt I got together with Mick and we had the inspiration to try something to improve security at O'Hare. Working thru the FAA bureaucracy was completely counter-productive, just bringing up new ideas could ruin your career. Mick and I developed a training course that we gave to the Precinct Commander of the Chicago Police Department that was responsible for O'Hare International Airport to try to give him some insight on how terrorists operate in the aviation environment. Mick focused on hand held weapons (guns and knives) and tactics while I talked about the terrorist profile, explosives and how they hide these weapons until they're ready to initiate their attack.

Turned out the Precinct Commander loved what we put together. We talked for a bit and he was astute enough to observe that what we gave him was a only a synopsis of what we had to offer. He asked us how many hours it would take to present our material to small classes of his police officers. We guesstimated that it would take 4-5 hours. The Commander thought for a moment and he set in motion a terrorism training class in which Mick and I would present this training session to small groups of police officers (about 8 to 10) on the graveyard shift at O'Hare Airport. Mick and I didn't even bother telling our management what we were doing. On our own time, once or twice or a week, we'd go to the police briefing room at the airport and spend the next four to five hours briefing the cops on how terrorists operate in the airport environment they worked in.

From my experience police officers aren't interested in any theory or academic treatise about anything, but are only interested in stuff that will help them do their jobs and keep them alive. So Mick and I would deliberately start off our little speech standing in front of the class wearing comfortable, normal fitting business casual attire with a sports coat or light jacket carrying a briefcase and a small bag containing our teaching aids and hand out material – trying to look like and talk like typical government geeks. The cops, of course, knew we were FAA and had sat through more than their share of droning briefings. After a few minutes I even heard some of them grumbling that "we're

Fortress of Deceit

supposed to sit here for half our shift?" It didn't take more than five or ten minutes when you'd start seeing some of the cop's eyes roll back in their heads or their eyelids start to droop. Keep in mind this was around midnight. Then after about ten minutes or so giving our introductory speech, Mick (who had fairly long hair) would scratch his head and pull a small razor sharp knife out of his collar and place it on the table in front of him. A few minutes later I'd let a switch blade fall out of my sleeve, feigning clumsiness and exclaiming "Oops!", placing the open blade on the table before them. Between the two of us, we'd take turns every few minutes and pull out another weapon and nonchalantly just place it on the table in front of them. After a few rounds off this we had their undivided attention. They were scanning us trying to discover where we were hiding these weapons.

After another thirty minutes there would be some fifteen or twenty lethal weapons ranging from small knives to a foot long bowie knife, non-metallic knives, small caliber pistols to a MAC-10 machine pistol. Even had the components of several bombs and demonstrated how easy it was to put them together and how the small explosive charges could have killed or wounded most of them in the room. All of these weapons were concealed from their scanning eyes – until we revealed them.

And so the rest of the night continued with their undivided attention. In the predawn hours the class would end and most of the time some of the cops would linger for another twenty minutes just jawing about terrorism. Then Mick and I would go to our respective homes, get a couple of hours sleep and arrive at our day job about 9ish.

This was the most satisfying part of the job while wearing our Special Agent hat, and we kept this a secret.

Inevitably, however, word gets around and our regional office found out about what we were doing. We heard rumblings that Mick and I were going to be subject to some disciplinary action for, I don't know what; but maybe for doing stuff that was marginally useful to the tax payers which is a big no no in the federal government. Somehow headquarters found out about it and thought it was pretty cool so our regional office back-peddled and added our nocturnal activities on their weekly activities report that they sent to headquarters to get some brownie points. Our managers even gave us time off to sleep after one of these classes.

Our briefings were extremely well received by the police. As we "trained" a growing number of them Mick and I couldn't walk anywhere at O'Hare without being stopped by a cop and just chewing the fat. They all said the same thing – all they were trained to do was fight traditional crime and had no concept or awareness of terrorism. We even started giving these briefings to some of the myriad federal law enforcement agencies that worked at O'Hare. While this was the happy time, all good things must come to an end. We briefed several hundred law enforcement types over some 6 months and were actually starting to get a little burned out. What I found curious, however, was not once did our own managers ask us to give this briefing to our own FAA Security colleagues, and they're supposed to be the experts in this stuff.

On another occasion in which I felt like I earned my salary, Sam (the same former agency agent Sam), as intimidating as he could be standing at about six foot, five inches, was actually just a great big Teddy Bear on the inside and always had room in his heart to help someone in distress. One day at work he pulls me off to the side asking for a favor. He explained that one of the Station Managers of

Fortress of Deceit

a small airline based at O'Hare Airport had a problem. Apparently one of her female employees was having a bad break up with a former boyfriend. Apparently the ex threatened to kill her and to do so while she's at work – at O'Hare airport. The Station Manager went to the police and they explained that since no crime has been committed [yet], there's nothing they can do. She also went to the FBI who also turned down any assistance. In those days the FBI rarely got involved in anything unless they could get some positive media coverage out of it. The Station Manager was extremely upset about this, concerned that not only could the female employee be targeted but other employees and possibly passengers could get injured or killed too.

So Sam asked me if I'd accompany him and pay the guy a visit to see if there was anything to this, and if so, put a stop to it. Of course I agreed. We quickly collected what information was available on the *suspect* including where he lived and worked, and when he got off work. The man's car mysteriously broke down and we saw an opportunity.

One late afternoon Sam and I dress up in our best agency type business attire, complete with our FAA credentials and pistols – just in the event things soured. We arrived in a government car at the factory where the gentleman worked, parked in an obvious spot up front and scanned the employees as they left the building for the day. Finding our man, we approached the suspect, identified ourselves and what we were doing and that we needed to talk to him. He was taken completely off guard. He even accepted our offer to drive him home.

So we took a long slow ride to his apartment engaging in a friendly conversation (no sarcasm whatsoever), and just feeling him out to see if there was any reason to be concerned. We agreed with him that women can drive you nuts, and although we didn't condone it, we certainly understood the anger he felt toward his former girlfriend. Well, there's no way of telling what he may have been planning, but it seemed to have sunk in that he wasn't the only one to have go through this type of pain and that violence wasn't the best approach to take to resolve this little problem. Plus, we emphasized, we knew where he lived and it wasn't worth ruining his life over this. We dropped him off at his residence and never heard of the guy again.

Of course, this went way outside the authority and bean counting protocol we were supposed to follow as FAA Special Agents but it may very well have prevented one or more innocent people from getting killed. That's the nature of security work if it's done with reasonableness and prudence. Sort of applying Ben Franklin's adage of, "an ounce of prevention is worth a pound of cure."

The big turning point in our office as well as in the FAM program occurred one morning while we're all just sitting around the office shuffling the mandatory paperwork. Mick and I shared a two-man office (as did everyone else). We're just sitting there doing our aviation security nonsense when suddenly the office reverberates with the deafening report of a small arms round going off.

Mick and I immediately go into tactical mode. Morale was fairly poor in the office and I figured someone just shot our office manager. Which I wouldn't have blamed him, but the survival instinct immediately over-took the situation. I unsheathed a combat knife I wore concealed hooked to my belt and Mick pulled out a small, small caliber pistol that he had strapped to his ankle, completely unauthorized. We looked out our office door into the larger foyer of the office – several people apparently left the office before the reverberating echo of the blast died away. The few remaining were frozen in place just staring at the open office door immediately adjacent to our office.

I fully expected my boss to be flopping around on the floor going through his last death throes, and maybe some screaming, but there was only dead silence. In a lot less time than it takes to explain it I figured I had a 50-50 chance of out-knifing most of the FAMs in the office – given what I knew of their shooting skills. Plus, I figured I could be a decoy for a fraction of a second that would allow Mick to get a bead on the shooter. During practice and qualifications Mick barely qualified, but he has shot people before in the line of duty. We had another FAM on my team who on qualification days was a nervous wreck, visibly shaking and chain smoking starting the day before. But when he was an Ohio State Trooper he shot an armed robber in the heart, killing him instantly.

This of course didn't apply to everyone – but everyone I knew that killed someone in the line of duty were terrible shots when it came to practice and qualifications; but when the shit hit the fan, they did what was needed to be done. I think it had something to do with thinking about it too much. Anyways, I wasn't the least bit concerned with Mick and considered him to be the right person at the right moment.

So the two of us are preparing to do a tactical entry to the shooter's office when a great big pall of blue smoke slowly drifted out of the door and the smell of burned powder was distinctive. Taking a quick glance in the room we see the perpetrator sitting at his desk, amidst the thickest part of the smoke, dismantling his firearm. He had all the requisite firearms cleaning gear spread out on his desk. There wasn't anyone dead or wounded in the room and Mick asked what happened. The short of it is that the shooter was going to clean his firearm and was taking aim at the building support beam opposite his desk and the gun went off by itself. Mick went over to the hole in the wall – which was dead center of the support beam and said, "Wow, _____ , this is the best shot you ever made."

It took a few minutes for the office to calm down and convince the manager not to call the cops. Mick did a quick forensic exam of the bullet hole in the masonry and could clearly see that the bullet hit the steel beam of the support girder and ricocheted up towards the floor above us. So Mick and I went upstairs to the office directly above us – which was some kind of interior decorating company. We entered their office stating that we just moved into this office complex and thought we'd introduce ourselves to our office neighbors.

The conversation drifted to how much we loved their carpeting and the painting on the walls. We asked if we could look around and they were only too willing to show off all their furnishings. Under their escort, and us bubbling with compliments and practically prancing around like a couple of psycho dandies, we made it to the same support girder to see if there was a dead body, none; so we gave the area a quick once over and there wasn't any sign of the bullet making an appearance. We thanked them for the tour and took off laughing, never to visit them again.

Reports had to be filed and one was sent to the building management to make repairs and the other sent to our regional office and thence to headquarters in Washington, D.C. Once the report got to the FAM branch headquarters, the illogic of the bureaucracy came to life again. Instead of disciplining the shooter (a minority), who shouldn't have been hired in the first place, headquarters made ALL the FAMs undergo extensive basic firearms familiarity and safety training – again. For those of us who were pushing the envelope on our tactical skills so that we could handle the best of the best that terrorists could throw at us – this was a major blow to our morale and operational capabilities. Reverting back to training that was about on the same level as how they used to train boy scouts to shoot.

It was also a big reminder of the federal government's failure based mentality – throw money at the programs and policies and people that don't work. FAM headquarters established a headquarters level training unit and the first manager of that unit had absolutely no operational savvy or tactical training experience whatsoever. She was just another sycophantic hack that worked her way up from being an FAA secretary, joined the FAM program, and was now a manager in the program.

One of the other potentially good things the bureaucracy did was establish Regional Training Officers. This was another great idea but lacked something in the execution. Instead of promoting Mick (who was in fact functioning as the unofficial training officer) to run this new training office for our region, they promoted another sycophantic hack that had no business being an air marshal in the first place, much less be in charge of training for the region.

This guy was late for everything, which wouldn't normally be a problem if they handled him appropriately. But instead of kicking him in the butt, they made everyone else wait for him. Well, this turned out to be one of his better qualities. His shooting skills were on a par with our own office wall shooter; but, better than that, when he was flying as an air marshal he literally would be asleep for three quarters of the flight or longer. A number of FAMs complained about him but management refused to do anything to him out of fear of getting hit with yet another EEO complaint. I don't know if our managers were the dumbest ones in the country but they would certainly be contenders for first place. During this timeframe we had two people in our region, one black one white (both of whom had the same lawyer) that filed EEO cases against these clowns. To make a long story short both these individuals ending up with getting a full government salary for the rest of their natural lives without having to do any work – they could stay at home and both only had about 10 years of government service between them. Just another way the tax payer is being taken to the cleaners on a daily basis. So anyway, management was gun shy about taking any action against our resident sleeping FAM (who was black) for fear of being it with another EEO case.

    I was on one lengthy overseas flight with the sleeper, sitting a couple of rows behind him and off to the side. He had his sunglasses on and was holding a magazine at the bottom with both hands – kind of like holding a hymnal in church. Not that I was keeping an eye on him, but about half an hour later I glanced back at this magazine and saw that he was still on the same page. Either that was a mesmerizing article and/or he's a very slow reader or, gawd-forbid, he's sound asleep – what with the sunglasses and all.

    By this time, the more operationally savvy of the FAMs just became inured to the dead weight we had to work with and pretty much looked at them as little more than extra gun and ammo toters in the event we needed refreshing. So I really didn't give him much thought. About an hour after I first noticed him *reading*, the top three quarters of the magazine sagged over his hands so that, even if wanted too, he couldn't read the magazine the way it flopped over. Just walking around to stretch my legs I pointed him out to other FAMs who made a point of walking past him and just snickering.

A full two hours went by and I started to get a little more interested in the sleeper. Not concerned mind you, just interested. He literally hadn't moved at all in over two hours. The magazine was still flopped over backwards over his hands, and I couldn't even tell if he was breathing anymore. Maybe he died and did the tax payer a real public service, probably the only one in his career.

I had been around dead bodies before as a criminal investigator but I never had to touch one, except once during an autopsy when the pathologist asked for my assistance, preferring to leave that chore to the medical types. So I was kind of curious if rigor mortis had already set in on this bozo. Most of the passengers were sound asleep. So I went up to him and jabbed my finger into the side of his cheek. He woke up with a snort and I just went back to my seat. After that he'd just go to one of the airplane lavatories for an hour or more. I did have to give him credit for that though. He probably spent more time, at any one time, in heavily used aircraft lavatories than any other jet setter above the planet. We always had people pushing the envelope in one category or another in the FAM branch.

So the sleeper is the clown they promoted to be our Regional Training Officer.

During this evolution of the FAM program, every six months we had to fly to the training facility out west and requalify on the shooting and physical fitness standards. Neither of which were particularly difficult. While it took a lot of effort to excel in these areas, I'm not aware of anyone that actually failed a qualification. This is typical of how our re-qualifications worked: Some thirty of us would start a timed two mile run. The gung-ho types would be busting ass trying to beat each other across the finish line – this was tough. Then you'd have the mediocre types gradually flop their way across the finish line. Lastly we'd have the tail end charlies, who either barely made it across the line or some that even seemed to have gotten lost on an idiot proof route through the base and never crossed the finish line. Then the next day they'd do a private re-test and miraculously cross the finish line with seconds to spare. The same applied with other components of the physical fitness qualifications and the shooting standards.

In between our biannual training qualifications our new regional training officer would arrange additional training challenges. O'Hare Airport, obviously, is one of the world's largest airports. It has huge aircraft hangars where jumbo jets are repaired and maintained. It is also a major training hub for flight attendants and pilots. Our training officer arranged that we go through an abbreviated flight safety class – basically the same thing flight attendants go through.

In groups of about forty, we went through the whole gamut of putting on life preservers, how to work the seat belts, the oxygen masks, how to open the doors, actually jumping down the inflatable rubber emergency exit slides and a few hours of briefings. The culmination of the training occurred in a large room which contained a full mock-up of the coach section of a jumbo jet. This contained about seventy airplane seats, complete with seat belts, escape hatches, etc; basically looked exactly like the interior of a large aircraft. So some forty of us enter the aircraft mock-up and we're told to scatter ourselves around the seats like real passengers.

Fortress of Deceit

The entire mock-up was seated on hydraulic stilts and other equipment to give the sensation of taking off, flying, and landing. At one point during our flight we encountered *turbulence*. This was something akin to a kiddy ride at an amusement park, but it was still cool how they got the whole mock-up to shake). A few minutes later the flight crew reported that we had to make an emergency landing. People starting screaming, really hamming it up. I had a bad feeling about this, it wasn't going to be pretty. The flight attendants (who were the actual instructors of the course) told us to get into crash position and we dutifully bent over placing our arms on the seatback in front of us with our heads wedged between our arms. Moments later the cabin shuddered to a stop and the whole cabin filled with a thick fog, simulating smoke.

When you get some highly motivated, physically fit guys together, most of whom have a decent sense of humor, throw in a heavy dose of fatigue and boredom, and you're bound to get some chaos. Instead of calmly filing out of the plane as we were instructed to do, one of them started screaming hysterically like a little school girl and rushing to get out the door first by pushing others out of the way – sparking off a *panic*. Just before he reached the exit door others grabbed him and pulled him back into the plane – resulting in a general melee and pile-up at the door. I managed to climb over the pile and was able to grab the outside bulkhead of the door only to find that someone grabbed my feet trying to pull me back in. For a few moments I was suspended horizontally over the fight but lost my grip and found myself in the middle of the melee. Through the din of combat I heard, "Stop it, stop it," bleating from our regional training officer.

I crawled out of the pile and went to one of those wing emergency exits. Red lights were flashing on the outside simulating fire over the wing but I started opening the exit anyway. An exasperated nurse Rachet type flight attendant/instructor screamed at me, "What are you doing, you're going to kill us all." I screamed back, "They don't deserve to live," while pointing at the pile of FAMs still clamoring to get out the door, and made my way out through the *fire*.

We had to be the only class in flight attendant school history to flunk their course. But politics being what it was, we were thoroughly chastised, and given another chance. This was now pushing 4 o'clock in the morning, most of us had been awake since the previous morning, and we lapsed into an adrenal dump. This time we went through the final emergency exit exercise in a calm but expeditious manner. Nursing our bruises along the way.

In another training exercise, a similar group of some forty to fifty of us were practicing different drills on a 747 jumbo jet while it was in the hangar at O'Hare. This was about three in the morning. Our illustrious regional training instructor, instead of running us through increasingly complex tactical drills using live ammunition (in a different environment of course); had us engage in increasingly stupid role playing exercises in which FAMs would be selected to play the role of FAMs, others would play the role of "bad" guys, and the rest would play the role of victimized passengers or flight crews, and we'd spend the night doing our version of the School for the Performing Arts.

We had a lot of comedians in the group and they couldn't wait to ham things up to at least have some fun doing these drills. But ultimately they proved to be a worse than useless waste of time – it gave those FAMS that were physically under par (which included almost all the females and a good portion of the males) an inflated sense of their own power when they could *manhandle* other FAMs who were instructed to go along with the scenario without resisting. If a situation deteriorated to the point of a FAM having to *shoot* a bad guy, they'd point their finger at him and yell, "bang bang you're dead." This was about one step above little kids playing cowboys and indians. If there was any value to this dribble it allowed folks to ham things up and resulted in a lot of jocularity in the middle of the night.

At one point I was selected to play the role of a drunken passenger and instructed to try to get into the cockpit. I just rolled my eyes when given this task, but then started thinking – which is always a mistake in the Tombstone Agency. I was seated near the very tip of the 747 jumbo jet on the main deck almost directly beneath the cockpit. There were five FAMs between me and the cockpit but I figured I had a pretty good chance of entering the cockpit or forcing the situation where one of them would have to point their finger at me and go "bang bang." Two FAMs were in the same first class section as me, and three were in the upper deck. The FAM closest to me was a bowling ball shaped individual who probably weighed close to 300 pounds (compared to my 185). He was in my FAM basic class and somehow he defied the laws of physics. He was the fastest runner on the two mile run over everyone in the class, and we had some really good runners in the class. He was also strong as an ox, I suspected he probably had Viking blood in him – given his features and the part of the country he was from.

The second FAM in this section was a petite Hispanic woman who, although spirited, would be way out of her league in any type of physical confrontation and was an irrelevant unit in my grand strategy.

Fortress of Deceit

The upper deck FAMs were Mick (our former unofficial firearms and tactics instructor) who I knew would fight dirty using anything he could get his hands on. The second one was a mid-western, tobacco chewing fellow, Billy Bob (not his real name), whom I believe was recruited right out of college. What he lacked in experience he made up for with the right attitude and would readily engage in a fight. In a previous scenario he shot a terrorist with his finger, who then dropped his dummy grenade. Billy Bob took a flying leap landing on the grenade yelling "save yourselves," nearly killing everyone around as we were laughing so hard. The third FAM was the potato who did absolutely nothing but sue FAA management. He was more irrelevant than the female below in the coming scenario.

My plan was to make it past the Viking, who although could certainly out-muscle me, and was fast on a straight run but wasn't particularly agile in the narrow aisles and seats of an airplane, get to the upper deck and take the potato hostage in a neck-lock, using him as a shield so they couldn't bang bang me with their fingers, and get into the cockpit.

Chances were that Mick would shoot the potato anyway and given the close confines of the passenger cabin the situation would result in a physical confrontation between myself, and Mick and Billy Bob. I was more than confident I could get past all of them. I never considered myself to be at a serious disadvantage unless I was outnumbered 10 to 1. This wasn't arrogance on my part, I figured I could be smart enough and physical enough to overcome the odds by doing the unexpected. In this case I knew how they trained – just do the opposite. Any odds greater than that would just be making a political statement and die trying.

Fortress of Deceit

So when the regional training officer gave the go ahead to start the scenario I waited a couple of minutes and rang for the flight attendant asking for some booze – hamming it up like a drunk might. But instead of a flight attendant the Viking sits down in the seat next to me and tells me that I've had too much to drink already. This was a totally bogus situation to begin with as FAMs wouldn't get involved with an unruly drunk unless requested by the crew, and I hadn't even gotten to the unruly part. But in this case the Viking was fully aware of my previous antics and was determined to stop whatever I had planned even before it started.

When I was in Officer Candidate School, the Commanding Officer of the school was a Vietnam era Green Beret officer. He apparently was wounded a number of times and in the later stages of his career he transferred to easier duty in the Coast Guard. But the one thing he beat into my head was the adage: "The more you sweat in peace, the less you bleed in war." And I kept this actively in mind for the rest of my career, including these BS training sessions; not only for my own benefit but I endeavored to push some of my own colleagues to the edge of the envelop too, as my life might depend on them at some point – to see what everyone is made of. Other FAMs did the same thing. In a previous martial arts training class the FAM program sent me to, I was getting ready to spar against an opponent when I overheard another FAM tell my opponent that "you can't hurt him." Which was far from the truth, I just learned to put pain aside within certain limits. The FAM who told him this was a Japanese American with a black belt in the traditional Japanese art of Karate.

So here I am sitting next to a 300 pound bowling ball, effectively closed in by the window on my right side, passengers occupying the seats in front and behind and a gorilla to my left. If the seats had been unoccupied in front of or behind me, I had a chance of rolling over the seats before the Viking could grab me, but no way with the bodies there.

After two or three minutes of verbal jousting it was clear that the Viking wasn't going to let me out of the seat for any reason. So I told him I had to go to the bathroom. After repeated requests to let me up he just kept insisting that the plane would land soon and I could go then. This was turning out to be one of the more boring training exercises we engaged in, until I started thinking like Mick. I told the Viking I was getting sick and had to go to the bathroom, his response was the same. In the meantime, I was slowly collecting saliva in my mouth and after a few moments leaned over in his seat and faked going thru the dry heaves, complete with drool. He shot out of the seat like a firecracker went off under his butt, cursing; but before he could turn around in the aisle I was walking down the aisle back toward the first class lavatories.

Instead of using the seatbacks for support, as a passenger would do while walking during turbulence, I was grabbing passenger's heads – trying to fire up somebody to react physically to add as much chaos to the situation as possible. But they were all conditioned to play the roles of polite and defenseless victims.

As I neared the open space where the lavatories were I made a couple of steps toward the lavatories and noticed in my peripheral vision the Viking was pacing me. I knew if I actually went into the lavatory he'd just lock me inside – a rather boring but fitting end to this scenario I was given. But I did a quick about-face and headed to the circular stairwell that leads to the upper deck. The female FAM stood in front of me and with her [well trained] command voice ordered

Fortress of Deceit

me back to my seat. I just walked through her and proceeded up the stairs. The Viking shouted upstairs to the FAMs not to let me up there so I found Mick and Billy Bob already waiting for me at the top of the stairs. Well, this wasn't exactly what I had planned but I figured I could still make it past them.

Just as my eyes cleared the upper deck floor I suddenly found myself immobilized on one of the steps. The Viking had reached through the steps and grabbed my right ankle in a vice-grip with both of his hands. I couldn't move what with a 300 pound weight on one leg. Mick and Bill Bob immediately descended the stairs, with Mick trying to hand-cuff my hands to the railing of the steps. As one learns in martial arts, for every move there is a counter-move, and a counter-counter move to that; so we engaged in a wrestling match for a minute or so. I actually had the advantage on the steps as the stair-well is only designed for one person climbing or descending at a time. I came close to hand-cuffing Billy Bob to the railing, using Mick's cuffs, when Mick started engaging in pressure point pain compliance attacks – which was a mistake as I could out-pain him. But the fight deteriorated into a general melee with neither side gaining an edge, but lots of yelling and screaming at each other. And I was still totally immobilized by the Viking. Through the din of battle some idiot was yelling, "stop it, stop it."

This went on for several more minutes, so long as I was immobilized by the Viking I couldn't advance. Every time I bent over to hit a pressure point on the Vikings wrist to rent my foot lose, Mick and Billy Bob would advance their attack. But it was clear that we had a draw. Mick then got me into a choke hold but he was only blocking off my oxygen, not blood supply, which gave me another minute's worth of time. I knew Mick had a four inch sheath knife

Fortress of Deceit

concealed beneath his jacket on his belt and I tried to grab it. He reflexively responded by trying to prevent my getting to it and I jabbed a pressure point in his thigh with my elbow which caused his leg to collapse. Meanwhile, Billy Bob, not knowing what I was trying to do was still fumbling with trying to hand cuff my wrist, I was able to fend him off with one hand and unsheathe the knife with the other.

Both Mick and I simultaneously called a truce as now things would have gotten really nasty, and everybody relaxed – fight over. If this had been a real fight instead of this totally bogus scenario I probably would have cut up Mick, Billy-Bob and the Viking and made my way to the cockpit only to be shot in the back by the petite Hispanic lady. The potato was hiding behind the seat. Typically these training situations were just a step away from sparing off in a dojo. When it was my turn to play a victimized passenger, I witnessed others of the more gung ho FAMs would similarly duke it out with the *terrorists* for control of the plane, testing not only their own prowess but seeing what other FAMs were made of. It was a great way to build a team, but not at all how FAA planned. The violence would continue to escalate in these scenarios until one side capitulated or a draw agreed on, or one side went "bang bang" as a last resort, to avoid serious injury. Well, the scenario was over, more ripped cloths, more bruises, and a cracked rib for me (from getting slammed into the railing) – this was the last of what remained of the happy times. Whatever minor damage we caused in the aircraft was pretty much covered up.

I discovered that these types of unscripted *fights* were actually better training than sparring off in a traditional dojo – a side benefit not designed into the training by FAA. It forced one to consider the type of cloths one wore on the street as an asset or liability in self-defense or attack, and more importantly, made one intimately acquainted with working within the close confines of an airplane cabin. Executing a roundhouse kick to the face of an opponent in a dojo or on the street may look cool, but you try doing that on a plane and you are liable to seriously hurt yourself. Plus, as in any close contact training, it allowed one to find out what one's teammates were made of as well as some of the advantages and disadvantages of physical action on a plane.

Shortly after this situation Mick got fed up with the training we were required to do and was very much aware that he should have been appointed as the new training officer instead of the goof sleeper FAM, so he just up and quit FAA altogether. He had enough sense to realize that working (and having anything approaching a successful career) in the Tombstone Agency was a futile endeavor if one pushed the envelope. I lingered a few more months before I made the same decision. This occurred at our next semi-annual FAM recurrent training out west in late 1992. The normal routine for this training was that Monday was a travel day, Tuesday would be the shooting and physical fitness re-qualifications and Wednesday and Thursday would consist of intelligence briefings and more advanced training, with Friday the travel home day.

What actually happened this week was that Monday and Tuesday passed like they always do but there was absolutely no training or briefings on Wednesday and Thursday. I literally spent both days sitting around the pool, going for the occasional dip, and doing lots of personal reading. The FAM branch now had more people working in the training sections at both headquarters and the various regional offices and collectively they couldn't drum up two minutes worth of training. The Tombstone Agency at its finest.

Fortress of Deceit

When I woke up Thursday morning and realized that it was going to be a repeat of the previous day I immediately decided I was going to resign from the FAM branch. I even drafted my resignation letter while sitting poolside. In the late morning one of the managers found me and asked if I'd give a martial arts session right after lunch involving the whole group. I said "sure" and for about five seconds thought this would be a great opportunity; but then reality set in – this was still the Tombstone Agency at its best. I figured I'd probably get sued for causing some bruises.

I arrived at the *dojo* at the appointed time and had the sorriest group of people in front of me. More than half were still suffering from the effects of the previous two nights of bar-hopping and partying in the closest town or the one bar on the base. The remaining sober – previously decent types had such looks of despondency on their faces, and then we had the group of folks that shouldn't have been there anyway. I ended up fore-going my moment of glory and gave little more than a quick talk about the importance of martial arts acumen in the FAM profession and that was about it. Proudly maintaining the mentality of the Tombstone Agency. I submitted my resignation from the FAM program that afternoon.

The only good thing the new FAM training section did cough up is that they contracted out to some company to produce some very sophisticated (for its time) "Shoot, don't Shoot" videos. These videos were composed of numerous films of live actors in an airplane passenger section *stage*. The stage consisted of a plane load of passengers and flight crew doing what they do on an airplane. At some point actors would engage in a drama on the plane and the FAM or FAMs would be sitting in an airplane seat watching this life size drama flashing on a wall in a specially constructed room. The actors would play the roles of everything from irate passengers, to out of control drunks, to various nefarious terrorist types. The test for the FAM was to make a judgment call on whether or when to use lethal force. If lethal force was required the FAM would draw his pistol from his holster and aim and fire his loaded firearm. The technology measured not only the FAMs judgment, but his accuracy and speed in shooting the target. Failures in either category required the FAM to under-go additional training to bring his skills back up to par. Repeated failures, particularly regarding judgment, and the FAM could be removed from the service, although this never happened that I was aware of.

In one of these scenarios I'm sitting in this training room with another gung-ho FAM, having watched and successfully resolved a number of these situations. This particular one started off like they all did, a normal flight. When suddenly five terrorists jumped out of their seats brandishing small submachine guns and hijacking the plane. My partner and I immediately opened fire on the hijackers and we were just as quickly chastised by the training crew for using poor judgment. This was a scenario, according to the script, that the FAMs should have ridden the situation out a bit more as we were clearly outnumbered and out gunned. We protested, however, and in the replay of the video which included our shots fired, the video clearly showed that in less than two seconds, each of the five terrorists was hit in the head with one bullet each. We, both individually and as a group (at least certain elements), were evolving faster than the ever increasingly complex and difficult training exercises could keep up. But this wasn't enough.

By this time I had pretty much had it with FAA Security altogether. While I wasn't a FAM any more I was still an FAA Special Agent doing the BS that that job required. As soon as I got back to the office I started drafting a letter to the Department of Transportation's Office of Inspector General (OIG). From my experience I knew the OIG was just another putz of a government agency. They investigated minor issues but out of political considerations with the bureaucracies they were chartered to *oversee*, they never engaged in investigations concerning managers – or if they did they whitewashed the final report to minimize any hard feelings, based on my own observations.

In this case, however, I thought they couldn't bury the fact that FAA was wasting tens of thousands of dollars sending FAMS to training in the middle of no-where and just let the party animals take over. I also added additional information about the nonsense we were required to do to support the Tombstone bureaucracy. I was so fed up with the agency I was daring them to fire me- I didn't want to work here anyway and it would have forced me to get a real job or start my own outfit (I was exploring the possibility of continuing the training of law enforcement types in anti-terrorism activities). The OIG didn't waste any time with doing an investigation into my allegations and every time I called them to find out what the status was, they just kept blowing me off.

As things happened, however, my timing of sending this letter to the OIG couldn't have been better. Turned out the river of life reached another major juncture. As a result of the various Congressional inquiries concerning the fallout over the bombing of Pan Am 103, two significant things occurred. The first was that they changed the position of the FAA Security section from a subordinate unit in another division and elevated it too a full Division within the FAA bureaucracy with the head of the Security Division listed as an *Associate Administrator of FAA*. There-by giving the security division higher status and moving it closer to the final decision maker of FAA – the godlike Administrator. Making it an area that the Administrator couldn't ignore anymore.

The second thing they did was appoint a gentleman by the name of Ort Steele to be the first Associate Administrator of the Security Division. Mr. Steele was a retired Marine Corps General. On that level he was one of the finest examples of leadership, honor, and dedication to country than anyone else I've been exposed too. I have nothing but high praise for the man. As I understand it, he only had a three year contract with FAA.

One of the distinguishing marks of his leadership style was that he would make unannounced visits to the field to find out what was really going on in aviation security and actually talk directly with the FAA agents on the front lines. Compared to the other senior managers in the Tombstone Agency (and especially the current TSA) who surround themselves with a coterie of sycophantic suck ups to avoid interacting with the field except under tightly controlled and scripted environments.

From my observations, this is how things progressed:

It took some time but my OIG contact told me that one of the first things put on the General's plate was the letter I sent to the OIG. The General slowly started making changes to the Tombstone Agency's mentality. During the first Persian Gulf War during the early 90's, I was sent to Berlin, GE to keep planes from being hijacked or bombed. I was given an official letter authorizing me to terminate any and all US air carrier operations in Berlin if the security wasn't up to match the anticipated threat there. This authorization was in effect at all US operations overseas. This in itself was a total reversal of the Tombstone bureaucratic mentality. One of my colleagues at the time, Motor-Mouth (not his real name, as he never stopped talking), was based in another European city and had apparently opened up some twelve to fifteen traditional type *cases* against the US air carriers operating there, demonstrating his acumen for uncovering all these security vulnerabilities, and expecting some big atta-boy from our headquarters. When the General found out about this he apparently went ballistic and sent the idiot home – with a strong message to all of us that the bad old days were over, finally. We were there to keep people from getting killed, not engage in endless paperwork.

Unfortunately, however, once the pucker factor started to dissipate as the war was winding down – the bureaucratic resistance of the managers started to manifest itself again. The General was trying to make changes faster than the managers would (not could, mind you) cope and they fought him tooth and nail just by dragging their feet. They knew he only had a limited contract and just waited him out until it was his time to leave.

One of the programs the General did make effective changes in was the FAM program. The short of it is that he got rid of most of the dead weight by instituting higher physical fitness and shooting standards with rigid testing protocols. He brought one of his own people on board to oversee the program. This guy was merciless in adhering to the standards. If a candidate was one second off a 2 mile run or a hundredth of a second off the upgraded speed shooting we were now required to do – they failed, period, and were kicked out of the program. We actually had equipment that would measure timed shots down to a hundredth of a second. This was a great time.

Fortress of Deceit

Much to my surprise and delight the river of life propelled me into one of the five FAM Team Leader positions. The program went from a maximum of some 400-500 FAMs down to between 50-60 comprising five 10-12 man teams (numbers fluctuating by injuries and folks entering and leaving the program). The basic philosophy of this new FAM program was to "train the trainers"; meaning the team leaders were trained to cutting edge lethality and we in turn would adapt the training to our unique operational environment and, in turn, train the rest of the cadre.

Of course, the new program was hit with the inevitable EEO lawsuit by a female who complained that the new physical fitness standards were discriminatory against women. She won the case and we had to establish standards that were "fair" to the fairer sex. She apparently received a nice cash award too, for the mental anguish she suffered. Somewhere it lacked the agreement with the terrorist union that she would only have to fight against female terrorists. Turned out she still failed the revised standards and was booted out of the program anyway. We had other females in the program and no one gave it a seconds thought.

Our approach was to train to beat the best that the bad guys could throw at us with clear rules of engagement: If one or more potential hijackers demonstrated the means, opportunity and intent to use violence or the threat of violence to take over an aircraft they would be dead in two seconds with a bullet hole in the head.

I returned from my first trip overseas with my new team on a cold February evening at our northern Virginia headquarters, there were several inches of fresh snow and ice on the ground. I hadn't met any of my team members prior to just a few weeks before we launched this mission. After I finished up my required post-trip paper work that evening I went to the parking lot to clean off the snow and ice from my car and discovered nearly half my team cleaning off my car with bare hands or credit cards. I told them I was very appreciative of their efforts and asked what this was about, complaining that I might be a lot older than most of my team but I'm hardly an invalid yet. What I discovered is that three of the other team leaders apparently never qualified with their teams. They had private qualifications which raised the question of whether they met the minimum standards that they enforced on the rest of the team's personnel. Killing off the old Tombstone method of operations proved to be impossible when no one in management was held to account for their actions. I made a point of not only qualifying with my team but was always the first one to jump into any new tactical situation that was thrown at us. Something they were greatly appreciative of. I knew at that point that I had a real team here.

The nearly three years I spent as a FAM Team Leader was the absolute high point of my entire federal career. I had the pleasure of being trained by and work with some of the most elite people and units that this country has; not only my own team, but both in the military and other civilian worlds. There are some things that should be kept secret and the units and mechanics of this training fits in this category. The basics of this training is that one hones the individual to a razors edge. If the candidate survives the individual training then starts the really important training – working as a team. Getting an elite group of individuals to function as a team is a force multiplier and the true value of a *team* – particularly in the life or death environment we operated in.

Perhaps one of the high points of this team building was a live shooting exercise in which we sat about twenty-five yards from each other, sitting inches from a metal shooting target and exchanging shots at the opposing target. Any subconscious or conscious bigotry a person may have had going into this exercise was quickly dissipated. All one cared about ultimately was competency and the team's esprit de corps. It also made a big impression on me concerning how small one tries to be both mentally and physically when being shot at.

The closest I ever came to shooting someone (not counting my law enforcement days) occurred on a long flight to Europe, this was right before I became a team leader (before they got rid of the dead weight): I was seated near the front of the coach section of a jumbo jet on the left side of the plane. A few rows ahead of me and on the right side was a FAM who had the moniker of *Terminator*, not only because he bore a slight resemblance to the movie character but because he had machine like shooting skills. He was probably the fastest accurate shooter in the entire FAM program. Considering that we measured shooting skills in fractions of a second, he was quite the shooter to observe.

Seated a few rows behind me but on the other side of the aisle was the sleeper FAM that I previously described. I was in the aisle seat and an elderly local lady was sitting next to me on my left. This was a late night flight. For the first half hour or so I engaged in polite conversation with this lady, always curious of tidbits of the local cultures. She was flying to Europe to visit her kids and grandkids.

Passengers slowly started turning their overhead lights off and nodding off to sleep. Our resident sleeper FAM was already in one of his rigor mortis level sleeps. A couple of hours into the flight even the flight attendants were zonked out, except for a couple of them on *awake* duty status. With virtually the entire coach section sound asleep, three men that looked to be in their late twenties or early thirties started making frequent trips to the same bathroom, even though others were vacant. Two of them would congregate in the bathroom area, one would go in and after a few minutes would come out and sit back in his seat and the second one would enter the bathroom and the third one would leave his seat and be the next to enter the bathroom. Then all three would congregate in the lavatory area for a few minutes and scan the passenger cabin.

This type of musical chairs show went on for nearly an hour. Both Terminator and I kept a close watch on this and we exchanged numerous looks of concern. Since we were about the only ones still awake in the coach section we also caught the attention of the three perps. One looked right at me and mumbled something to his colleagues who also took a glance in my direction.

By this time, the old lady next to me (who had previously fallen asleep talking to me) had apparently been awake for a while and when I turned to look at her she had an obvious look of fear on her face, not to mention her white knuckle grasp of the arm of the seat. I had the feeling that she'd been through something like this before. I followed her eyes as the third perp walked back toward his seat but instead sat down right behind me in a vacant seat. By this time the pucker factor was getting intense. A look at the Terminator and I could tell that we both thought this was going to be the big one.

I made an obvious move in my seat to look behind me at the perp as well as the sleeper FAM – who was still fast asleep – not watching my back.

There were still the two perps in the lavatory area. One went into the lavatory – they all used the same one even though the others were mostly vacant except for the occasional passenger usage. Even the still conscience flight attendants stayed away from this area, not wanting to be involved in this. Perp one came out, exchanged some words with the second one who then entered the bathroom. The first one sat down in his seat. The guy behind me got out of his seat and went to the same lavatory again and entered it right after the second one left. Then the other two met in the lavatory area while the third one was in the lavatory. They then sat down.

Terminator and I kept exchanging looks – I had the feeling that the same wide-eyed looks of concern on the three perp's faces were also on our faces.

In martial arts one learns that typically a fighter is at a split second advantage when he acts as opposed to when he reacts to an action by an opponent. In our training, time measured in fractions of a second can mean the difference between success or failure – or life and death. So I decided to push them into a *reaction mode*, and put all my expensive training to the test. Even at this era of history I knew that the face of terrorism had evolved; that terrorists were changing their tactics from hijacking a plane for the benefit of the news media circus and manipulating government and possibly killing a passenger as negotiations dragged on and failed, to now just killing someone outright to get everyone's attention and abeyance. Was also very much aware of the possible use of a dead-man switch (push a plunger on an explosive but the bomb doesn't go off till the plunger is released), would cause a good guy not to shoot till he was very far away – or someplace else besides the inside of an airplane. There was also the strong probability of "sleeper" terrorists that weren't directly involved in this drama, at this stage anyway. They wouldn't reveal themselves until any law enforcement types took action first.

Fortress of Deceit

When the individual that previously seated himself behind me opened the door of the bathroom to exit it, I got up from my seat and walked toward the same bathroom. When we passed each other in the aisle we'd have to touch each other to squeeze past, and at that moment I quickly ran my hands lightly up the front and back of his torso, feeling for a possible weapon – none. It took less than a second. Before he knew what was going on I was already past him.

I went into the same lavatory they had been using all this while, and quickly ran through a cursive search of the garbage can, paper napkin bin and even unscrewed the cover beneath the sink. Nothing was amiss. Either they already have what they wanted – not the first time weapons or contraband were hidden in these lavatories, or what? I expected to be met by one or more of them as I opened the lavatory door, expecting and prepared for the worst, but no one was there. As I left the restroom I glanced at all three of the perps sitting in their seats and they all met my eyes. One could feel the adrenaline in the air.

I thought for sure this was going to be the big one. So I sat down in my seat, sort of diagonally so that I could keep all three of these guys in my peripheral vision – especially the one sitting behind me. I pulled my semi-auto pistol from its holster and pointed it right through the middle of my seat back (concealed beneath my jacket) pointed directly at the perp sitting there. I knew that whatever slight deflection of the bullet blasting through the seat back would be negligible at this range.

If any one of the three made the requisite hostile act my plan was to fire three rounds into the guy behind me – directly through the seat back. I knew that the Terminator, should the need have arisen, would kill the two other guys before they could blink twice. I was very painfully aware of how the best plans can go awry. I even gave half a thought to *losing* a round and hitting our sleeper FAM – not so much out of contempt for him, but to keep him from doing anything dangerously stupid when he wakes suddenly in the middle of gun fight from a deep slumber. I was more concerned about ruining another jacket than I was of killing him. The margin of error is slim on an airplane, which is just a bit more than a flying gas can. Assuming we survived this, I'd deal with the legal consequences later. After about another half hour, the antics of these three petered out and they kept out of sight for the duration of the flight. In those days FAA didn't have the slightest interest or the mechanics to obtain the names of these guys and run them through any type of intelligence or law enforcement data base. Typically clueless Tombstone mentality. So we couldn't do any checking from the passenger manifest to see if there was any official intelligence interest in these characters. I figured they either got spooked by the Terminator and me, or this was a test run.

One of my favorite memories of the FAM days occurred after an evolution in which a number of groups of FAMs were converging on a New York City airport on the last leg of a two week trip around the world. We arranged ahead of time, for those who were interested and had the time, to meet at one of the popular airport restaurants. As much as I enjoyed the international travel one couldn't wait to make it back home on American soil and imbibe in some good old American beer, an airport hotdog or hamburger, or pig out on pizza.

I arrived late for the rendezvous, but had a later connecting flight back home. Several FAMs had already come and gone but there was a constant influx of FAMs as the afternoon wore on. In spite of the problems in the FAM branch, we actually had a lot of camaraderie in the program

Fortress of Deceit

– if for no other reason we were all in the same boat and had a vested interest in surviving the elements. And it was good just to blow off steam and have a good laugh with folks from around the country.

The restaurant was a typical very busy airport eatery for a late Friday afternoon, it consisted of about a dozen small tables and booths with one large table in the middle. Unfortunately there was only one waitress servicing the whole restaurant including bussing the tables. The waitress was middle aged and I guessed that she was from Nigeria based on her features and accent (with all the worldwide travel I was doing I became pretty adept at identifying what part of the world people came from), and she was clearly frazzled and stressed out with her work load. Actually felt kind of sorry for her, and she was the subject of some conversation amongst us FAMs – very thankful for our government jobs as a lot of us did our share of grunt work before the FAM program. Without any prodding, as FAMs would leave our table to make their connecting flights home, in addition to paying their lunch tab and a usual tip, they'd throw in a few extra bucks just to balance out the stress the waitress was under. We put all the food and drinks on one tab so we had a growing pile of money on the table.

As if this wasn't bad enough a group of eight kids whom I assumed to be of college age came into the restaurant and occupied the large table in the center. They were all impeccably dressed and the leader of the group had his sweater draped over his shoulders, as of some sign of being of the filthy rich caste. They were also very boisterous and obnoxious and giving the waitress a hard time; complaining of bad service, cold food, flat beer and anything else they could whine about. Their leader was by far the worst one of the group. One couldn't help but hear that they just came back from a month long cruise in the Mediterranean on the ringleader's daddy's yacht. Trying to impress everyone in the restaurant. The waitress was having a fit just trying to keep up, much less having to deal with their attitude.

The last of us FAMs had to leave and make our connecting flights. With three of us left, we counted the money on the table and made sure we covered the tab with a more than generous tip; then we threw in another handful of bills to make up for the assholes she had to deal with at the center table. I was the last one in line as the three of us filed out of the restaurant and we had to pass the center table. The FAM immediately in front of me stopped adjacent to the ringleader at the center table, picked up his glass of beer which was about three quarters full, poured it on the chest and lap of the ringleader, gave the glass a couple of extra shakes just to get the last drops out, put the glass back down and walked out of the restaurant. I was right behind him the whole time. As I left the restaurant I turned around just to see if anything more was going to come of this and all the kids at the table just sat there with their mouths gapping open, but totally silent. It looked like this was the first time they had ever been spanked. Directly above their heads and behind them my eyes focused on the waitress who was holding the large wad of bills from our table, our eyes met. She had the biggest grin I'd ever seen anywhere, not sure if she was grateful for the money or putting the center table in its place, but I couldn't help but to smile back.

On multiple levels, the elite of the FAM branch were way beyond the capabilities of anything the bad guys could throw at us.

On another occasion four of us were walking back to our hotel after dinner during a stint in South Korea. It was night time but the streets were reasonably well lit. We happened upon a darker little side street short cut to the hotel that had

Fortress of Deceit

at least half a dozen Taekwondo training facilities, and the classes were just getting out. There must have been thirty adult students just milling around (some still practicing on each other) until they saw us walking down the middle of the street. The Korean's take their martial art very seriously, as a national pride. About fifteen of them surrounded us, and the leader roughly muttered something in Korean but I could understand the word "American" thrown in – it was pretty clear we were going to get our butts kicked. This wasn't a mugging, it was something more. There were elements in Korean society that didn't particularly like the American military presence in their country (primarily because of the crime, which was mostly rape), and we could have passed as military what with our reasonably short haircuts, age, and demeanor. Without giving it a seconds thought, I instinctively fell back on my judo training, and I bowed to these opponents just as I would in a dojo, as a prelude to combat. I guess the symbolism really did mean something. Two of them exchanged a few quick words, and they immediately made a hole for us to pass, motioning us through.

After I returned home from a couple of weeks of international travel, I had a pretty set routine. Aside from the jet lag, I was usually pretty exhausted from two weeks of little and broken sleep, as well as spending every spare minute of down time exploring whatever part of the world I was in. So when I got home, I'd check to make sure my townhouse was still in one piece, check my mail and phone messages, then in order to recover from the jet lag as quickly as possible I'd force myself to stay awake until my normal bed time. I'd stay awake by doing some jungle therapy for a couple of hours – which was usually a combination of kayaking and running, regardless of the weather. I got in the habit when I was in college working more than full-time and going to school full time that forcing myself to run for a few miles would keep me awake and alert for four or five hours no matter how exhausted I was.

On one particular occasion, however, as I was sorting through my mail I happened to find a letter from my oldest [biological] brother Steve. This was always a big treat. Every few years I'd receive some correspondence from him, usually mailed from a western or gulf state, and giving me an update on his adventures down the river of life.

After he returned from Vietnam, he joined the thousands of other Vets that were homeless. He continued working for a living and paying his taxes, but could never find it in himself to settle down. Often times he wouldn't even have a return address as he was living on the street. Other times he'd be in temporary housing at a Mission for poor folks, or one of those inner city dirt cheap hotels. If his letter had a return address I'd quickly scratch out a note trying to encourage him to settle down so we could continue to have some communication – we missed about 99% of brotherly bonding while growing up.

There wasn't a return address but he stated that he was living under a bridge near Athens, Ohio; trying to get a job. He described how the police weren't particularly friendly in Ohio. Normally the local cops would pick up a homeless person and drive him to the next county, make him someone else's problem. In this case, however, Steve cleaned up the garbage under and near the bridge he was living under and the cops would pretty much leave him alone. He still had money he saved from some day laborer work so he was able to buy food in the meantime, at least enough to keep him alive for a limited period of time. He explained that once a week some of the local college kids would treat themselves out to dinner at a local fast food restaurant and every week they'd buy him a meal and deliver it to him. Something he greatly appreciated. And here I thought that this generation of kids were just self-consumed semi-educated brats. I always kept learning new things, made a point of it.

This was an opportunity. Instead of bothering with a letter I quickly calculated that I could easily drive to Athens from Washington, DC and hopefully track him down before he moved on again. So I put in for leave for the rest of the week and drove to Athens, putting my hunter instincts in gear again. On the first day I discovered about half a dozen bridges in the vicinity of Athens. Two of them were particularly clean so I focused my efforts on those. On one of the main roads near-by I found one of those thrift shops where folks can drop off cloths and such. I kept an eye on this as I drove and walked around town looking for signs of my brother.

It didn't take too long when I found my brother rummaging through some free books at a stand in front of the thrift shop and I pulled into the parking lot and just sat in my car for a moment. Turned the engine off, and leaned over on the steering wheel with my eyes shut. I was glad to finally see my brother, but saddened to see him in this situation. I think the last time I saw him was ten to twelve years previously. He carried every-thing he owned in a couple of medium sized packs. We greeted each other as long lost brothers.

So for the next week or so the two us of drove all over Ohio. I was trying to get him situated in some housing and maybe a job. And he gave me a hard lesson on what life is like for the working poor. Just trying to get a state identification was a nightmare. The decreasing number of street pay phones just exacerbated the problem. One couldn't get a state identification without an address, but you couldn't get an address if you didn't have the money to pay the rent, and you couldn't get a job to pay the rent if you didn't have a state identification. It was a bureaucratic monster that just beat these folks into remaining in this circumstance. I observed that we treat our own poverty stricken citizens worse than we do illegal aliens. This was a crazy situation. Fortunately, however, more charitable organizations are being set up to help these folks.

Aside from our respective efforts to educate each other and catch up on a life time apart, we spent more time that week than we had our whole lives just bonding as brothers. And I came to understand that we both suffered from wounds that never healed, and in his case, his Vietnam war experience crushed any chance he had for some semblance of a normal life.

Ultimately, we couldn't find any place for him to settle down, and I had to get back to work. In Toledo, I put him on a train back to a western state where there were lots of poor folks, where he blended in and was most comfortable. As the train pulled away, he put his hand on the window and I gave him something of a salute. And it occurred to me that he wasn't doing anything I wasn't doing. The two of us just followed the route that the river of life meant for us, and while neither of us could eliminate the pain, the respective courses we were on would at least provide some distraction to put the pain aside and forget about it for awhile.

My experiences with my brother that week also made me realize some of the other incongruities of our government. Our government spends more money, more research, more debate on building a small damn or some other building project than we do when we engage in idiotic optional wars (wars that clearly don't meet the Constitutional criteria). You engage in a major building project in a woods or wetland and you have to jump through hoops producing an environmental impact statement, and gawd forbid there's a threatened worm in the vicinity. But when our politicians get us involved in unnecessary war there is little real debate on its impact and certainly no formal impact document produced – not least of which is the impact it has on the lives of those who dutifully fight those wars, not to mention the enormous financial costs of the war, and the costs of caring for the veterans, nor the scale of collateral damage involved. This seems a bit on the insane side to me.

I spent a total of about seven years in the FAM program and must have a hundred of these little anecdotes from around the world; about four years as a team member minus a few months when I resigned, and another few months taken off operational status while recuperating from a back injury; plus a little under three years as a Team Leader. But all good things come to an end. If I remember correctly, General Steele's tenure as Associate Administrator for Security ended in 1994. Before he left, however, he instituted operational changes, not only in the FAM program but in the more mundane aspects of aviation security. I truly believe that had he continued as Associate Administrator up to 2001 that 9/11 could have been avoided entirely or at least greatly minimized in its severity. But he was fought tooth and nail by the managers that ran the bureaucracy. And things he was able to force past their thick heads they just waited him out – knowing that he was only there for a limited time.

As an example; under the pre-Steele days, FAMs were not allowed to fly armed in US skies except when operating as a team and on a flight going to or arriving from a foreign location. So a FAM flying from point A to B in the U.S. to undergo the frequent training (as an example), had to lock his fire-arm up in his check-in luggage just like any other civilian. And yet every local, state and federal law enforcement agency's personnel were allowed to fly armed. So here we were, the only law enforcement agency specifically trained to use lethal force on an airplane, and we were the only law enforcement entity specifically prohibited from flying armed in routine travel. This Tombstone Mentality permeated everything FAA security did. So Steele changed that with the stroke of pen. The day after he resigned, however, the Tombstone managers rescinded this directive and prohibited us from flying armed on routine positioning flights. And things soon got worse.

Steele's replacement in 1995 (there was an acting in the interim) was Cathal Flynn, a retired US Navy Admiral and was the highest ranking SEAL in navy history at that time. But I had a bad feeling about Flynn from the get-go. He was at the top of the administrative heap when I was a criminal investigator for the agency – and I don't have many fond memories of that time. So it may have been just guilt by association.

Back to FAA: Flynn didn't create the Tombstone Agency mentality within the Security Division but he certainly maintained and enhanced it within the security division. In addition to returning to business as usual in the various aviation security mission areas, the FAM branch didn't escape his notice either. To make a short of it: We, in the FAM branch, went from an elite group of operators with extremely clear rules of lethal engagement to an elite group of operators with a very confusing operating mission. Under Steele, the unit cohesion was so tight that you could tell with a glance what your teammates would do in any operational situation; under the new regime you'd have to debate all the parameters for a half hour to figure out what to do. But that would have to wait till the afterlife as we'd all be dead.

At one point in 1995, FAA sent the entire FAM branch of some sixty or so FAMs and staff to some air force base out west to have our new lethal force engagement rules explained to us. We were now instructed that we were prohibited from taking any action on an airplane unless someone had already been killed or is suffering grievous bodily injury. We also had to take into consideration where the hijackers wanted to take the plane. If it was to a friendly country we were instructed to ride the situation out. In spite of having a fairly large intelligence unit in their bureaucracy, FAA management was completely ignorant of the evolving terrorist methodology. Noticeably absent was any discussion on what the terrorists will do to an armed FAM sitting on his butt when they find out he's a representative of the Great Satan. One of my team members suggested that management used the *Airplane* movie starring Leslie Nielsen as its basis in conducting security operations, and their comedic show would have been hilarious except for the deadly consequences.

Needless to say, we were all somewhat in shock and disbelief. Management was somewhat remiss in explaining the mechanics of how all this was to take place. It was left up to us to figure out. Subsequent discussions with my team about this and we quickly devolved into making a big joke about it.

We had a fully qualified emergency room medic on my team and under these rules he's supposed to ask permission from the terrorists if he can take the vital signs of a passenger they're beating to a pulp to ascertain when the poor sap has suffered grievous bodily injury. As the FAM team leader, I pictured myself drawing the terrorist's team leader's attention by yelling, "You Hoo, if you could let us know where you want to go that would be just peachy."

Fortress of Deceit

My assistant team leader just up and quit that afternoon. A handful of other folks from different teams also quit that day. Other folks gradually quit over the next few months as they arranged other employment. For the umpteenth time in my federal career I was fed up with the federal government and did another round of soul searching on what I wanted to do when I grew up, drawing blanks. In this place of my journey down the river of life I found myself in a stinking swamp, trying to muck my way out of it. Images of Bogart in the *African Queen* came to mind. I had about fifteen years in the federal government – another five and I might be able to take an early retirement with at least some modicum of benefits, if I could gut it out. So I lingered for a few more months.

The last straw for me though was when I had to take another team out on a two week overseas mission. The persons on this team already had a reputation of being the party animal team. A week prior, that team's team leader was apprehended by the state police for a drunk driving offense but due to professional courtesies he wasn't formally charged but had to quit the FAM branch – due to, apparently, flashing his credentials to the arresting officer trying to get out of the bust. He ended up having a glorious career under TSA – no surprise there.

So just a week or so before his team was scheduled to go overseas I was tasked to lead the team in his stead. To make a long story short, this was my worst trip ever. While the team members were competent when sober, on every flight we were on in the Mediterranean theater at least 90% of the team were unconscious on all the flights sleeping off the effects of their hang-overs. My attempts to force them to show up for work sober and alert were futile as this apparently had been their modus operandi for years. Half way through the trip I contemplated terminating the rest of the trip and sending everyone back home. But it would have taken months of paper work to do this. There was an incredible amount of administrative work involved with sending a FAM team overseas. Not only with mundane things like arranging lodging and ground transportation but liaison and courtesies with the foreign governments and our own embassies as well as our State Department headquarters. So I gutted out the trip and upon my return to FAM headquarters I wanted to initiate disciplinary action against almost the entire team, but management wouldn't have any of it. Under Steele and his merciless #1, these folks would have been keel-hulled, but under the current management this was SOP. I quit the FAM branch right after that but was still in an employment limbo at FAA headquarters.

As the 9/11 Commission documented, there were only thirty-three FAMs on that fateful day – and this is the story behind the story as to how that number came about.

And then, it wasn't any surprise to me; the river of life manifested itself again. Another current reached out and carried me along. The FAA Red Team was greatly understaffed, no one there but the manager, a secretary, and an idiot team leader with the name of Motor Mouth (not quite his real name). They were looking for someone who would "hit the ground running", who had lots of international experience and could operate independently. Turned out I was their ideal candidate, and signed right up with no hesitation. Just like in the *African Queen*, at the point of total despondency in the swamp, a new adventure beckoned.

CHAPTER SEVEN
The Red Team

+

He can best avoid a snare who knows how to set one.
Publilius Syrus

+

+

One of the other fallouts from the bombing of Pan Am 103 was that FAA was ordered to have a Red Team. A Red Team, by definition, is an *adversary* team designed to give the good guys some realistic training against how the bad guys operate. I don't know who initiated this endeavor but whomever it was should have been awarded a medal for intelligent thinking – which is a rarity in the federal government. If the program would have been given its appropriate emphasis and follow up – which is also a rarity in the federal government, 9/11 wouldn't have happened.

The basic operating parameters of the Red Team were three fold:

First; to use the tactics and equipment that terrorists would use against the US commercial aviation industry both domestically and overseas.

Second; the Red Team reported directly to the Associate Administrator of Security there-by by- passing all the bureaucratic layers and influences in between.

And third; *to project what the next most likely terrorist attack will be so that appropriate countermeasures can be taken to prevent the attack.* My emphasis.

So simple in its design but so profound in its realistic and expected impact. But unfortunately, this was still the FAA and it was still the Tombstone Agency. Nevertheless, I jumped into this program with a burning fury. It was right up my alley and exactly what I was looking for ever since my post college days reading Sherlock Holmes. The GAME was finally afoot. Everything previously was just a warm up to this.

While I loved my time as an air marshal team leader, I knew the overall impact of the FAM branch was negligible. With only five teams we weren't even a token force. Something which was proved on 9/11 when the air marshals only had thirty-three personnel according to the 9/11 Commission Report. At their new facility they were little more than a dog and pony show so the visiting Congressmen and bureaucrats could see their lethal prowess. But they weren't even a factor to be considered when the terrorists made their plans for that horrible and fateful day.

But the Red Team was a different story. This was like having a neutron bomb in your back pocket. While I knew from personal experience that the FAA version of security was a total joke, proving that point to a recalcitrant bureaucracy was another matter. But I relished the opportunity. I spent most of my career as one of the good guys fighting the bad guys, now I was being paid to be one of the bad guys fighting the good guys. This was exactly what I was looking for; and maybe, just maybe accomplish something for the taxpayer for the first time in my career.

In typical Tombstone mentality, during the seven years I was with the unit FAA staffed it primarily with people whose main interest was to travel overseas on the tax payer's dime. We had some decent folks in the unit but the bureaucracy was against decency. This was a weird environment, by this point in my career I was picking up waves that FAA actually liked misfits in important positions.

Fortress of Deceit

When a misfit stepped out of line so far that under any normal situation they'd be subject to severe disciplinary action; under FAA, however, management would not only turn a blind eye toward the miscreants behavior but would often reward the bastard. I saw this early in my FAA career beginning with the sleeper FAM, continuing on through the drunken FAM team leader, and a host in between. But it wasn't until the Red Team that I felt that this was more a matter of standard policy. The end result of this *policy* was that once a misfit is taken care of you have a guaranteed loyal employee for life – the misfit knowing they couldn't get a decent paying job anywhere else. It also made me wonder if the entire FAA security management gene pool was staffed entirely by loyal misfits. After I filed my whistleblower disclosure against FAA in late 2001, the Office of Special Counsel made the public statement that there was a "substantial likelihood" that the Red Team was grossly mismanaged and ordered the Department of Transportation to investigate my allegations, officially reinforcing my suspicions.

Operationally, however, Red Team work was actually a very tedious and monotonous exercise involving countless hours standing in passenger lines at airports waiting to see what happens at the screening checkpoint. Some of it involved staging operations breaching security at various points around the airport and observing and documenting how the local security and police responded, if at all. A third major area was positioning one's self at some point in an airport and just maintain endless hours of discreet surveillance and document what happens. We did this worldwide, almost. This wasn't unlike the surveillance and testing of security that a real terrorist team would engage in prior to initiating an attack. We never actually executed any simulated attacks. For one thing we were instructed not to do anything that would disrupt flight operations, endanger lives or break equipment. Plus, we had a vested interest in not getting shot or beaten up by cops, particularly in third world countries.

While the work was tedious and monotonous, it wasn't boring. When I went on a mission my adrenaline went through the roof. This was nothing short of a hunt. It was reminiscent of the adrenal rush of my earlier dear stalking days – the patience and persistence of the hunter. On top of that, at least when I started with the Red Team, I felt I was actually making a major contribution: Behave the same way a terrorist would when conducting surveillance for an attack and do some quiet testing to ascertain the feasibility of the success of such an attack, and sneak away without anyone noticing. The essence of Red Team work.

If I were a bad guy, this would be crucial information to start planning the attack. As a good guy, however, this was an opportunity to fix or change security so that attack could be foiled even before it began. This was the theory anyway, but there's a big difference between theory and execution of same in the Tombstone Agency. With all the flying around the world I did as a FAM, I knew security was a joke. Now I was documenting that fact in a manner that the bureaucracy was forced to eat.

During my first year on the Red Team I observed and documented that terrorists could pretty much do whatever they wanted to do anywhere they wanted too, whenever they wanted too. By the second year (1996) I started to go back to some of the same airports around the world that I had been to the year before and discovered the same security problems that I had previously documented. By 1997, my third year, this was confirmed. No effort was being made to fix the problems we identified.

Fortress of Deceit

What made the situation even more disturbing was that I discovered that the security problems the Red Team documented in the early 90's were the exact same problems at the exact same airports that I was identifying in the mid to late 90's. This information came about due to another confluence of junctures of the river of life. When I was an air marshal working overseas I had a tendency to wear out a lot of shoes by walking all over the place during my free time. I'd mix with the locals as much as possible, eating local food, drinking local drinks, and just generally having a keen interest in how people lived around the world. Didn't make any difference if I was in the Arab world, the deepest darkest jungles of south and Central America or the Far East, or the modern metropolises of Europe. It was a fascinating time of my life. I also frequently got sick drinking and eating the local cuisine. In some places just breathing the noxious air would get one sick. As incredible an experience as the worldwide travel was, whenever I returned to US soil I would momentarily pause and mentally kneel down and kiss the home ground. But as it turned out, getting sick from eating indigenous food and drink particularly from third world countries actually saved my life.

In 1997 I became sick enough that my home remedies and *mind over matter* healing efforts weren't working any more. I went to my family doctor and ended up getting blasted with several heavy artillery barrages of antibiotics trying to kill off the multiple invading bacteria that I was incubating. After months of this treatment I was still having some discomfort so the doctor ran me through an MRI or a CT scan to see if there was anything else he could detect that might be causing my discomfort (turned out to be an old martial arts training injury). However, unrelated to my symptoms he happened to find a particularly lethal form of cancer that was growing on one of my kidneys. The immediate *treatment* was to undergo surgery and have this cancer shaved off my kidney. I happened to be heavily engaged in a yearlong project in which I was spending about ten days every month working at San Francisco International Airport (SFO) assessing the effectiveness of the latest bomb detection equipment for checked baggage. If everything worked according to plan it would be two or three months before I would be able to go back to work; so a replacement had to be found for me to continue this project through its projected funding cycle.

Turns out Steve Elson (the same from the first few pages of this book) was available and willing to take my place. So the next scheduled trip to SFO I showed him the ropes as to what we were doing out there and a bit on the technology involved. He was a quick study and instinctively grasped the situation.

Steve and I immediately hit it off with each other. Within minutes of working with him one is impressed with his integrity, professionalism and dedication to duty. He even carried a miniature copy of the oath of office we were required to recite in his wallet and a copy of the U.S Constitution was never far from his grasp. Definitely a kindred spirit here.

When I first met Steve in the early 90's I was a new FAM Team Leader and he worked in the Red Team, we had very little interaction with each other however. Occasionally our respective offices would get together and go out for lunch. Lunch conversation would swiftly drift into how screwed up FAA management was, literally all over the country. What I experienced back in Chicago was only a microcosm of what was going on nationally in the Tombstone Agency. Out of all the stories we shared back then I can't say that my own managers represented the finest examples of stupidity and gutlessness but they were

Fortress of Deceit

certainly near the top. I did get the unofficial award though for having the funniest true story.

At our regional office in Chicago, a couple (a male and a female) staff members would periodically work late at night together and engage in sexual activities in Yogi's (the division manager) office after everyone else went home. Apparently on one of these evenings during what was a particularly physical encounter the male broke an artery in his twang with blood spurting around all over the office. Well, they couldn't keep this little tryst quiet. The following day Yogi was moved to a different office while his old office had to get new furniture, new carpeting and a new paint job.

A couple of days went by when I happened to be walking in one of the terminal buildings at O'Hare and one of the cops that Mick and I had previously briefed in one of our terrorism sessions came up to me with a big grin on his face. He explained that he was on duty "the night of the broken twang" (his words) and apparently the call that came over the 911 dispatch was so hysterical and horrifying that a dozen cops showed up just to see what all the hubbub was about. He described a *crime scene* in Yogi's office that would have made Jack the Ripper envious.

Not long after that, the man with the broken twang was fired and the female was promoted. Years later, when TSA took over, the female had a glorious and rising career into senior management. No surprise there.

Back to Steve Elson in SFO: Prior to this office lunch, I was convinced that Yogi and Booboo and company had to be the most incompetent managers in all of FAA Security, but Steve related that in his current office out west literally all the employees filed grievances, EEO complaints, or sent letters to the Inspector General's Office complaining of gross incompetence as well as a litany of other wrong doings against the manager. Nothing was ever done to correct these problems. Apparently the main manager involved received a sizeable cash award for having to deal with extremely difficult personnel issues in her office. Later she was promoted under TSA. Again reinforcing my maxim that misfits tended to get promoted. Our tax dollars hard at work. Never imagining at the time, that these folks were the elite, compared to the new managers TSA coughed up years later. One never appreciates what one has till it's gone. While the FAA managers I came across were buffoons, some of the TSA managers I knew were outright evil. If it weren't for their cushy government jobs they'd probably be on some type of government watch list.

With all this BS going on, I was somewhat starved of the intellectual challenge I was seeking, so I tried my hand at writing: In keeping with the habits of my mentor, Sherlock Holmes, who wrote a number of monographs on different aspects of crime and some of his investigative principles and methodologies, I tried my hand at doing the same.

One of Holmes' greatest attributes was his observational skills. He'd walk into a situation and observe the minutest of details that could be of the greatest use to solve the case but that most everyone else either ignored or simply did not notice even though it was there to see. Was this ability just a fanciful skill attributed by fictional liberties – kind of like Superman's ability to fly, Spiderman's ability to climb up walls, or Obama's ability to tell the truth? Or was there really something to this?

When I was an undergraduate student one of the most fascinating psychology courses I took was mnemonics. The basic gist of the course was learning the ability to memorize essentially any amount of information by associating the things to be memorized with some rote mechanical device such as numbers (although numbers certainly aren't the only device). Since the human brain remembers and learns primarily through the sensory input from the eyes, the emphasis of this course was on visual memorization techniques.

This skill I learned in college lay dormant for years, until I started working as a Special Agent for the agency. At that time I noticed a very practical application for this, thanks in large part to Sherlock Holmes. I practiced this system whenever I walked into a crime scene. In a matter of a minute or two I would go through this series of mental steps and memorize all the pertinent details of the scene as well as the individuals involved. Later, back at the office I'd write down a detailed report of what I had observed. The methodology essentially involved taking a series of mental photographs of what one was looking at, incorporating the smallest of details. During this time frame I was still just experimenting with these mnemonics techniques and developing and enhancing my own skills in applying then. As with any skill – practice makes perfect.

When I was a criminal investigator, my supervisor, as part of his supervisory pin headed duties, asked to see my investigative notes. I told him I don't have any. "Oh, you don't have any", as he started making an obvious point of jotting down this little tidbit in my personnel folder. I told him I keep this stuff in my head. He picked up the latest investigative report I put on his desk (which was fortunate since I was most familiar with it) and proceeded to quiz me on various details of the report. I was able to regurgitate everything he asked me and more. Down to the distance between footsteps in the lawn and dimension of the window that was broken into. This really was a fascinating system.

He never bothered me again about my lack of investigative notes.

Still later, when I was an air marshal, I became rather adept at applying mnemonics in a more *tactical* environment. As a FAM in those days, one would occasionally travel around the world with a group of ten to twelve folks. You get to know them fairly well. Not only during normal conversations, learning about their likes and dislikes, their family lives etc., but it's only natural to develop bonds of friendship with some, and avoid being around the misfits like the plague.

One also develops a tactical assessment of one's teammates; who you would rather have around when the guano hits the fan and those that are just toting ammo around. Basically dividing up the team into the mental carnivores (those who were in hunting mode) and the mental herbivores (those that were just grazing away in the meadows, taking in the sun, and were essentially oblivious of the other carnivores that could threaten them). A pissed off rhinoceros was certainly a dangerous animal to be around, but you had to beat it over the head to get it fired up. A hungry tiger, on the other hand, was always looking for something to kill and eat. The latter were the type of FAMs I made a point of being around when operational.

Using my mnemonics technique I quickly divided up my teammates into carnivores and herbivores. This distinction was not only obviously apparent during training and observing how folks reacted under stress and fatigue but there were also very subtle signs the members of each group gave off. One of those signs, but certainly not the only one, was how they walked, particularly going up a flight of stairs. Initially I was just practicing my mnemonics on my fellow team members, but I soon observed some

Fortress of Deceit

amazing commonalities in each group that distinguished one group from the other.

I noticed that when an herbivore walks up a flight of stairs, as they placed their foot on the next step their ankle would sag a bit and the heel of their foot moved slightly below the level of that step. On the other hand (or foot in this case), when a carnivore walked up a flight of stairs, as he or she placed their foot on the next step they kept their calf muscles tensed, with the heel of the foot raised slightly above the step level. Almost as if they were walking on their toes. The action was so subtle, you wouldn't notice it unless you were deliberately looking for it. This walking trait was universal between the two groups based on my own observations. I had other observations too, but I don't want to divulge all my little secrets – just in the event someone finds this a useful skill to carry on. Unless you were specifically looking for trifles (just as Holmes would), you'd never notice this. (Advertising specific details of what one is looking for when conducting profiling is a big mistake, any nefarious individual paying attention to these would just change his profile so as not to give off these warning signs.)

So I started using this same methodology as a FAM, when observing my fellow passengers while in the airport terminal building and memorizing every pertinent detail of the passengers who gave off all the signs of being a mental predator (IE: the most likely characters who were mentally engaged to resort to immediate violence – a possible terrorist). One might call this "profiling", but in the federal government, particularly in TSA, you can't even use this word without being labeled a racist and ruining one's career. This "p" word is only a couple of steps behind the "n" word. TSA even has policy memos about this politically correct nonsense. Which is really unfortunate, as an erstwhile *good guy* is missing out on a lot of tactical information available but TSA is conditioning their employees to not think pre-emptively – remarkably similar to the Tombstone Agency mentality.

In all the nonsense that TSA does, the one program that actually seemed to make some sense (when it first started) was the training of Behavior Detection Officers at airports. But TSA screwed up this program too. Lots has been written about this program, but the New York Times summed it up succinctly on March 23, 2014 in an article titled, *At airports, a misplaced faith in body language*. What the Times stated is that TSA is looking for "liars" and they don't do a very good job at it. Furthermore, they state, there isn't any scientific data which supports this program anyway. And TSA already spent, according to the article, one billion dollars on this nonsense already. Looking for "liars", they must be kidding! What they should be looking for are terrorists.

So anyway, I wrote up my little monograph and had it published in the *Police Marksman Magazine* in the late 90's. Called it, *Tactical Memorization, or Mnemonics and the Law Enforcement Officer*. I actually forget the month and year it was published, this stuff only works if/when one actually uses it. Fortunately, the publisher sent me a book titled, *The Best of Police Marksman*, Volume II 1995 to 2000. Copyright 2002. My article is featured starting on page 234.

I received a number of letters and phone calls from folks around the country congratulating me on the article and describing how much they use it. Most of these were from cops of course. One in particular, however, came from a lady who was teaching children with learning disabilities and adopted my methodology in her classroom describing how the kid's academic performance increased significantly

– her husband was a cop which is how she came across the article.

One example of my own successful use of this system occurred after arriving in Paris on an air marshal mission. As my FAM team was queuing up going through customs and immigration with hundreds of people in multiple lines, I started taking mental snap shots of anyone that seemed to give us anything more than a passing glance. Took a dozen snapshots of folks by the time I made it past the government officials. I happened to notice a couple of individuals paying us some unusual attention – just watching us from a distance. Later, they were in the baggage make-up area. I noticed that they noticed that I noticed them. I didn't give them much thought, though, at the time, until I saw them waiting for us at the hotel, amongst a crowd of guests. Taking mental photos of them every time I saw them. I just figured they were with the federal cops given their ease of getting through the airport checkpoints and in the baggage makeup area they didn't appear to be even looking for their luggage on the carrousel, it's not the first time things like this happened and I just kept them in mind, not particularly concerned. After we checked in at the hotel, myself and a FAM colleague of mine were still wired from drinking coffee and staying alert on the flight to France – the adrenal crash and jet lag hadn't hit us yet. So we just walked around the local area near the hotel, dropped in on a French bistro to get a bite to eat and something to drink. This was in the late afternoon when it's a common habit for Frenchmen to drop in at the local pub after work for a quick snippet before they head home. By total coincidence one of these guys was having a drink at the far end of the bar. So I mentioned this whole situation to my colleague and the two of just stared at the cop at the far end of the bar, with totally dead-pan faces. It took a couple of minutes, but just as the cop was about to take another sip of his drink, he noticed us in the crowded bar and literally spilt his drink all over himself - must have thought we were a lot more operationally savvy than we initially appeared, what with reversing the surveillance.

The routine of Red Team work was further interrupted during this time frame with the explosion of TWA-800 just off the coast of Long Island. This situation brought me in closer contact with another very unique and gifted individual working within the FAA Security Division. I'll call him Sal (not his real name).

Sal was one of FAA's Bomb Investigators. Previously, Sal found himself in the middle of unraveling what later became known as the *Bojinka Operation*. This was a January of 1995 attempt by terrorists to bomb a dozen or so US commercial aircraft over the Pacific Ocean killing several thousand people. The plot was foiled when a fire broke out in the apartment in Manila, Philippines where they were constructing the bombs. Somehow Sal found himself in the Philippines during this situation.

If I didn't know any better, I'd swear that Sal had some sort of hypnotic ability on people. To persuade people to do things that they would not normally do. He missed his calling in the State Department where I have no doubt that he could, with relative natural ease, bring any long term feuding parties together to the peace tables and coax them into a genuine ceasefire of hostilities. Typically in any type of major terrorist situation or major intelligence coup by an organization/country, that organization is extremely xenophobic of any outside rival organization or country. Part of this is simply due to the usual bureaucratic forces to protect one's own turf, but there is also the perceived need to protect one's own sources and capabilities. Well after the situation successfully resolves itself is when the respective bureaucracies like to brag about its successes or hide their failures. But rarely while the situation is on-going are they very open with even allied but competing services.

So Sal is in the Philippines as the Bojinka plot is unfolding. He was already recognized in certain professional circles as one of the world's leading experts in bomb investigations. He didn't just manage to *sneak* his way into the Philippine's intelligence and law enforcement efforts investigating this attempted wide scale terrorist attack but was actually involved with helping direct their investigative efforts. He provided real-time up to date information to FAA headquarters on reconstructing the bombs and which planes were targeted. Long before the terrorists had any chance to regroup and try again, Sal almost single handedly provided crucial information to various intelligence, law enforcement and security services in this country to thwart that attack. One of the unsung heroes of that day. I was still a FAM team leader at the time and had little interaction with Sal at that point.

However, on July 17, 1996 TWA-800 exploded off Long Island, NY killing all 230 people on board. Scores of federal, state, and local agencies as well as commercial aviation experts descended on the scene to participate in the recovery operations and slowly piece together the plane to determine what happened. Eventually it was officially determined that the cause of the explosion was most likely due to some faulty wiring in one of the fuel tanks.

I was doing Red Team work, per usual, while this was going on, but during my down time I paid close attention to the news on the daily developments of this tragedy. I had a vested interest in this since I was flying a lot and in fact frequently flew on that very same aircraft when I was a FAM. Typically in any domestic airline crash it is the National Transportation Safety Board (NTSB) that is the dominant investigatory agency. If/when the NTSB determines that foul play may be involved then it's the FBI that becomes the dominant agency and they handle the situation like a crime scene. Even though there wasn't any hard evidence of a crime that destroyed the aircraft, in the immediate weeks and months after the crash its very nature arose the appropriate suspicion: airplanes typically don't just blow up on their own so there was reasonable suspicion that foul play was involved. So the FBI became the dominant agency with scores of other government and industry groups playing a supporting role. The most popular suspicion was, obviously, that a bomb destroyed the plane. But there were also growing reports of a possible missile that brought down the aircraft.

As I read and collated all the news reports I could get my hands on, there was something about the news articles of a possible involvement of a missile that just didn't sit right with me, although I couldn't quite put my finger on it at the time. So I ended up calling Sal who was in the middle of the recovery efforts.

We both agreed that there was something amiss with the missile angle but neither could describe it. I made an off the cuff comment that if I could get my hands on the FBI statements they took of the witnesses who claimed to describe something resembling a missile then I'd probably be able to sort this out.

Sal said, "Are you serious?" I explained that I'd love to go up there but our own headquarters wouldn't let me up there as I don't have any experience in these types of crash scenes and certainly the FBI wouldn't let me take a crack at their investigative files. "Stand by, buddy", was all he said. And we hung up the phones.

Fortress of Deceit

I don't know what Sal does, but whatever it is, he smoothed the way not only at FAA headquarters but with the FBI in New York City. Within a few days I found myself working at the FBI Command Post and at the hangar where they were putting all the aircraft pieces together. He also got me access to some of the reports of witnesses that claimed to have seen something like a missile streak toward the aircraft right before the explosion.

So I'm sitting in the FBI Command Post going through a small pile of these witness reports describing a streak of light heading toward the jumbo jet followed by a big explosion and my first reaction after reading just a few of them was shock. These were the most poorly written witness statements I'd ever seen. They were little more than hand-written agent's notes. Having flashbacks to my agency days, we'd have more detailed witness statements concerning the theft of a can of beans than what was contained in these reports of a possible missile strike. Here I was, participating in what I assumed to be the largest investigation in the entire history of the FBI and this is what they call an investigation!

Well, this was what I had to work with. The witness reports were just as confusing a mix of conflicting reports as what appeared in the news. Some witnesses reported the streak of light moving from east to west, others from west to east and some from south to north; but all toward the aircraft and preceding the explosion. At first glance I could understand why the government discounted these reports. They all conflicted with each other. But I tried to apply a bit of Sherlock Holmes' reasoning to this problem.

The short of it was that I fabricated a little map of Long Island and plotted the location of each of the witnesses when they claimed to have seen the streak of light. I then divided up Long Island into three sections: the west, middle, and east. As it turned out, all the witnesses in the western part of Long Island described seeing the same thing: that the streak of light went from right to left across their field of vision heading towards the aircraft. Those witnesses on the eastern side saw a mirror image from those on the western side: that the streak of light went from left to right across their field of vision and intercepted the aircraft followed by the explosion. And lo and behold the witnesses in the center of Long Island described the streak of light heading towards them, intercepting the aircraft followed by an explosion.

If you plot this on a map it makes a fairly clear image of the alleged missile flying directly toward Long Island from the south, hitting the aircraft and destroying it. Essentially the origin of the missile was further out to sea than the aircraft and headed directly toward Long Island on a track almost perpendicular to the coast line.

As Sherlock Holmes might have said, "Elementary, my dear Watson", and yet the FBI and all the other federal agencies involved failed to conduct such a simple analysis. I wrote up a report concerning my methodology and conclusions and sent my report (on September 20, 1996) through my chain of command to the Associate Administrator of FAA for Security as well as a copy to my FBI contacts in NYC, and infoing Sal. In the final paragraph of my report I recommended that a follow up analysis of ALL the witness statements be conducted in the manner I described. I also suggested that it would be prudent to re-interview the witnesses to get more detailed statements. I never received any feedback from my own agency. None!

Prior to this memo I also had a pretty good working relationship with the FBI guys involved in this. A few weeks after I submitted this memo all of a sudden the FBI refused to return my phone calls and emails. It was plainly clear to me that the powers that be had already decided, long before the evidence was in, that a missile was not the cause of the explosion of TWA-800.

After 9/11, Jack Cashill, an award winning author, did a story on this little sidebar to the TWA-800 tragedy titled, *FAA Special Agent Exposes FBI TWA-800 Cover Up, dated 30Aug03;* adding additional evidence that I wasn't aware of. He and a number of other good folks have been trying to re-open the TWA-800 investigation as none of them trust the official government line.

One of the other unusual anomalies of this situation is that the CIA also got involved in this dog and pony show. The CIA has no legal authority to participate in domestic aviation crash investigations, yet to help tout the government line they produced an animated video shown on national TV demonstrating how the center fuel tank blew up (due to an internal wiring problem) and its dramatic flight characteristics after the explosion in its final moments before hitting the ocean. Check "cia twa 800 video" on the internet and you can still the video. There are also a lot of hits from various experts involved in this claiming that the video is mostly hogwash, a major whitewash of the facts, and is basically a big fat lie. Just a continuation of the Hollywood themed illusion based government cartel?

I don't know what destroyed TWA-800. All I had was a glimpse of a handful of witness statements. What I do know, however, is that the government made the decision before the investigation was complete that there wasn't any foul play involved, and they didn't give any evidence a fair assessment that conflicted with their own political objectives. It was my opinion at the time that the FBI took control of this investigation not to find evidence of a crime, but rather to make sure that no evidence of a crime was found.

I know from personal experience that there are outstanding field agents in the FBI, as well as other agencies, and I'm sure the FBI does excellent work when it comes to its bread and butter investigations (IE: kidnappings, bank robberies, etc.); but when it comes to really sensitive or potentially explosive investigations they are just the strong arm of the government dancing to the tune of its masters and blowing gas with the political winds of the times (in my opinion). Whatever doubts I had about the FBI prior to TWA-800 were removed after the event. I don't trust them. And 9/11 was still years away.

Unfortunately, Sal, the miracle worker of Bojinka and who assisted me in the TWA-800 work, couldn't work his magic on the FAA bureaucracy. He quit FAA shortly after this. Last I heard he was working in a grocery store. A big loss to the taxpayer and to this country.

Back to FAA in the mid/late 90's:

Turned out, I discovered, that Elson was already heavily involved in fighting the managers in the Tombstone Agency. He was a magnet for other concerned employees who were sending him a growing mountain of documentation from around the country proving that FAA Security management was grossly incompetent and negligent.

Wow, there was real potential here, I thought. For the first time in my approximate 16 years in federal service I didn't feel like a lone wolf hunting a huge monster bureaucracy, and one that was proving accountable to no one. Together we could start taking bites out of this beast.

Unfortunately, however, I had to direct my immediate energies toward getting rid of the cancer which set root in my body. As a cancer victim/survivor I had it easy compared to most. Surgery removed the cancer and only a small part of one of my kidneys. Took about six weeks to recover enough to get back to work but another couple more months before I could do any more travel – what with all the follow up medical visits and tests I had to undergo. Fortunately I didn't have to undergo any chemo or radiation therapy (apparently this cancer was so lethal that there wasn't any treatment other than surgery) and have been cancer free since.

Perhaps one of the more memorable moments of this adventure was when I had to go to the oncology section of the hospital for follow up tests. I was sitting in the patient waiting room in my hospital gown minding my own business and reading a book when some kid of about twenty was wheeled in and sat down in one of the chairs.

I couldn't tell if the patient was female or male, he or she was in the advanced stages of cancer, no hair, skinny as a rail, and a terribly gaunt look about the face. Our eyes met for a moment and we just nodded at each other – in seconds exchanging unspoken communication of sympathy, empathy, well-wishing and the hope that the suffering will soon be over, one way or the other. Definitely found a kindred spirit there.

Well, I survived the cancer without too much ado and was soon back at work doing my usual Red Team stuff. Involved a lot of international travel continually documenting how screwed up security was and how management did absolutely nothing when confronted with this information. While in country, I was also working very closely with Elson in compiling and collating all this information to organize it into some type of meaningful package that someone in authority could read and understand.

Elson, in the meantime, got so fed up with FAA that he just up and quit too. He had his retirement pay from the Navy and his wife was still working so he wasn't hurting financially. But this freed his hands considerably. He started writing to various members of Congress that were on the various committees that oversaw the FAA bureaucracy and commercial aviation industry, trying to get them interested enough in doing something about the Tombstone Agency before lots of people get killed.

I was working with Elson, in between my international travel, primarily in a support role and providing additional documentation. This was a slow and tedious process: Send a letter to Congress, follow up with phone calls, finally talk to someone over the phone – but what to do about it? Due to Elson's persistence more and more folks in Congress were starting to be made directly aware of the issues within the security bureaucracy of the Tombstone Agency. The fighting I had done against bureaucratic incompetency and unaccountability paled in comparison to what Elson had been doing, but working as a team we became a force multiplier.

While this was going on, however, I was for the first time in my federal career having second thoughts about endlessly fighting the federal bureaucracy. I still supported the effort, but I was getting tired of beating my head against the wall. Maybe it was my little bout with cancer, but I came to realize that for my entire career, if not my entire life I

Fortress of Deceit

totally neglected my personal life. My entire focus was on some notion of duty, honor and country; or maybe just figuring out what my route was on the river of life. Maybe it was time to get a job as a shoe salesman and settle down.

I was about forty-five years old at this point and never took a vacation lasting more than a long weekend, maybe once or twice before. So I decided to take a couple of weeks off and join some family and friends on a vacation to the old country. My father was born in Montenegro in the waning days of World War I, so for the first time in my life I was visiting the country of my paternal ancestry (which I still referred to as Yugoslavia even though it had split apart by this time). Montenegro was politically aligned with Serbia, which as the 1990's history has demonstrated was rife with various wars including a brief spat of NATO/US bombings. The family and friends I was traveling with were primarily Croatian. I couldn't distinguish the two sides and everyone pretty much looked the same to me. I was mystified and extremely somber, if not saddened over the violence and cruelty that overcame this area for much of the 90's.

In keeping up with my previous habit of just walking, I found the country to be one of the most beautiful parts of the world I've ever been too. Mountains on one side and the Adriatic Sea on the other. During peacetime the area is one of the favored tourist destinations of western Europeans.

One day during this vacation adventure I was walking near the Croatian coast, gradually making my way down one of the coastal hills. I passed what appeared to be a still functioning Roman Era aqueduct that was used to water a hillside garden over-looking the ocean. This was the most ZEN like place I've ever been. I had a bit of lunch there and continued walking down toward the coast.

Fortress of Deceit

After a short rout I happened upon a cove that was sided almost entirely by land except for a small break which opened directly to the sea. The cove and its beach were occupied by hundreds of kids doing what kids normally do on a beach on a perfect summer day. I walked right through the middle of them and nobody paid me any attention. I made the observation that there were only about four to six adults in this swarm of hundreds of kids that ranged in age from toddlers to kids in their late teens. Some of the adults could have been just older kids - I couldn't tell as I was some distance from them. There also weren't any life guards around. I just figured they must do things differently over here - all it takes is one kid to drown and the lawyers will be all over the place, if there were any more alive over here.

About half way across the crescent shaped beach I heard some little kid screaming behind me at the top of his lungs; I paused walking and turned around to see if I could discover where and whom this was coming from. I thought it odd that no one else seemed to notice this. Through the din of all the beach noise I couldn't tell where the screaming emanated from, just that it was some distance away. But this was a scream like none I've heard before, and yet deep down inside it was familiar. It wasn't the scream of some kid that just stepped on a bee, or because he was told to get out of the water. It was something more elemental.

A few moments later I passed another kid of about four years old that started screaming with everything he was worth. He was in the fetal position face down in the sand but with his hands covering his face, the scream being muffled slightly. I was about to stop when an older sibling (I assumed) picked him up and wiped the sand off his face - the kid was still screaming as he was carted off. I was actually starting to get a little light-headed and didn't know why, but I continued walking. About a minute later I approached a girl of about twelve who was just sitting on a towel, with her legs straight out in front and her hands resting on the ground. A baby of about two or three was playing at her feet with some beach toy – a shovel or something and flicking sand around.

As I passed the girl I saw that she was just staring blankly ahead of her across the water, non-blinking. Her eyes were glazed over and filled with tears. I barely made it a few paces more when my legs almost buckled beneath me. For the only time in my life I experienced the expression of being *weak-kneed*. I had trouble walking and almost collapsed in the sand. I made it to an empty bench and sat down. A feeling of absolute horror came over me and I had trouble breathing. It dawned on me that all these kids were orphans – made that way due to the *collateral damage* of the various wars that overcame this place. I couldn't move and just sat there staring at all this.

I drifted into a reverie to an earlier time. I was eight years old and living at St Aloysius Orphanage in Cincinnati, Ohio. My father had died about a year and half prior to this and my mother died just weeks before. During this phase of life I vaguely recall being somewhat stoic throughout the ordeals. Not quite understanding what or why these things were going on but waking up every day and enduring.

At the Catholic orphanage we had a lot of religious services which provided some degree of comfort. It was also a very regimented environment. After an afternoon benediction at the chapel, as we were filing out of the building I felt something starting to well up inside of me. I couldn't explain it but knew I had to get away. When the escorting nun turned away I stepped out of line and ran around a corner of the walkway unseen. I beat feet to a corner of the orphanage grounds and sat down at the base of a large tree. A few yards away was a fence and on the other side a road filled with the normal afternoon vehicle traffic. A family on the opposite sidewalk walked by. I started crying.

The crying turned into a torrent of tears and wailing. Moments later I involuntarily started screaming as loud as I possibly could. I just kept screaming and screaming as the weight of the loss of my family, and routine, and life path just totally crushed my spirit. I don't know how long I kept this up, but at some point I fell asleep from total exhaustion and defeat.

At the cafeteria at meal time they had those tiny little chairs that one sees in kindergarten classes, one each for each child and surrounding the tiny little dinner table. As children would arrive at or depart the orphanage the nuns would add a chair or take one away as necessary. So when I missed dinner they could easily tell that one of their charges was missing.

I awoke a little before dusk and found one of the nuns standing above me with her arms akimbo. She held her hand out to me and I stood up, grasped her hand and the two of us started walking back to the main building. While walking with the nun, I started to have a flashback to a previous time. After my father died, my mother was in and out of the hospital undergoing cancer treatment. When she was gone my four siblings and I were split into foster homes or were sent to a public institution called the Allen House, I went to the latter. This place provided three square meals and a warm dry place to sleep but it seemed to be lacking in other areas.

Fortress of Deceit

The way they handled minor discipline problems was to take a kid's clothes away, by force if necessary. So they had to remain in bed under covers with meals delivered to their rooms. This could last several days depending on the offence. Any behavior requiring a more severe punishment resulted in the police carting off the kid, kicking and screaming, never to be seen again. The day after I arrived at the Allen House was the dreaded shower day. I was ushered to a large shower stall room with a dozen or so spigots sticking out of the wall. There must have been thirty or more kids crammed into the adjacent *dressing* room. We were ordered to strip and enter the shower room where some big fat black lady was standing in the middle of the room with a long piece of a hula hoop. She yelled at us to grab a bar of soap and start washing ourselves. Problem was that there weren't enough bars of soap for each kid nor were there enough spigots, so we had to wait for a kid to finish washing, pass an inspection by the fat lady and then she'd throw the bar of soap in the middle of the washroom where whomever was bigger and faster got the soap. Those of us unlucky enough not to get a bar of soap were whipped with the hula hoop because we weren't washing as directed. As a six year old I was one of the smaller kids in the group and one of the last ones to get a bar of soap. I don't know how many times I was hit.

During the winter, when the kids were allowed outside to play in the snow, they'd pile all the winter coats, hats, gloves and boots on a large table in the recreation room. All this cloths came from charitable donations; old, well-worn and torn as they were. The kids would stand against the wall until they blew a whistle which was our signal to engage in a free for all to grab some winter cloths and run outside. The bigger kids would get the best clothes. Along with my small like-bodied colleagues, I'd manage to get a light weight jacket if I was lucky. Run outside and play until I couldn't take the cold any more then come inside to warm up. Then repeat the cycle till they blew the whistle for us to come back inside.

Later, some older black guy (I don't know if he was one of the older kids there, or a volunteer or a staff member) would grab one of the best coats on the table and give it to me, wait to make sure nobody stole it from me and then I'd run outside. The bottom hem of the coat reached nearly to my feet, so I'd frequently run around, trip on the coat and fall flat on my face, but it was warm. Think I saw him driving a city bus when I was in high school. As I was sitting in the bus he seemed vaguely familiar but I couldn't place him. I noticed that he kept looking at me in the mirror. As I stepped off the bus he said, "Have a nice day, John" (my middle name that I used growing up). As the bus pulled away I finally realized who he was, and I just stared at the bus as it disappeared down the long street. Normally I'd ride my bicycle eight miles to school every day rather than take a bus. But I kept bussing it for awhile in the hopes of running into him again. Never saw him again. One of my life-long regrets was not being able to thank him for taking me under his wing; a simple gesture that had a life-long impression on me.

On one of my subsequent visits to the place, one of my older brothers (Peter) and I snuck into the maternity ward (apparently the place used to be a hospital) to see my little brother, who wasn't yet a year old. We looked through the window and saw about a dozen or so babies in cribs, all of whom were crying. We spotted our little brother screaming, with dried mucus caked all over his face. I immediately started kicking at the wall and banging on the windows till one of the staff chased us out of there. Peter escaped from the place shortly there-after but was nabbed by the police a few days later when they found him wandering the streets looking for food, and was returned to the Allen House. They took his clothes away for several days, while I'd sneak his favorite foods out of the cafeteria and give it to him. Its weird how life can be, this was probably my first real Red Team activity.

This was my first introduction into government sponsored institutional life. I checked the name of this place on the internet in preparation of this book, just to verify the spelling, and discovered websites where former inmates described their experiences there. Apparently lots of child abuse of various types occurred there.

I was never really impressed, except for a few individuals, that government employees weren't particularly the most well-read of the population; in this case the only book these people must have read was *Lord of the Flies*. Recently I couldn't help but wonder, what with how prisoners were treated at Abu Ghraib prison, that there must be some kind of official training facility on how to humiliate prisoners – kids or otherwise. I wondered how many lives they ruined at the Allen House. Take kids that are sent there because of broken homes, physical abuse at home or, as in my case, no parent at home; kids already stressed out to the breaking point, and totally destroy their spirit in this place. The joint eventually closed down and is now a neighborhood recreation facility.

So this experience at Allen House went through my mind as the nun, gently but firmly holding my hand, escorted me back to the main building. As strict as the discipline was at the orphanage, I expected the worst. As we were walking, I made the commitment to mama and papa that I would endure what this, and life, would bring, and make them proud of me; even if it was only to be a decent person in the midst of all this madness.

Fortress of Deceit

Since I missed the evening meal, the nun took me to the cafeteria and walked me to the sink. I wasn't tall enough to reach the faucet so she got a hot soapy wash cloth and cleaned my face and hands. She sat me down in my personal tiny chair and served me up a bologna sandwich on *Wonder Bread*, a cookie and a glass of milk. As I devoured this I looked up at the nun and saw the saddest look on her face. I don't recall if I thought the same words- but my reaction was anger, "what the hell does she have to be so sad about!" It was more a statement, not a question. This was before I understood what empathy meant. Empathy, more than an emotion, maybe even an instinct; something that would rule my life, my behavior, and my conduct as a public servant – and served as the motivation for my subsequent whistleblowing activities. Over the years I learned to despise orphans, not because of who we are, but because there were too many of us. I made the decision back then to do what I could to minimize man's inhumanity to man, to prevent the further growth of the orphan population – "collateral damage" as the talking heads use to mask their violence. The seed was planted here.

After I finished dinner, the nun escorted me to the lavatory where the *junior boys* cleaned up. I brushed my teeth and changed to my pajamas. By the time I got to our ward it was already lights out and a serious offense to be wandering about. But she escorted me to my bunk, saw that I was tucked in and left. Throughout the entire evening neither one of us said a word. This was the second act of kindest I remember in my life, but certainly not the last one, which set me on the proper course in the river of life, which directly led to where I am now. Looking back on it, I don't believe the nuns had any discipline at the orphanage. They led by example, and us kids just naturally fell into step – for the most part.

Fortress of Deceit

On the beach, after I stopped feeling sorry for myself, I recovered from my own thousand yard stare and left this minefield of orphans, praying to God that these children would have folks in their lives that would show them a bit of kindness and empathy and give them a chance to live decently. This certainly wasn't what their young parents had in mind when they started their families.

I had it easy compared to most orphans, eventually made it to a decent middle-class foster home for a few years, then lived with my sister and her husband for a while; and became completely independent at nineteen. Perhaps the single person I owe the most too was Tom Burnside, a social worker from the local Catholic Charities. He spent an inordinate amount of time with me when I was growing up, as something like a *big brother*. Years later, after he saw me testifying on Capitol Hill regarding 9/11, he told me that when I was a new kid in their system I was "voted" by the staff as the one with the least bit of hope. It took me another twenty years to recover enough from a life in which I was seriously debilitated on a daily basis. Overtime, as I was growing up, I discovered that my only real fear in life was falling in love, getting married, having kids and putting my kids (and spouse) though the same thing I went through. It was a phobia actually. I didn't even know what my real first name is until after college.

After I left the cove I did some checking and discovered that some anonymous philanthropist paid the expenses for 300 war orphans to spend two weeks at this cove. This went on all summer long, 300 kids every two weeks for months. This was the day I decided to become a whistleblower, although I wasn't really aware of the official connotation at the time. There was too much at stake to stay on the sidelines.

Fortress of Deceit

When I returned back to work I changed my whole approach. If I could prevent just one innocent person from getting killed, then all this BS would be worth it. Instead of just sending endless reports through my chain of command I started to confront management directly, not in an aggressive or nasty way, but just asking questions and pushing them on answers. Eventually I was written up for being potentially violent prone and subject to being fired. Fortunately the charges were dropped as being nonsense but it was a fine example of the increasingly deteriorating situation between myself and management. After a while I started to get a pat retort from management: "We must be doing something right, we haven't had a terrorist attack since the last one", referring to PanAm 103. This proved to be as idiotic a statement as the managers that made it. No matter what evidence was presented to management they made comments similar to this. All I did at this point was ruin my career. The Human Resources division mysteriously lost all my job bids and requests for transfers. All one had to do to ruin one's career in this outfit was to question the Tombstone Mentality – it proved you weren't a team player, that you were a malcontent and a disgruntled employee, a person to be avoided, if not ostracized completely. This was nothing, yet.

Working with these clowns was totally futile. If this was how they wanted to play, it was time to elevate the game. While all this was going on Steve Elson's wife was transferred back to Washington, DC – so Steve was back into what he would eventually term "the Centrum of Evil." So I renewed and enhanced my work with Steve.

In August of 1998 I sent a letter to the Administrator of FAA Jane Garvey (through my chain of command) trying to convince her that there was "a dangerous culture of mismanagement" in the Security Division. I also told her that the United States "faced a potential tidal wave of terrorist attacks." Garvey didn't even have the courtesy to acknowledge receipt of my letter much less do anything about it. But I already knew she was the epitome of the tombstone mentality, which is why she was appointed to the top of the heap. So simultaneously I sent a copy to the Secretary of Transportation Rodney Slater. He at least had the courtesy to acknowledge receipt of my letter and copied me on a letter that he sent back to Garvey. He basically stated that Garvey ought to look into my allegations, but there wasn't any follow up and ultimately nothing was done other than to put me into an even deeper shit list with these clowns.

Several more months went by and Steve was continuing his pursuit. He put together a binder of documents that he collected from FAA Security employees from around the country proving that the managers in FAA were dangerously inept. The documents were about three inches thick which he placed in a big blue binder and labelled *The Big Blue Book of Death*.

CHAPTER EIGHT
Analysis of the Threat

+

Everything becomes common place by explanation.
Sherlock Holmes

+

+

I should probably digress a little here, again.

There are two sides of the security coin. The first is security, the actual systems that are in place and their effectiveness or lack there-of. The flip side of this coin is the actual threat, which has traditionally been defined through *intelligence* analysis. In the intelligence field there are basically two types of intelligence, referred to as *tactical* and *strategic*. The names may change based on what school of intelligence one was trained in.

Typically, tactical intelligence is information obtained from waterboarding prisoners, or electronic eavesdropping in which the listeners stumble upon an operation in the planning phase. The results are usually pretty clear and it doesn't take much analysis to report the obvious. The other type of intelligence (strategic) is the real work of intelligence analysis. This is the process of looking at all the various indicators one has access to and trying to foretell the future. Unfortunately, our collective intelligence agencies are terribly inept at making predictions. I'm convinced that if the President ordered our intelligence community to predict the timing of the next sunrise they couldn't do it without first spending a million dollars on contractors to tell them what to do, then they'd have to debate the subject for a week, pass it through the lawyers, and make sure that no one was offended by whatever conclusion they coughed up; by which time the sun rise in question would have long since come and gone. Makes the whole process kind of moot.

Look at the history of our modern intelligence apparatus which officially started shortly after World War II but its fore-runner was formed during the war: They failed to predict the Japanese attack on Pearl Harbor; they failed to grasp the significance of the German build up which preceded what came to be known as the "Battle of the Bulge", which was the largest single battle fought by the US; they failed to predict the dissolution of the Union of Soviet Socialist Republics and the fall of the Berlin Wall; they failed to "connect the dots" (as the 9/11 Commission mentioned) which preceded the September 11, 2001 terrorist attacks; they failed to predict the Arab Spring in which the people of numerous Arab countries short-sheeted their own governments; they failed to predict the spawning of ISIS and its mayhem in some of these same countries, and they grossly underestimated the capabilities of the USSR, China, Pakistan and India to make and deploy nuclear weapons (and Iran is just around the corner). Makes one wonder what we're actually wasting more tax dollars on this yet another failure based government program, and yet now they feel they have the God-given right to get into everyone's knickers through the NSA electronic eavesdropping program and the ever growing surveillance state programs. And yet, maybe elements within these intelligence bureaucracies actually did predict these events but were thwarted by the same bureaucratic and political obstacles that crippled FAA. According to whistleblowers from these agencies, it appears likely they suffered from the same bureaucratic problems that I witnessed in FAA as well as some problems unique to their own organizational environment. Regardless, the end result is that they have an abysmal failure record that rivals the Tombstone Agency. In either case, failure prone is failure prone. And lots of people died that didn't need to.

I dare say that the system I developed for analyzing intelligence (ie: information) is a much more prescient predictor of major terrorist attacks than the combined capabilities of the billions and billions and billions of dollars we waste on the intelligence, law enforcement (which is primarily the FBI) and security agencies combined.

This is how I did it:

First, I took another lesson from my mentor Sherlock Holmes. He had his own filing system of the criminal element in and around London, card indexed and cross referenced. Something he used to great effect in helping him solve his mysteries. I modeled my system off of his.

Prior to every air marshal trip I took overseas, the team received a one or two hour top secret intelligence briefing by some idiot from the FAA intelligence branch. By the time the "intelligence" was sanitized and filtered to make it dispersible to those of us in the field it was virtually useless. Just another bureaucratic anomaly which guaranteed failure. These briefings were so ridiculously poor they were a worse than useless waste of time. We would have been better off taking a nap.

Prior to my second FAM trip in the late 80's I started intensely reading up on the sections of the world we would travel to from completely open sources (newspapers, magazines, books, etc.); and would take notes from listening to radio news reports and television news shows and documentaries. For those that would listen, I would give an unclassified intelligence briefing that was much more useful than the official classified briefings we received. Turns out

Fortress of Deceit

that I actually had a bit of a jump start in understanding the terrorist mindset going back to my intense study of Soviet Spetznaz special forces when I was in the Coast Guard. Some talking heads blamed the Soviets for the training and equipping of many of the anti-western terrorist groups that manifested themselves during the turbulent 80's and 90's. This would have been accomplished primarily through their own special forces.

As time went on, I started to accumulate so much terrorism information on a world-wide basis that my own manual filing system couldn't accommodate it (my initial concern for studying terrorism was merely survival – one ought to know as much as possible about the jungle one intends to wander into). Cutting clippings out of the newspaper soon overwhelmed me. So on my own time I started to input my collected information into a regular word document in my computer. But even this was overwhelming me as there was so much information out there on terrorism. Instead of writing detailed reports in my computer I shifted to just writing bullet points of terrorism activity from around the world. I carried a little 3x5 notebook everywhere with me and whenever I came across new info on terrorism I'd jot it down. Even when I was overseas I'd pick up an English language newspaper or periodical on the subject and take notes – absorb a local spin on the subject. Gave me a good grasp of how foreigners view terrorism. Nor did I consider politics in evaluating the information I incorporated into my data base. So long as a situation crossed the threshold of violence associated with my understanding of terror, I used it – the 1993 FBI massacre of the Branch Davidians in Waco, TX, for example, carried as much weight in my analysis as any other terror killing(s).

By the time of 9/11 I had approximately 500 pages of notes on terrorism, single spaced. Initially when I started this, I would just input this information chronologically in my file; but with so much information this proved to be too unwieldy to use. So I re-organized my file into countries, groups, individuals, modus operandi, weapons, tactics, and over a score of other categories. I also cross indexed all this information so that any commonalities in one category would be easily referenced in another section. Just inputting all this information was a very labor intensive process, but that process itself helped get me very acquainted with the pulse of terrorism. I used this information as a basis for the lectures I gave to elements of the Chicago Police years before. About ten years after 9/11, Jeff Stein, a reporter working for *Congressional Quarterly* (a major periodical read on Capitol Hill) wrote an article titled, *Obama Faces Gaping Holes in U.S. Intelligence.* One of the theses of this article was that the CIA experimented with a unit that only looks at unclassified open source material and discovered that this unit had a better track record of predicting major events than the rest of the intelligence community combined – which obsessed over classified material. No secret to me there. Unfortunately, in an intelligence agency, one's status is based on one's access to classified material. Just another bureaucratic anomaly, examination of open source material therefore isn't a priority, even though it was officially demonstrated as a better predictor than the classified nonsense.

While working on all this did greatly assist me in getting into the terrorist mindset, it did not necessarily point to the impending attack on the scale of 9/11. There were other key indicators which should have raised a red flag and fireworks in front of the faces of our overpaid and sleeping intelligence, law enforcement and security agencies. The first of these indicators was the use of suicide tactics by terrorists. Based on the open sources I had available to me at the time, the first modern terrorist/guerrilla group to use suicide tactics in its operations were the Tamil Tigers in Sri Lanka. Their basic modus operandi (MO) was to engage in a standard guerrilla style attack against an airport or government facility but they would reserve one or a few of their operators to rush a target and light themselves off with explosives in a backpack.

It took a little time but the next group of people to adopt suicide bomb tactics were Palestinian terrorists within the borders of Israel. Their typical MO was to carry explosives in a backpack or a vest and casually walk onto a bus, into a religious ceremony or a bar and then light themselves off. There were so many of these attacks during a phase in the 90's that I had to stop even making bullet notes in my terrorism data base. Instead I'd make a generic entry every month or so simply stating that "Israel was hit with a rash of suicide bombings, scores of casualties", or words to that effect.

This type of attack remained fairly uniform until they started using females. Another milestone of some note. However, the really big indicator concerning the suicide nature of terrorism occurred on December 24, 1994 when terrorists hijacked an Air France commercial aircraft departing from Algeria. Somehow the French intelligence/law enforcement/security apparatus deduced that the terrorists were going to crash the plane into downtown Paris or blow it up over the city. They passed this info to the pilots who convinced the hijackers that they didn't have fuel to make it to Paris so they rerouted the plane to Marseille where French commandos re-took control of the aircraft.

I have nothing but high praise for the political fortitude, the command and control, intelligence services, and operational capabilities demonstrated by the French authorities during this incident. Seven years before our own 9/11 attacks the French managed to avert their own. Its something our own government could have learned a lot from – and we did have the opportunity. I was still a team leader in the FAM program when this hijacking was successfully resolved and I happened to be at our headquarters when a French official came to FAA headquarters to provide an in-depth briefing on how all this transpired. As an air marshal I was intensely interested in the French assessment of the capabilities, tactics and weaponry of the terrorists. But the French authority had no more success in educating the managers in FAA Security than anyone else did. The French also briefed other bureaucracies within the federal government. This is just another crucial fact that the 9/11 Commission thought little of. After 9/11, when the French publicly rejected the rationale for the US engaging in ill-begotten wars, the Congress thought it important enough to change the name of *French Fries* to *Freedom Fries* in the Congressional cafeterias, when instead they should have gotten on their hands and knees begging the French for guidance in fighting terrorism after waking up from a deep slumber – just like after Pearl Harbor.

    Well, this wasn't the only major indicator which presaged a 9/11 type attack. About a year later another group of terrorists attempted to blow up a dozen U.S. commercial aircraft over the Pacific Ocean. This plot was foiled when the apartment in Manila, Philippines caught on fire while the terrorists were making their explosives. This was subsequently referred to as the "Bojinka" operation (which I previously mentioned involving Sal). This should have been another major eye opener to the managers in the Tombstone Agency. It was now clear that the face of terrorism had evolved. It went from the occasional hijacking or bombing where a handful of people would be killed for the purpose of engaging a worldwide media circus to clear evidence to cause massive casualties. You take just these two major indicators: the suicide component of terrorism entering the commercial aviation field, and the effort to cause massive casualties; the obvious deduction should have been, well, obvious. Instead, we were hit with the same refrain when we confronted management with the implications of these latest major indicators, that "we must be doing something right blah, blah, blah."

But there was still more to come. In 1996 I was made privy to a document that was written by several brilliant authors working at the Pentagon. They went through a brief history of warfare, effectively dissecting it's stages and types, including the funding, logistics, tactics and long term strategies. The various types of warfare included: guerrilla, low intensity conflict, conventional and nuclear. However, the primary focus of the study was on terrorism, or rather the projected iteration of this type of warfare. They called it "asymmetrical warfare." Post 9/11, this term has been totally misused by many talking heads in Washington and elsewhere that I've heard use the term. They use it as a synonym for terrorism when they want to prove to their listeners they know a few big words or two. Terrorism has been with the human race almost as long as the oldest profession has been, asymmetrical warfare has not.

What these incredibly gifted authors presented is that the next phase of terrorism will change from the occasional act of violence primarily for the benefit of getting temporary 24 hour news coverage, to acts of violence that will *use the infrastructure of the target country against itself* and cause as many casualties as possible. This was a paradigm shift in reasoning this problem out. The authors didn't predict the methodology of the next attack, however, leaving that chore to others. This official Pentagon report wasn't of any import to the 9/11 Commission either.

This was another WOW moment in my career. These guys were way ahead of my understanding of terrorism, and I arrogantly thought I had a pretty good grasp of the subject at the time. But I incorporated what I knew about terrorism with this new assessment of the trend its taking. Basically terrorists, by definition, have very few resources and their tactical capabilities are extremely limited; anything more and they would be classified as guerrillas, and their MO would change accordingly. So how would a small group of suicidal fanatics, with very limited resources and dubious tactical capabilities conduct an attack to get the most bang for their buck?

I spent a considerable amount of time studying this issue and went through every conceivable target scenario I could think of. From nuclear power plants, to oil storage depots, to vacation cruise ships, liquid natural gas containers, school yards, professional sporting events, shopping malls, the White House and Congressional buildings, the use of chemical or biological agents or a small nuclear bomb, and everything else that came to mind. I'd actually wake up in the middle of the night in a cold sweat visualizing some new methodology I hadn't previously thought through only to discount it after reasoning it out in the light of day as totally impracticable. In fact, I ruled out every single one of these alternatives. Major federal government buildings are too well protected for anything short of a full scale guerrilla type attack. Same with nuclear power plants. Oil storage facilities were a possibility but they'd need a hundred teams scattered about engaged in simultaneous attacks to really impact the country – way out of their capabilities. They could shoot up a sports arena, shopping malls or grade schools but this would only result in a brief flash fire in the news, and bore a huge risk of failure what with the then current security structure at these places and the law enforcement response capabilities to contain the assault. Chem/bio weapons – stuff they could only dream about on the scale they required. Furthermore, most of these scenarios didn't fit within the definition of asymmetrical warfare. The destruction of the Bamiyan Buddhas in Afghanistan in March of 2001 was yet another big clue as to the changing evolution in their thought processes.

The terrorism compass kept pointing back to commercial aviation as their most likely target, and this attack would be accomplished in one of two ways: Multiple simultaneous hijackings in which they'd crash their planes into pre-selected targets or place bombs on as many commercial planes as they had operatives. I didn't really give any thought as to where they would crash their planes in the former scenario or where or over which cities they'd blow up the planes, the trick was to stop them at the airport.

What I knew of the joke of aviation security both of these options were equally plausible, and it scared the hell out of me. This was well above the heads of the managers in the Tombstone Agency, and apparently above the heads of the entire intelligence, law enforcement, and other security agencies combined too. Once I evaluated the intelligence, combined with what I knew of aviation security, the simple deduction was that it was time to start working even more intensely with Steve Elson again. Frantically might be a better word for it.

And, as Sherlock Holmes might have said (yet again) in deducing this new terrorist methodology, "Elementary, my dear Watson".

CHAPTER NINE
Jaws

+

Fools are more to be feared than the wicked.
Queen Christina of Sweden (1626-1689)

+

+

Steve made numerous copies of the *Big Blue Book of Death*, spending a small fortune doing this. In between my international travels I'd accompany Steve to various government offices that had some oversight responsibility over FAA and the commercial aviation industry in this country. One of the first offices we visited was the Department of Transportation's Office of Inspector General (IG). We were granted an audience with a Mr. Todd Zinser who was in charge of their criminal investigations division and was, to my understanding, the third highest ranking official in the IGs office. He readily accepted a copy of the *Big Blue Book of Death* and seemed interested in what we had to say.

Over the course of the next few months I had several more sessions with Mr. Zinser and provided him additional information proving FAA's malfeasance. But his bureaucratic instincts eventually took over. In one subsequent meeting, out of exasperation he exclaimed, "Unless you give me a dead body and a smoking gun, there's nothing I can do against the managers in FAA because of the political situation between the FAA and the IG's office." This was a not so veiled reference to a previous Inspector General (Mary Schiavo) who rocked the bureaucratic boat, which I'll get into later.

In a subsequent meeting, after I presented him with additional documentation, he threw the document into the air and shouted, "FAA is so fucked up, I don't know where to begin!" This was my last meeting with Zinser as I realized that working with the IG was a pointless waste of time for anything other than relatively minor BS issues. After 9/11, Zinser was made acting head of the DOT IG's office and later still was made THE IG of another federal agency. A reward for keeping a lid on who knew what, when they knew it and what they did about it? None of which made it to the 9/11 Commission, or at least wasn't included in their report. Still, I have to give Zinser some credit. Federal agencies would frequently revoke an employee's security clearance who asked too many questions or rocked the boat too much. Virtually guaranteeing they'd get fired and make it impossible for the person to get another job. Zinser, I was told, pressured FAA not to use this ploy against me after 9/11. In fact, I think this *power* is one of the main reasons the government has such wide sweeping use of security clearances. I've had a Top Secret security clearance for nearly all of my federal career, until TSA recently took it away from me, but I don't ever recall even being around any legitimate top secret stuff except on extremely rare occasions (none of these situations are included in this book). It costs the tax payer tens of thousands of dollars to do a single background check and the periodic refresher checks on each individual with a clearance; but I'm convinced it has little purpose other than as an employee control tool – with some legitimate exceptions.

Steve, however, was relentless. Even though he was retired, he pointed out that there is no expiration date on the oath of office he took to defend this country from all enemies and to abide by the Constitution. This was when I first observed his spiritual association with the great white shark in the movie *Jaws*. Just when these clowns thought it was safe to go back into the water, he'd show up again.

Fortress of Deceit

Next, he started to badger the General Accounting Office which is the official investigating arm of the U.S. Congress and is their primary means of oversight of the executive branch, which includes virtually all the federal agencies. After 9/11 they changed their name to the General Accountability Office, which is a big joke of a misnomer. Eventually Steve was able to arrange an audience with the manager in charge of the commercial aviation section of the GAO. This was a black gentleman, a scholar, and dedicated public servant whom I refer to as Mr. Joe. He was another one of those real leaders one sometimes stumbles upon, not just a paper pushing bureaucrat; someone I had great respect for.

In between my travels a date was set for Steve and me to brief Mr. Joe on what we were alleging. Steve already convinced him of the preliminaries so I took four hours of annual leave from work which I figured would be more than enough time to get to the GAO in downtown DC, spend an hour or so briefing the official (which was our standard time frame), have a quick lunch in one of the Congressional cafeterias and get back to work.

Turns out when we arrived at the GAO office, Mr. Joe had his entire staff sit in on the briefing – some fifteen people. These GAO folks were some of the most professional people we briefed and they were intensely interested in what we had to say. With very detailed questioning and interrogation from them, our normal one hour briefing turned into a four hour session. I had to get back to work so I left in the early afternoon but Steve continued briefing the staffers for the rest of the day. The following day Steve took a handful of the staffers to National Airport in DC to give them an up close view of what we were talking about.

We subsequently had frequent communication with the GAO from that point on to just a few days before 9/11. In my case, the main thing they were interested in was how I did the Red Team assessments of security as they were contemplating setting up their own Team. But well intentioned things move slowly in the federal bureaucracy and certainly not fast enough for Steve and me. We both were having terrible feelings of dread that something horrendous was just around the corner and the sooner we motivate people to fix the problems in the Tombstone Agency the better. So we kept badgering Mr. Joe and his staff on the progress they were making.

Mr. Joe at one point admitted that he doesn't have the authority to do anything, as he gets his marching orders directly from Congress, but that he is trying to persuade the key elected personnel in Congress to take a serious look into our allegations. Well, this still wasn't good enough for us. Since Steve now lived in the DC area he started to go to Capitol Hill directly and bang on the doors of the individual Congressmen themselves. No surprise here, but we found out that if you go to Capitol Hill without a briefcase full of money and expect to have an audience with an actual elected official, forget it (with a few exceptions).

But we did start having meetings with their staff members – and the staff are the eyes and ears of the politicians (and in some cases, their brains too). Bob Monetti, whose son was killed on Pan Am 103, joined us at some of these meetings. Most of the staff members we spoke too were medium level folks who really didn't have much authority but were very interested in what we had to say, and they were a direct conduit to their respective Congressman. We also gave each of them their own copy of the *Big Blue Book of Death*. One of the documents that we added to the book that was filtered to Steve was an email exchange between several of the senior managers in FAA Security in which they were making jokes about pulling the wool over the eyes of Congress in a recent official Congressional hearing. The medium level Congressional staff members were aghast at this blatant display of arrogance and they thumped their chests and stated that when their bosses find out about this their heads will roll. Somewhere in this discussion was the serious ramifications of lying to Congress – ultimately though, nothing ever materialized about this little tidbit. I think Congress, when it engages in its endless C-SPAN covered Congressional hearings, expect bureaucrats to lie them – so long as the lies fit within the established parameters of the mechanics of running the government. These hearings are usually nothing more than a big dog and pony show which gives the Congressmen a little face time on TV for their constituents.

In one of these C-SPAN covered hearings I attended, I made a mental note over the fact that out of some twenty Congressmen on the committee (based on their displayed name tags on their benches), only four Congressmen were actually present during the whole hearing. The rest would come in for a few minutes, get their face time asking questions, and leave. Whatever decisions were to made by Congress, were already made, I suspect, based on the lobbying that is conducted off-camera prior to these hearings.

It was Senator Chase, who [apparently] sarcastically exclaimed in one Congressional hearing during the Vietnam War words to the effect, "If I can't trust you on the little lies, Sir (addressing McNamara), how will I ever believe you on the big lies." Nothing has changed since that era. Due to Steve's unflappable persistence, however, we did get the attention of several senior staff members on both the House and Senate sides of the Congress and from both parties.

Fortress of Deceit

These were the puppet masters of our elected officials, the one's that set the agenda for these hearings and tell the Congressmen what to say – the brains behind the facade.

Most of these guys were great and were very interested in what we had to say as well as the documents we threw on their laps. With repeated visits to their respective offices they assured us that they had discussions with our elected officials about these very issues. But Steve and I were both becoming jaded about this whole process though, and neither one of us felt that any of these clowns were going to do anything. But Steve was relentless anyway. He continued collecting internal FAA documents from a score of insiders providing more current and damning evidence of FAA's growing malfeasance. He put these new documents in a red binder which he titled *Better Read than Dead*, and we delivered this book (all two inches thick of it) to the same folks who received the blue book as well as new folks we were visiting.

In my visits to the Congressional Offices I never paid any attention as to whether they were democrats or republicans. I just figured, albeit naively, that they'd put the interests of their country above their party affiliation or the continuity of the bureaucracy. We did have meetings in the offices of a number of nationally recognized Congressmen, some of whom would later run for President – just picking one from each party:

On March 6, 2000 we had an hour long session with the Chief Legal Counsel for Senator John McCain. She graciously greeted us and escorted us to a back room in McCain's office and sat us down on one side of a large wooden table, she on the other. Steve always did most of the talking, with me interjecting comments every once in a while or to help clear up any confusion I saw in the recipient's eyes. So Steve goes into his usual spiel and offered our collective documents to the Chief Legal Counsel. She was sitting back in her chair and was writing voraciously on a legal pad of paper, occasionally looking up at Steve or me as we made a particular point, then she'd go back to writing.

Wow, I was impressed. Most of the time a staffer would write down an occasional note when we briefed them but she was writing furiously the whole time. If we could get someone of McCain's stature on our side maybe we would have a chance at preventing the calamity of 9/11. As we wrapped up our one hour briefing she put her pen and paper down and said, "This is all very interesting, but what do you expect us to do about it?" There was a long pause, like literally 12-15 seconds where no one spoke – just staring at each other across the table. She wasn't even paying any attention to us, probably working on a speech or a recipe for tonight's dinner at home – where she probably should have stayed, would have been much better for the country if she stayed home baking cookies.

I could sense that Steve was getting ready to explode. There is no doubt that he would have reached across the table, grabbed her scrawny neck and pulled her over the table and physically beat the briefing into her empty head. I still had to keep my job, however, and put my hand on Steve's shoulder in a symbolic gesture to hold him back (Steve once said in a joint press briefing we gave after 9/11, that he was the *Id*, and I was the *super-ego* of this team) and I immediately went into a grade school level course (which was still above her head) on our system of government: That there are three branches of government, Senator McCain is part of the legislative branch, and one of the responsibilities of the legislative branch is to engage in oversight (ie: maintain accountability) over the executive branch of which FAA is part, and furthermore the esteemed Senator McCain is one of the ranking members in this set up.

She just glared at us.

We got up and left, I recall one or both of us just saying under our breath, "fuck this shit", and left the building. This was the first time I started to think that if the terrorists targeted Capitol Hill they'd probably do the country a favor rather than killing lots of innocent folks in Main Street, USA.

On the other side of the House we had some communication with Senator John Kerry (of Massachusetts) – the same who subsequently ran for President and is the current Secretary of State (as I write this). Senator Kerry was the first Congressman that either Steve and/or I went to that wouldn't have anything to do with us since neither of us were one of his voter constituents. In my naiveté of the time I thought this was a pathetic excuse especially since he has the nerve to vote [in his capacity as a Senator], on things that effect the whole country. But he just slammed the door shut in our faces.

At another Capitol Hill session some no-name Congressman assigned two new interns (a female and male) to *interview* us. They both looked like they were still in college, or maybe even high school, but they were very enthusiastic and bubbly. I had the impression we were the first members of the public they ever talked to in their official capacity and they wanted to do a great job to kick off their career in politics. They escorted us to the usual big oak table in one of the back rooms of the Congressman's offices. As we sat down Steve and I just glanced at each other quickly – it was like maybe we should go easy on them. But we decided to blast them with the usual briefing.

Fortress of Deceit

We went through the whole gamut of what we'd been though: the evidence of zero security, the terrorist threat we faced, beating our heads against the wall working through the various bureaucracies, talking to a seemingly endless series of Congressional staffers and a few Congressman themselves, listening to a bunch of lame promises and nobody was doing a god-damn thing but playing politics, and that a lot of innocent people are going to get killed because the clowns we elect into public office aren't doing squat but getting rich from lobbyists.

During the course of this briefing the bubbly demeanor of the two interns slowly started to deflate. They both had a pen and pad of paper to take notes but they just stared at us the whole time, frozen in place. At the end of the briefing they both had red eyes and were visibly palpating, it appeared we totaled eroded their illusion of what this republic was supposed to be – already turning into the worst traits of a democracy. If it weren't for the bars on the windows I thought for sure the girl would have jumped out. The male intern was ready to stab himself in the neck, but building security previously took his pocket knife away.

It was clear we were batting zero dealing with the bureaucracies of the FAA, the Inspector General and the General Accounting Office; but it was a major blow batting zero with our elected officials. But Steve persisted. If these clowns don't want to listen then we'll go totally out of the government chain and try to get the press to take an interest in this brewing calamity. Typically when the press claws into an issue then the politicians jump on the band wagon to get their own little sound bites in the news, and it might even force their hand into actually doing something productive. So Steve spent a lot of time trying to get one news outlet after another to do a story on the sorry state of aviation security and the terrorism threat we faced. But none were the least bit interested in the evidence that Elson dumped on their laps. The press had no more prescient demeanor than our politicians and bureaucrats; with a couple of exceptions.

The first was the reporter Jim Morris of *US News and World Reports*. He saw something in the evidence Steve presented him and subsequently had an article printed February 19, 2001 titled *Since Pan Am 103, a Façade of Security*. Morris had hoped the story would have been the front page feature article of that issue but the magazine's own bureaucracy pushed it back to a one pager on page 28. Still, the article went into some detail of the "façade of security" and the threat, quoting Steve Elson by name, and one of my comments – anonymously (I had not yet become an official whistleblower and was still working behind the scenes). It even mentioned Osama Bin Laden, named by the CIA director as "the most immediate and serious threat to the United States." And yet, we still couldn't get Congress to do anything.

Then followed the second reporter. Quite independently of us, however, another former FAA Security employee was doing his own fighting, trying to fix the Tombstone Agency before 9/11 happens. This was Brian (Sully) Sullivan – his real name. Sully is a Vietnam veteran, retired army Lt Colonel and had worked for some time as an FAA Special Agent in Burlington, MA, and lived in MA. So he was certainly a constituent of the not so honorable Senator Kerry. He retired from the FAA in January of 2001 with a determination to address aviation security vulnerabilities he'd witnessed during his career with the Tombstone Agency. He too tried to address his concerns within the FAA chain of command to no avail and could hardly wait to secure his retirement so he could work with the media on these issues. Sully and Steve then worked with a local TV reporter (Deborah Sherman of Fox 25 News in Boston) to plan an undercover sting (hidden camera and all) of the poor security at Boston's Logan Airport (where two of the terrorist teams began their fateful foray into history). This story first aired May 6, 2001. As usual the FAA, airlines and the Massachusetts Port Authority paid no attention; but Al Qaeda, in the person of Mohammed Atta, did, as he was seen 5 days later (May 11, 2001) conducting surveillance, videotaping and taking photographs of the very same checkpoint he would pass through four months later on 9/11.

Sully was an unusually prescient individual, particularly since having no Red Team experience. The day after this TV special aired he sent a letter to Senator Kerry accurately describing the probability of multiple eventual plane hijackings and suicide terrorists crashing planes into selected targets. (Sully's letter can be found as the link to an article by Paul Sperry, titled *Official: Kerry Failed to Act on Pre-9/11 Tip* which can be found on the internet, as well as the *9/11 Digital Archives*.) He asked me to hand deliver a VCR copy of the Fox 25 report to Kerry's office so they couldn't claim it got lost in the mail. So I went to Kerry's office the following week, re-introduced myself to the secretary (since I had previously been there in a failed attempt to get an audience – with anybody) and asked to speak to their senior staffer. After a half hour of sitting on my butt it was clear he still didn't want anything to do with me. I got up and feigned an interest in the various photographs and plaques decorating the senator's office, peeking down the corridor looking for the senior staffer, while engaging in small talk with the secretary making glowing comments about the esteemed Senator in the photo's and the plaques; while holding down the dry heaves. When I saw him traversing the back halls of the office I advanced toward him, shoved the tape into his face, explained what it was and who it was from and left. Couldn't have taken more than ten seconds. Before the secretary could even stand up to chase me down I was gone. Around the same time frame, Elson hand delivered the tape to FAA Administrator Jane Garvey's office.

Kerry did the usual Congressional shuffle dance and forwarded Sully's letter to the Department of Transportation's Office of Inspector General, despite the fact Sully warned him in his letter that going to the DOT OIG would be a waste of time because they were part of the problem. When confronted by the press after 9/11, the Senator said he contacted the GAO about the matter, but a check by Sully with the GAO showed no record of that contact. Basically, he absolved himself of any responsibility by passing the buck to someone else. We had repeatedly warned all of these clowns that working through the IGs office and GAO is a total waste of time.

I should point out that although we didn't speak to the actual elected officials, except for a few no-name not popularly nationally known folks; each Congressional office had its own personality, reflecting the atmosphere and mood of its master.

I can't speak for Elson or Sully; but by this time – which was the spring of 2001, just months before 9/11 – I had changed my motivation from actively trying to prevent 9/11 by lighting a fire under the collective butts of our elected officials, to fatalism. These bastards don't do crap unless you bribe them. But I continued contacting them just because it was the right thing to do. To stop fighting was to be a part of the problem. In late August of 2001, my last Red Team assessment of aviation security occurred at the New York City airports with the usual abysmal results.

But Congress did know about these problems, and not only from us.

I'm not asking you to take my word for this. In a letter dated March 11, 1999; Congressman Frank Wolf, Chairman, Subcommittee on Transportation, informed Jane Garvey (Administrator of FAA) of the following, in part: Regarding "...the state of security at our nation's airports...", "...I appreciate the fact that it is the FAA, working with the OIG, that is doing the 'red team' testing of airport security...", and, "...I also know you have requested significant increases in civil aviation security appropriations over the past several years...and Congress provided those funds. We now need to get the payoff from that investment", and continuing later with, "...I'm sure you agree that our citizens have the right to expect a consistent and high level of security at all of our major airports, and this is apparently not the case today..." Of course, the honorable Congressman is in error about the Red Team working with the OIG – it never happened, other than my informal contact with them. And what he doesn't state is that the OIG, when confronted with the Red Team results decided to bury its head in the sand just like FAA did.

And in June of 2001, just months before the 9/11 attacks, the US House Appropriations Committee report stated, in part: "...Five years after the effort began, the Committee concludes that FAA's personnel reform has been a failure. The most recent employee attitude survey showed severe levels of employee dissatisfaction, <u>EVEN AS COMPENSATION LEVELS HAVE RISEN TO MAKE DOT THE HIGHEST-PAID CABINENT LEVEL AGENCY IN THE FEDERAL GOVERNMENT</u> (my emphasis). Fewer than one in ten employees felt the agency rewards creativity and innovation-even though personnel reform allows the agency great flexibility in this area." This EXACT same activity is currently going on within the DHS/TSA, by the way. DHS and TSA had been rated the worst of government agencies to work for in employee feedback surveys AND the DHS/TSA managers are the highest paid in the entire federal bureaucracy. Starting with the already inflated pay grades of FAA, TSA, taking advantage of the post 9/11 hysteria, super inflated its salaries and bonuses.

And the report continues with:

"The Committee remains disappointed over management issues which continue to surround the civil aviation security program. The organization failed to meet a majority of it's performance plan goals for fiscal year 2000, YET PAID SIGNIFICANT BONUSES TO EXECUTIVES (my emphasis). The Congressionally-directed strategic plan, recently submitted, was little more than a statement of core principles, and offered no indication of planned resources, management focus, or schedules for accomplishment…In all, last year's Committee report directed the agency to address these concerns expeditiously; however, THERE IS NO INDICATION THAT THE AGENCY HONORED THAT REQUEST. THE COMMITTEE CANNOT CONTINUE PROVIDING SUCH SIGNIFICANT RESOURCES IN THE FACE OF SUSTAINED MANAGEMENT PROBLEMS." All my emphasis. And yet Congress did nothing but continue to throw more of our tax money at these failure based managers.

Furthermore:

After the bombing of Pan Am 103 which killed 270 people, a Presidential Commission ordered the FAA to start a Red Team (back in 1990). Additionally, in 1997, the White House Commission (resulting from the TWA-800 explosion off Long Island) stated, in part, "...frequent, sophisticated attempts by these Red Teams to find ways to dodge security measures are an important part of finding weaknesses in the system and ANTICIPATING (my emphasis) what sophisticated adversaries of our nation might attempt...." I fulfilled ALL of these mandates and was subsequently punished for it by TSA, more on this later.

And the icing on the cake:

The problems in the FAA mismanaged aviation security system as well as within the FAA Security tombstone bureaucracy itself had to be one of the most heavily documented program areas in the entire federal government. The Department of Transportation's Office of Inspector General had scores of official reports they developed over the years and through the 90's documenting the Tombstone Agency mentality. A former Inspector General herself, Mary Schiavo, had nothing but absolutely scathing criticisms about FAA in the early to mid-90's. Some attribute her as the person that coined the term, "Tombstone Agency" in referring to FAA.

While I didn't know it at the time, even the General Accounting Office (the official investigating arm of Congress) had scores of official reports documenting how screwed up FAA management was. And still Congress did nothing except continually dump tons of tax dollars on FAA, and the more they failed the more money they got.

But it got even better:

In early 2000, I was contacted by two investigators who were with the Surveys and Investigations Unit of the Appropriations Committee of the House of Representatives who were tasked to investigate FAA Security's alleged malfeasance. This is THE primary committee that is responsible for deciding how our tax dollars are spent. This was the most tangible result of the repeated and endless pounding on the doors of Congress by Steve Elson, with me in a support role. Finally, it seemed at the time, Congress was going to do something.

The investigators explained to me that they needed my help to do this investigation. I had previously heard complaints from Congressional staffers that it was easier to get information from the Central Intelligence Agency (CIA) than it was from FAA, particularly its Security Division. The CIA was only trying to minimize the exposure of its legitimate secrets, the FAA was hiding its gross incompetency, and now was no exception.

Unbeknownst to FAA management, I provided Red Team documentation to the Congressional investigators, but the documentation I provided to the investigators didn't mean doodly unless it came through official channels. So I'd provide them a document, the investigators would make a veiled request to FAA (to not make it appear that they actually had the document in hand) for a certain type of document, FAA would insist such a document didn't exist, the investigators insisted it did and demanded its delivery. This kind of nonsense went on for most of the year 2000. I was still doing a lot of Red Team work around the world during this time frame and would coordinate my down time with the investigators.

Even the investigators I spoke to were appalled. They had clear evidence that FAA Security was lying and withholding information from them. The US Constitution mandates that Congress has oversight responsibility over the executive branch, which included the managers in FAA. But since none of these managers in FAA were ever required to read the Constitution, lying to Congress or withholding documentation, so what. This was all just part of the game.

In early 2001, the Surveys and Investigations Unit of the House of Representatives completed its report. I asked for a copy of the report but one of the senior investigators explained to me that their reports are so "highly classified" that even the Congressional staffers are not allowed to see them; that they are "eyes only" for the Congressmen themselves. The investigators assured me, however, that they corroborated everything that Elson and I have been saying for years, and then some.

Again, this was early 2001. And still Congress does nothing but dump more money on the Tombstone Agency. Just another little tidbit the 9/11 Commission had no interest in. What they did know, when they knew it, and what they didn't do about it. And they knew it all, and did nothing at all except continually contribute more tax money and support to the failure prone Tombstone Agency. One has to keep in mind that FAA Security was funded in its entirety to prevent terrorist attacks against the commercial aviation industry. In spite of all the excuses made by the talking heads in government, the bottom line is that FAA failed to do it's job. All the millions or even billions of tax dollars spent on FAA Security over the years was a total waste, and Congress and the Executive branch knew it.

About a year before 9/11, Michael Canavan, a retired army general with a heavy background in special forces took over the reigns of the Tombstone Agency. He was another real *leader*, not just a manager. He talked directly to the front line troops to find out what was really going on and both Steve Elson and I had direct communications with him. He was beginning to make positive changes within the bureaucracy (albeit in slow motion as he still had to contend with the ubiquitous Tombstone managers), but time was against him.

CHAPTER TEN
The Predicted Attack

+

Ever tried. Ever failed. No matter. Try again. Fail again. Fail better.
Samuel Beckett

+

+

And so, 9/11 happens....

And in keeping in line with the Tombstone mentality, I (along with, I assume, every other headquarters based FAA Security employee and manager), received a very expensive looking plaque months after the attack signed by Administrator Jane Garvey which states in its entirety:

*Superior Performance Award presented to _____
In recognition of your excellent performance on
behalf of the Federal Aviation Administration in the
months following the terrorist attacks of
September 11, 2001*

And continued with:

*During a time of national distress, your personal caring, commitment,
and dedication assisted the FAA Task Force in providing excellent
customer service to the traveling public and contributed to
renewed confidence in government*

I'm not sure how much this crap cost the tax payer, but not even a drop in the bucket as far as other waste tally's up. But it does highlight the maxim of the Tombstone bureaucracy, instead of punishing those responsible for failure to do their jobs, they reward everyone after the fact. I did hear that sixty-six FAA Security people were promoted after 9/11 and before TSA took over, and many received cash awards for maintaining the tombstone standards. Most were promoted again under TSA.

CHAPTER ELEVEN
Retribution

+

We can't solve problems by using the same kind of thinking we used when we created them.
Albert Einstein

+

+

And all the government talking heads in Washington clambered aboard the political train to infamy by denying any culpability or knowledge of the sorry state of aviation security or of any of the obvious intelligence indicators, just blaming non-entity unaccountable bureaucracies themselves for having "a failure of imagination." And the tax payer gave these clowns tons of money to prevent a 9/11, and they failed miserably, and not one person was held to account. Even the President's national security advisor (Condo Rice) said that "no one could possibly have imagined such an attack would take place." I thought I was going to heave, wondering what planet she was from. I was reminded at the time, of the apparent surprise Japanese attack at Pearl Harbor, which kicked off our involvement in World War II. Later history claims recount that our government was clearly aware of the planned attack but let it happen for political reasons. We couldn't declare war on the belligerents without them attacking first – essentially our troops and sailors at Pearl Harbor were sacrificed. Couldn't help but wonder if the 9/11 victims were sacrificed for the same political reasons. But the worst was yet to come as far as the bureaucracy was concerned.

It was no surprise then, that right after 9/11 Congress immediately reimbursed the airline industry with billions of tax dollars for lost revenue when commercial aviation was impacted by the attacks. All that lobbying money from the airline industry that they used to bribe Congress had to be one of the best investments ever, avoiding not only the financial loss, but all accountability as well. And later, Congress, using more tax money, bribed the 9/11 victim's families by offering them tons of money in exchange for not engaging in any law suits against the airlines, there-by escaping the airing of all the dirty laundry of their own culpability in this game.

On September 28, 2004 Elson wrote a fifty-seven page *White Paper* (titled: *9/11, Yes, There is a Smoking Gun*) which is the single best indictment of who knew what, when they knew it, and what they did about it concerning the pre 9/11 tombstone agency, including most of the critical names both within the bureaucracy and within the hallowed halls of Congress. He provided this document to numerous government, news outlets and other organizations and individuals. The 9/11 Commission had little interest in it. (Its now available at http://911digitalarchives.org/items/show/97082).

Meanwhile the FAA Red Team, namely Elson and myself, the one unit in the entire federal government that accurately predicted the 9/11 attacks, was immediately grounded right after 9/11. Never to see the light of day again. For months I was repeatedly shifted from one temporary administrative duty to another.

Minutes after the attacks, however, the Washington bureaucracy was effectively shut down with government employees told to go home for the day. I, along with a handful of other FAA security employees, stayed behind to staff the operations center where details of the attack had to be collected and disseminated. Things like the aircraft involved and their routes, passenger and cargo manifests etc. An auxiliary operations room was set up in a classroom sized room at FAA headquarters. On each of the four walls of the room were large sheets of paper taped to the walls and each of the four walls contained information specific to each of the four planes involved.

In the late afternoon of September 11, 2001, FAA Administrator Garvey requested a situation report (SITREP) of everything we had at that point. After the individual that wrote this report was finished with the draft, she asked me to verify the report for accuracy. So with the report in hand I went to each wall and confirmed every single detail contained in the report. The report included information that on one of the planes a hand gun was used by the terrorists. When I saw this detail on the wall and contained in the Administrator's SITREP, I didn't give it a seconds thought. If you want to hijack a plane, why not bring a gun, I knew from my red team work how easy it was to do.

The detail of the gun was also contained in the next day's SITREP. Weeks later the SITREP was leaked to the news media. The consequence of a gun on the plane was only significant for purposes of law suits against the airlines – as irrefutable proof of their poor security. It would also kick up a lot of dirt concerning FAA's poor oversight of aviation security.

Once it made it to the news media, Congress stepped in to resolve the situation and ordered its investigating arm, the GAO, to find out if a gun was used on the plane or not. Weeks later the GAO publicly reported words to the effect, "We found no evidence that a gun was used in any of the hijackings." Well, I don't know if a gun was used or not. What I do know, however, is that the GAO did not interview me about the gun report and they did not interview the person that wrote the SITREP which reported the gun.

Fortress of Deceit

While I was already suspicious of these *high level* investigations prior to 9/11 (based primarily on my involvement with the TWA-800 explosion); suspicion segued into confirmation after the attacks. Whenever some high level (IE: politically sensitive) investigation is conducted by Congress or some other anointed special investigative committee, if they don't want the dirt to be exposed they usually come out with a statement such as, "We found no evidence that an ugly slimy bug was beneath the rock." What they don't tell you is that they never bothered to look beneath the rock in the first place. Technically they are telling the truth, that they found no bug beneath the rock, but their investigative techniques are somewhat lacking. This was confirmed in my mind as a result of the GAO investigation into the gun SITREP. In any type of investigation like this there are three simple questions that must be asked: What did you know? When did you know it? And what did you do about it?

What they should have done is go to the person who wrote the SITREP and find out where that information came from. Then my name would most likely have turned up as the person who verified the information. Then they'd go on down the line finding out where the information originated. One of the failures in this bogus system is that no one (except in rare situations), in these high level political investigations, is required to take an oath, either orally or in writing. I even testified before the 9/11 Commission and I wasn't required to take any oath.

When I worked as a federal criminal investigator for the agency, if I was tasked with investigating the theft of a can of beans, I would have to obtain a verbal oath from witnesses and suspect(s) that the information they provided is the truth to the best of their knowledge. I then was required to have them write down the oath along with their formal statement and they'd have to swear to the accuracy of the statement. Even if a prospective witness had nothing relevant to say about the bean theft I would still have to go through this process; one, to be able to document that a thorough investigation was conducted; and two, to obtain an oath or affirmation as to the truth of the information, with severe legal consequences if its later demonstrated they lied in their official statement.

In these high level political investigations, however, they don't even have to document who they talked to (or more importantly, who they didn't talk to) nor which rocks they failed to turn over, much less obtain an oath or affirmation from anyone just to make it official. I'm convinced that the next time one of these special committees is established to investigate the latest national level tragedy such as another 9/11 attack or Presidential assassination (ala: Kennedy), that the best chance to obtain irrefutable truth of the circumstances of the incident so as to curtail any lingering conspiracy theories is to task the latest graduating class from any of the FLETC criminal investigative agencies, or even some state or local police academy. The brand new investigators most likely wouldn't be soiled by politics this early in their career and they would do an amazingly thorough job of documenting who knew what, when they knew it, and what they did about it. If for no other reason than to prove their new found investigative skills. But, alas, not in this day and age. One might surmise, that given we have essentially a two party system, that one party would balance out the other and ensure that a fair and impartial investigation would be conducted – but in this case both parties had vested interests in keeping a lid on things. Both parties received tons of bribe money (I mean lobbying funds) from the aviation industry. And things continued to get worse.

Fortress of Deceit

About two weeks after 9/11 I had two separate meetings on Capitol Hill. One on the House side and one on the Senate side, involving very senior staff personnel from both parties. The gist of these meetings were that they acknowledged that what Elson and I had been telling them was obviously accurate; but where do we go from here? Elson accompanied me to one of these meetings and adamantly protested against the formation of any type of super-agency (as was subsequently created, namely the TSA and its mother agency the DHS). He explained that all its going to do is be a massive syphon of tax dollars, be a contractor's paradise, and with the already over-inflated salaries of FAA Security, would be a huge feeding frenzy of incompetent sycophantic bureaucrats all fighting against each other for choice high paying government jobs. And this is exactly what subsequently happened.

We both went into the need to focus on the basics and not waste money on high-tech equipment. That well trained, well led people at the front lines at airports were the single biggest deterrent against aviation related terrorism and it didn't make any difference if the screeners were government employees or contract employees working for the airlines or the airports. I emphasized that it made more operational sense to have screening personnel work directly for the airports rather than the airlines (where the pressure to rapidly process passengers and their luggage would soon take over as the hysteria of the moment subsided). We also mentioned the need to bring some accountability for those in charge who thwarted security improvements in spite of the evidence presented to them. A lot of the middle FAA managers who just played the system to their advantage had a lot of valuable institutional knowledge and could be of valuable service with the right leadership and discipline – if nothing else, to learn from their mistakes and not repeat them.

I, of course, highlighted the need to have a specialized small Red Team made up of specially trained and dedicated personnel doing what a real Red Team should be doing: pointing out once again the obvious fact that in the entire federal intelligence, law enforcement, and security agencies combined it was the FAA Red Team (namely Elson and myself) that was the only organizational unit that accurately identified the vulnerabilities, the threat, and ultimate calamity of 9/11.

For the first time in our protracted struggle it felt like they were going to finally do something in the interests of the people of this country, at least initially, and well after the barn doors were closed. But one had to start somewhere.

We even forecast the knee jerk reaction of the government's efforts to violate the Constitution and the steps it's taken to lead us closer to George Orwell's 1984 type of government, as well as the need to guard against this behavior. This was hardly any special analysis on our part. In the latter half of the 20th century there were numerous examples of countries that experienced internal strife in the form of terrorism, guerilla warfare or low intensity conflict. These were primarily in Central and South America and in Africa. The governments in each of these countries gradually minimized human rights, became increasingly domineering and paranoid in every day affairs and in some cases became a bigger terror than the groups they were allegedly fighting against. All in the name of national security. The leadership in our own government is just as narrow minded and predictable as the pillars of leadership in these third world countries. I'm actually a little surprised that things haven't digressed even further in this country, but time and bureaucratic momentum are on their side.

Fortress of Deceit

The dark shadow of bureaucracy and unaccountable government manifested itself in these Capitol Hill meetings. At the end of both of these I asked the senior staff members when they anticipate commencing an investigation into all the government failures which contributed to the ease of the terrorists executing their attacks and formally document who knew what, when they knew it, and what they did about it. Both the House and Senate staffers said almost the exact same thing; that, "our bosses (meaning the elected officials themselves) will do everything in their power to prevent an investigation into 9/11, as it's a big can of worms that they don't want to open."

After the second meeting, when I realized that both the Senate and House were intent on avoiding accountability, I decided to file a formal whistleblower case against the FAA with the United States Office of Special Counsel (OSC). So in my free time I put together a few hundred pages of documentation, wrote up a thirty page narrative and submitted it to the OSC on October 31, 2001 (OSC File # DI-02-0207). In my continuing naïveté about the workings of the hallowed halls of our federal government, I wrote my whistleblower disclosure directed entirely against the FAA, thinking the OSC would bring about some accountability. I didn't include any information on who else we talked to (namely the IG, GAO, and members of Congress). Additionally, the authority of the OSC is fairly limited. They can't investigate Congress and they can't even investigate something as fundamental in our government as allegations of constitutional violations. Technically, I suppose, the IG and GAO didn't break any laws by keeping their mouths shut at this point in the game.

So for nearly four months the OSC stewed on my allegations. In the interim, I enlisted the assistance of Tom Devine, the head lawyer for the Government Accountability

Project (GAP), a non-profit group on K Street in downtown Washington, which assists government whistleblowers and tries to influence Congress to enhance whistleblower protection laws. He, and they, were a great help in my survival of this bizarre arena.

In mid-February of 2002, I was contacted by the OSC and they asked me if I would attach my name publicly to this document. They explained that it would carry more weight and be more productive if my name was attached as opposed to just being an anonymous disclosure. I naively said, "Yes." A week later the OSC publicly announced details of my disclosure along with my name stating publicly and for the record that it was likely that my allegations against FAA were correct: "That FAA executed its civil aviation security mission in a manner that was a substantial and specific danger to public safety." Tom Devine arranged for the reporter Blake Morrison of *USA Today* to break the original story, and for a brief period my tale was a leading feature on the entertainment evening news and even made it to the international press. Months later a former FAM colleague of mine told me that he was flying around the far-east at the time and found my face on the front page of a local newspaper.

Which brings me back to the opening paragraphs in the introduction of this book.

On the Monday morning that this story broke, I walked to my third floor office at FAA headquarters on Independence Ave in Washington. Outside the office some clown was supporting the wall with an earpiece and wire hanging from his ear, I assumed he was from the DoT Inspector General's Office. My office mates were in shock seeing my story in the news and most refused (or more likely, were afraid) to talk to me. A short while later I went to the restroom down the hall. Another individual with an ear piece and wire dangling from his ear followed me into the bathroom. I didn't know if they were there to protect me from physical retaliation or were concerned that I'd go off my rocker and shoot the place up. A formal whistleblower process where-by a federal employee reports various forms of gross malfeasance through official channels (via the OSC), the actual mechanics of this process hadn't been exercised to any great degree and no one knew what to expect of this; least of all me. I never even heard about the OSC or the whistleblower rules and laws until after 9/11 when a like-minded colleague informed me of the option.

I could tell by the looks of folks in the office and their reaction to me that there was some fear that I was going to go ballistic and start shooting up the place. Like, I'm going to go through this whole tedious formal process and as an after-thought I think I'll start killing people in the office too. I couldn't believe their reaction to me. I happened to bump into my immediate supervisor when I went outside for a cup of coffee (a third individual followed me to the coffee shop); there was fear in his eyes. I assured him that I wasn't going to go berserk and shoot up the place. He said he was glad to hear that and will pass my message to senior management – who will also be relieved to hear this. None of this made any sense anyway, like if I really was intent on killing people, these clowns are dumb enough to believe me that I wasn't going too just because I said I wouldn't? They suspected me of being a potential killer, but not a liar. And these were some of the intellectual elite of the agency.

While I was outside talking to my boss I noticed yet another individual milling around nearby with a wire dangling out his ear. This was state of the art technology back then. I had previously used this stuff before. You have the ear piece with either a narrow, clear plastic type wire or flesh tone colored wire dangling from your ear and routed beneath one's collar to a battery pack and transmitter/receiver usually clipped to one's belt. A similar wire that is routed through one's sleeve with a microphone clipped to the end of the shirt sleeve. To talk into the microphone you had to bring your hand, normally the one you don't shoot with, close to your mouth and just whisper whatever you had to say. If you were the least bit observant, or knew what to look for, these guys, and a few females, stood out like a sore thumb in spite of their efforts to be somewhat incognito. Every time I made a movement, in the bathroom or otherwise, I'd see one of these clowns talking to his hand as I quickly turned around after I passed them.

While all this was going on, when I arrived at my office first thing in the morning I had twenty-eight messages on my work phone from one news outlet or another from all over the country, all wanting to do interviews. I remotely checked my home answering machine and had even more of them there. And they were still coming in. I couldn't do any work, not to mention the fact that my adrenaline was pumping to the maximum. I was previously warned by Tom Devine to expect some media coverage but I wasn't ready for this.

I had spent my entire federal career working behind the scenes and was most comfortable in this environment, so getting all this attention had me exasperated. I had to go see my lawyer, Tom Devine, and see if he could put this stuff into some perspective. So I put in for leave for the rest of the day and most of the rest of the week. Packed up my work back pack and left the building with a small entourage of official looking geeks talking to their left hand (mostly). I still didn't know if these guys were shadowing me to protect me against physical retaliation from pissed off FAA folks, or make sure I didn't go ballistic, or if it was an effort to

Fortress of Deceit

intimidate the latest notorious government whistleblower. I considered each of these equally plausible. Asking them directly I knew would be pointless. If it was the first option to protect me I could have saved them a lot of time and money if they would have just let me know why they were here. Heck, just chewing the fat with a couple of Cro-Magnon body guards would have been a welcome relief the first few weeks of my new public status when almost everyone at work avoided me like the plague. I would have even bought them a coffee. I wasn't particularly concerned about any type of physical attack at work, for one thing these people weren't quite that stupid, for another reason most of these people were a bunch of gimps, the relatively few at headquarters that might have caused me some concern probably agreed with my actions and information that made it to the press at this point.

Under the circumstances, however, I was becoming increasingly uncomfortable having them around, and so many of them. I left work and walked to Le Enfant Metro Station with several of them tailing me but at a discreet distance. I don't know if they knew if I knew they were tailing me. As the doors to a subway train opened up I entered the car and noticed that one of my tails entered the car at the next set of doors. There are three sets of doors on each of the DC metro trains. Right before the doors shut I hopped off the train and my tail was left sitting in one of the chairs. As the train passed I waved to her and she simultaneously was talking to her wrist. I lost one of them but she was definitely talking to someone. I just milled around the tracks waiting for the next train to get there and kept looking for my next tail among the growing small crowd of metro riders. Found him lingering about twenty feet away. One of the problems with this profession is that a lot of these guys take themselves too seriously. Trying to look too stern or macho, probably from watching too many cop shows. I entered the next train and sat down and he sat down at the opposite end of the car. As he pivoted to sit I noticed the proverbial earpiece.

I took a long circuitous train ride to Metro Center, which as its name implies is the central metro station in DC. It has several layers of underground tracks and a small labyrinth of walkways for the passengers. I figured I didn't have a whole lot of time left before they were able to reorganize their little army that got scattered about on different trains and re-converge on this metro station. It also occurred to me that I could understand them sending a couple of guys over to FAA headquarters to keep an eye on things, and I was actually a little grateful, but following me into the metro station seemed a bit much and went way beyond an interest to make sure FAA didn't retaliate against me physically. So that left the other two options, either they were concerned about me engaging in some violence or this was an effort at intimidation – to demonstrate the long arm of the government. It also made me wonder if these clowns were with the FBI. The FBI has virtually unlimited resources and an army of available agents to mount an operation like this, and I wouldn't put anything past them.

As I was sorting this out I was meandering around the underground like a mouse in a well-run maze. Waiting for a lot of passengers to disembark from a train then mingling with them as they moved about the station. Periodically taking my jacket off and later putting it back on, as I knew any tail would report this while I looked for the tell-tale signs. Even stood in the shadows for a while, near one of the stairs, out of sight. At one point I happened upon one of these guys standing near one of the ends of the train tunnels with his back facing me. I of course couldn't hear what was coming in over his ear piece but I caught the tail end of his end of the conversation. He said "… he's not here." It was apparent that they had lost me. But I figured I'd fuck with them anyway. I gently patted the guy on the shoulder and asked him how he's doing, and walked off, not waiting for a reply – this was easier than my early deer stalking days. I eventually made it to K Street near the GAP office, continuing my counter-tailing techniques – walking down the sidewalk then turning around and walking in the other direction looking for any one talking to himself, as well as observing anyone looking in my direction on the opposite side of the street, etc. I must have memorized the faces of fifty people during this chase. Anyone I saw twice, I paid extra attention too.

Later I went into a restaurant, moseyed back to the restrooms, went out the emergency exit in the back, which alarmed, immediately shut the door which turned the alarm off and walked down the alley arriving at the GAP office shortly thereafter. As far as I could tell I lost them some time ago. If they thought I was violent prone I doubt that any one of them would have followed me down this alley.

As I was standing in the small lobby of the GAP building waiting for the elevator I realized how calm I was. In fact, I felt great. This little distraction, since I left FAA headquarters, took my mind off the growing storm my whistleblowing started. I realized being hunted like this was similar to the hunter's adrenal rush. Hunting or being hunted was the same to me.

What really had me stressed out was dealing with the press and wondering if I'm going to be able to keep my job, and if not, if I'd ever be able to get another job. That was terribly stressful. I spent several hours at the GAP office talking to Tom Devine and some other staff. He even arranged a number of press interviews for me while I was at his office. Well, the game was set and put in motion, I figured if there was anything positive to be accomplished by all this I had little choice but to pursue this action as aggressively as possible (while remaining within the law), and to hell with their efforts at intimidation – I'd throw it right back in their face. At this stage of the river of life I was tossed about in intense rapids and was paddling as fast as possible to maintain some degree of control on the trip downstream rather than try to reach shore or change directions. The system was broken and I was determined to do what I could to fix things.

While still at the GAP office, I called my home number and Steve Elson picked up the phone. On September 16, 2001 he was featured in a segment on *60 Minutes* (interviewed by Steve Kroft) and went through a similar rigmarole with the press at that time. So he was a lot more prepared for this stuff than I was. He previously came out to watch my house when I was at work and other wise serve as a body guard if needed. He reported that there were several news vans parked outside my townhouse. While I decided to aggressively pursue this course of action with the press since Congress doesn't do jack shit (for the public good, not their pocketbooks) unless they get press coverage for it. I drew the line with them getting too close to home however. I had a lot of news interview requests over the phone that first day and even a taped TV interview. But I didn't go home till the press vans left the neighborhood later that night. Drove the neighbors nuts.

I ended up doing a lot of press interviews that first week. But the following week I had to go back to work. It was still total bedlam there. The Red Team was effectively killed off, never to be revived. Just as in the old "Tora Tora Tora" movie dramatizing the Japanese attack on Pearl Harbor, a Japanese admiral exclaims that he fears all they did was, "awaken a sleeping giant." I found it amazing how the government learns nothing, and how history endlessly repeats itself.

Our government, in spite of the billions of tax dollars spent annually since that fateful Japanese attack, never figured out how to stay awake. Yes, now the sleeping giant was awake again, and it was on a rampage. A rampage of spending tax dollars with very little thought on how the money was spent. Starting TSA was the first black hole absorbing tax dollars. There was a litany of blatantly wasted tax dollars the first few years of TSA's existence, a half million dollars spent on the agency's first anniversary party, screener recruitment drives in resort vacation hotels, tons of money spent on decorating offices and operations centers, etc. TSA managers were spending money like oil sheiks on a buying binge. I visited a TSA Category X airport office (one of the larger airports) a few years after 9/11 and discovered *holding cells* (essentially small jails) built into their office space located in a commercial office park. I'm not sure who they expected to lock up there, nursing mothers were a big threat at the time though. When I observed this holding cell (reminiscent of my law enforcement days) a co-worker gave me the history – it was built into the office space at quite a sum of money right after TSA took over security but once the original management nut jobs left, the room has since been used for stationary storage. Nobody is ever held accountable for wasting tax dollars – which is little more than theft in my opinion. This doesn't even count the 'legitimate' moneys spent on dubiously effectively technology and program areas that were poorly thought out.

I attended the TSA's first anniversary party located in a hoity-toity hotel in downtown Washington, DC in the largest room I've ever seen and enquired at the front desk how much this extravaganza cost. The clerk wouldn't give me the billing amount for this party but said rental of the conference room cost $50,000 just for one day; everything else is extra (food, decorations, setup, etc). A huge set of tables loaded with food and drink were in the back of the room (no alcohol that I noticed) to cater to the thousands of TSA headquarters employees and other invited guests. However, I did see in the back of the conference room a door in which hotel staff were wheeling in carts covered with white sheets. Standing outside the door was another government goon with an obvious ear piece dangling to the side of his head. I acted like I belonged there and just tried to walk into the room following another caterer, but he did a very thorough job of checking the required ID everyone had to wear at this event, literally shoving his hand toward my face (not touching me, but coming awfully close) and told me this was a private room and I didn't have the appropriate coding on my ID badge. I did get a quick glimpse into the room though since I was right behind the caterer as he opened the door, saw a room about the size of a school classroom with a table in the middle loaded with gourmet food (compared to the over-priced expensive crap the rest of us had) and what looked like a lot of bottles of wine and hard liquor artfully placed on various stands. I kept a periodic eye on the room but no one entered it other than the caterers and a few goons doing their security checks. The big party outside was for the worker bees, while this smaller room was for the elite of the agency after the big party was over. I didn't eat or drink anything and left after a half hour – part of me was hoping the place would be hit with a contagion and cordoned off by the CDC. A reporter later determined the afternoon event cost the taxpayer half a million dollars. Peanuts as far as government waste goes.

This was also the time of the planting of the seeds in the government where everyone in this country was suspect until they proved themselves otherwise – all in the name of political correctness and sensitivity to diversity issues instead of focusing on who or what the real threat was. A number of operations centers were set up to examine all the terrorist indicators. At these operations centers every little pimple was investigated to determine if there was a threat, instead of reasoning the situation out and focusing on the most likely probabilities. Since the Red Team was no more, I was assigned temporary duty at various operations centers and was bored out of my mind. There was no doubt in mind that the next substantial attack was years away in spite of the government's hysteria of the moment. What we should have been doing was engaging in a serious investigation into the government failures and correcting the problems before we started throwing more time and money at failure based programs, equipment and people, and do so before the evil doers could regroup and attack again. But this was not to be. After TSA, the next big siphon of tax dollars was the Department of Homeland Security (DHS), not even counting the unconstitutional wars we started.

A couple of years later, after a lot of bureaucratic problems made it to the news media, one of my exasperated Congressional staffer contacts told me that TSA was a mistake, it was not the intention of Congress to establish the huge TSA as it developed, but that the bureaucratic momentum just kept growing. Another of the senior Congressional staffers, when the plans for TSA were still on the table, told Elson that, "the new organization would be unlike anything we've ever seen", inferring some degree of uniqueness and greatness, and that "none of the former FAA managers would be transferred to TSA." A couple of years later, the same staffer told Elson, "Well, things didn't turn out like we planned." Most FAA security employees were automatically transferred to TSA, including management personnel. Those that wanted to stay with FAA could do so. Instead of killing off the virus, Congress incubated it, made it copulate with the newly hired goof managers of TSA, and the resulting organism metastasized into the TSA/DHS tumor.

Congress was in a panic, they had no idea what to do to fix the aviation security problems that countless reports had previously documented; so they effectively told TSA, "We don't care what you do, just do whatever it takes to prevent another 9/11"; with virtually an unlimited amount of tax dollars and virtually no oversight. The bottom line of all this: I previously reported that working for federal law enforcement was like shoveling a never ending pile of manure around, working for FAA was the equivalent of playing in the manure, in TSA, we produced the manure and expected everyone else to play in it.

Before 9/11, Congress stuck its head in the sand and didn't want to do anything about the bureaucratic problems in FAA in spite of the obvious warning signs of a terrorist attack; the dumbest thing they did was give a bunch of bone-headed bureaucrats (who knew nothing of security or terrorism) cart-blanche to do whatever they wanted to do. The first head of TSA lasted about a year before he was relieved of command. Then they gave the second head of TSA the same vague instructions and unlimited funds with virtually no oversight but with a suggestion not to be so nuts as the first head. This type of *Congressional oversight* continued ad infinitum to the present administrator.

It didn't actually begin with TSA, but certainly TSA brought it into the light. This country now has unelected bureaucrats that are essentially establishing law in this country – not least of which is TSA's literal strip searching and groping of passengers, essentially some bureaucrat decided that we give up our 4th amendment rights against unreasonable searches as soon as we step onto airport property with absolutely no debate in Congress except for the occasional dog and pony show hearings.

Well – back to February of 2002. TSA started off as a one cell cancer in the government. I don't know exactly when it started but I suspect it was within a week or two after our elected officials cleaned their underwear after the 9/11 attacks. And it was no surprise as to Congress' treatment of government whistleblowers, they pretty much allow government bureaucrats to treat whistleblowers any way they want.

While TSA hadn't formally taken over the aviation security functions from FAA in February of 2002, the cancerous cells were already starting to metastasize in the guise of the new managers that slowly started exerting their influence in the FAA security bureaucracy. One of the first things they did during the very same week that the OSC publicized my whistleblower disclosure was to take away all my job duties, and I mean this quite literally. My supervisor at the time came up to me and told me that he was told to tell me by our new masters, "When we want you to do something we'll let you know."

Well, they didn't let me know for an entire year. I went from February of 2002 to February of 2003 with absolutely no assigned work to do whatsoever. I volunteered for a couple of months, just to have something to do, to help put the training binders together for the hundreds of newly hired Federal Security Directors and their senior staffs that were being sent to all the commercial airports around the country. This at a salary of about a hundred thousand dollars a year at the time.

Otherwise, I'd come in to the office first thing in the morning, go get a leisurely coffee and a belly bomb at the local deli, come back to the office and continue working on my terrorism data base. Then go have a leisurely lunch, work on my data base some more and go home at quitting time.

I was figuring during this time frame, that once the hysteria of 9/11 died down that some wiser minds in the TSA leadership would acknowledge the fact that if my assessment of FAA security hadn't been correct, then they wouldn't have their overpaid government jobs in the first place, and perhaps they would give me a job in which I could contribute to the national security efforts. But this was not to be. Wiser minds in government management? I should have known better by this time.

During 2002, the Office of Special Counsel ordered the Secretary of Transportation (Norman Mineta by this time) to investigate my allegations. Mineta in turn ordered the DoT Office of the Inspector General to investigate my allegations – in effect, it was the same group of folks I had visited in the lead up to 9/11 – who in turn conducted, what I was later told, was the largest and most expensive investigation ever conducted by the IG in its entire history, when in fact they should have been investigated themselves for what they knew ahead of time and why they refused to take any action against FAA. In spite of this effort and expense, both myself and Tom Devine (my lawyer with the Government Accountability Project) felt the IGs report was a shameless cover-up and protested to the OSC. A follow up effort was made. Their report was submitted to the Office of Special Counsel and in February of 2003 the OSC made a public statement on their conclusions of this bogus investigation. They stated words to the effect that, "....FAA Security executed its civil aviation security mission in a manner that was a substantial and specific danger to public safety..." (Effectively reiterating their initial support of my allegations.) There was also an itemized listing of various other details of my allegations that they also agreed with. Even though their investigation basically corroborated my allegations, it should have been a lot stronger. The one item that they did not agree with was my allegation that FAA engaged in a cover up of their own malfeasance. Well, this latter conclusion was just a bunch of bureaucratic guano. If it weren't for my whistleblower disclosure none of this stuff would have made it to the light of day. It wasn't offered to them (by FAA), documented by, or even of interest to the 9/11 Commission when they allegedly investigated the failures in aviation security. And yet they claim there was no cover-up.

In addition to their public statement that the OSC made regarding my case, they had previously sent a letter to the Administrator of TSA expressing their concern that I wasn't being assigned a job commensurate with my background. They didn't accuse the TSA of retaliation against me for filing a whistleblower disclosure against the FAA, just expressing concern about my employment status with them. This was in spite of the fact that both myself and my lawyer, Tom Devine, had told the OSC that TSA took away all my job duties.

The entire marching orders of the Office of Special Counsel consists primarily of only two critical mission areas. The first is that they can order an agency head to investigate cases of "gross" waste, fraud, and abuse within the executive branch ('regular' waste, fraud and abuse is investigated by the respective agency's IG) as well as gross threats to public safety caused by government malfeasance, and the second is that they are supposed to protect government whistleblowers from retaliation by the same bureaucratic machine that caused the problems in the first place. This is the theory behind the laws anyway. But the practice of the law deviates somewhat from the principle behind it.

The way the system actually works is that the OSC sends a formal letter to the agency that the whistleblower disclosure was made against. In this case I filed the case against FAA, but since the government terminated FAA's involvement in aviation security and created the TSA to take its place it was the TSA that had to respond to the OSC's letter. And there are only two things that the agency has to respond too. The first is that the TSA has to identify how it corrected the problems that I identified in my whistleblower disclosure, and the second is that they have to address the issue of my allegations of retaliation for filing the whistleblower case – which is against the law, in principle.

Once the OSC receives the response from the agency, they put a nice cover letter over it and forward that response, along with other documentation (foremost of which the OSC makes a determination on whether the agency's response "appears reasonable" or not) to the Office of the President of the United States – who was still Bush at this point. And from there it enters a black hole where it's never seen again. Case Closed. I'm not directly blaming the OSC for this nonsense, Congress and/or the President severely restricts what the OSC can do.

What happened in my case: the same week (in February of 2003) that the OSC made a public statement corroborating my allegations against the FAA, the TSA transferred me from my non-job, to an operations center located near Dulles Airport. I was assigned to the graveyard shift and my entire responsibility was to wait by the phone and when I hear it ring, pick it up, write down a one sentence narrative documenting a particular type of flight operation, type one sentence in a computer log and hit the send button. This operational activity occurred 4 to 5 times a night. Even by government standards this seemed kind of lame, but I guess compared to doing nothing for a whole year, this was a major step forward. This was my sole job, now at a bit over a hundred thousand dollars salary a year (ever increasing salary due to cost of living adjustments and other across the board increases rewarding failure based bureaucracies). The one thing that kept me from going berserk was that I read a lot and it gave me the time to catch up on personal reading. But I hated graveyard shift work with a passion.

About a month or two after I started doing this crap, I received a phone call from the OSC asking me if I wanted to read the letter the TSA sent them – effectively wrapping up my whistleblower disclosure – and write a rebuttal if I so desired, and both letters would be forwarded to THE President. Of course I accepted.

Fortunately, Tom Devine had previously briefed me on how federal government whistleblowers are typically treated. If TSA doesn't just fire me outright, he stated, they will make my employment situation so miserable that I'll just up and quit, and I'll hope to get another job as a fast food cook. If I don't quit they will try to set me up in an untenable situation where I'll react emotionally and be charged with insubordination or better yet, I'll punch some one's lights out. In either case, particularly the latter, it would be grounds for TSA to fire me for cause. Never to get another decent job. Being labeled a federal government whistleblower is as bad as receiving a dishonorable discharge in the military. One's livelihood is effectively ruined, all for abiding by the Constitution and the oath of office we take.

Fortress of Deceit

So I kept these words to heart whenever I was confronted by a seemingly endless parade of idiot managers and supervisors that TSA found under the slimiest rocks where they did most of their recruiting.

With this in mind, I went to my supervisor and explained the situation to him and that this coming Friday I was scheduled to work at the OSC and even though I had the day time off (since I worked the graveyard shift) I'd need to take Thursday night off so as to be reasonably alert on Friday. My supervisor wouldn't give me the time off, explaining that my job is so crucial and that he'd need more advance warning to get a replacement for me. This, even though the operations center was over-staffed with half a dozen other folks doing little more than the BS I was doing and could easily have them do my *job* for one shift. In his defense, my supervisor was so stupid that I half believed that he believed what he told me and the other half was deliberate retaliation.

I called up the OSC and explained the situation. They apparently went ballistic and called up the TSA Administrator's office and I suddenly found I had Thursday night off. I was impressed with the OSC. But this official interference didn't exactly endear me into the hearts and minds of TSA management.

So the first thing Friday morning I arrived at the OSC office on M Street in downtown DC. They place me in an office with the TSA document, sat me down in front of a computer, and one of the OSC staff members sat across the room staring at me. He explained that I can't have a copy of the TSA document nor can I take any notes. Furthermore, I have to type my rebuttal on their computer and I can't even have a copy of my own rebuttal. I wasn't even allowed to have my lawyer present or available. And furthermore, an

OSC staff member will be sitting in the room with me to monitor my adherence to the rules for the duration of my stay. He further explained that this is not part of their normal routine. He stated that given the unusual nature of my case (I was not attacking a little bit of waste, fraud, abuse or minor threat to public safety; but instead I was attacking the efficacy of an entire agency, not to mention the extensive press coverage I received) that they were giving me the courtesy to make an official response for the record. Later Tom Devine explained that the reason for this was that TSA marked their document SSI (or Sensitive Security Information), which was treated at the time as not subject to public release and even congressional oversite (there-by reinforcing government paranoia and secrecy, as I understand this nonsense). These rules were loosened years later, somewhat.

Over the course of the day I had about half a dozen different staff members spell each other watching me as they got bored or had other things to do. What a bizarre way to run a government, I thought at the time. But I was grateful for being given the opportunity to read and rebut the dribble that TSA coughed up in response to my allegations as to how they corrected the problems in aviation security.

Retired Coast Guard Admiral James Loy actually signed the document (dated February 24, 2003) as the second Administrator of TSA. I have since referred to him as *Lying Loy*. In my rebuttal I explained that all TSA was doing was using the failure based FAA template of security and multiplied it at least a hundred times in terms of tax dollars wasted; but failure based is failure based, no matter how much money you throw at it. My letter was later vindicated by the series of amateur attacks such as the shoe bomber, under wear bomber and various cargo related incidents like the nut job that shipped himself cross country in a big box.

All of these made it past TSA's vaunted failure based security systems and were thwarted only by passengers and crew members while in flight or by pure dumb luck. We only found out about the nut job in the box caper because he broke out of the box in front of the destination house when the delivery person was still there.

Lying Loy also explained that TSA was getting rid of the Red Team concept so as "to avoid that little problem." Unfortunately, when the OSC wrote up its evaluation of the FAA Red Team, it wasn't very clear. Depending on one's point of view you could interpret their remarks as the FAA Red Team was responsible for the problems in FAA Security, when in fact it was the Red Team that identified the problems in management and security. I emphasized in my rebuttal that there should be a more rigorous Red Team and more importantly that the agency should have to take action based on their assessments of security – unlike in FAA, we'd spend a lot of time and money flying around the world, send our reports to management, and our reports would go into the circular file. Well, I should have known better by this time. Genuine Red Team work is as much a reflection of the agency's senior management as it is of front line security – and no high level manager in this post 9/11 world I ever came across would tolerate an *uncontrolled* Red Team documenting how screwed up a job they were doing. Another part of Lying Loy's report is that he stated that I'm gainfully employed and "that TSA is making full use of my talents and abilities." All of which was a blatant lie, so I went into some detail correcting that little item, emphasizing that I was entombed in an entry level staff job. The only benefit to the crap I was doing was that the intellectual *nothingness* of TSA headquarters really enhanced my study of ZEN, and to top it off TSA was throwing away all my job bids.

Fortress of Deceit

While I was writing my rebuttal, every time I got a change of the guards (to make sure I didn't do anything dastardly) I'd engage in a little chit chat with the on-coming guard and pick their brain. What I gleaned from them is that what I was doing there (contributing to the OSC final report to the President) wasn't only highly unusual; this was, in fact, the first time anyone there had witnessed this event. Furthermore, and the main reason for this, is that the OSC knew that Lying Loy's report was a bunch of hogwash, but they weren't about to tell the President of the United States that his new super agency TSA was little more than a refried beans version of FAA nonsense, except for the size and expense involved and the amount of gas expelled – with an undertone of a serious conflict with the Constitution.

Shortly after that day, the final OSC report, with my note as an attachment, was sent to the White House where it met its final resting place – the *first* circular file, never to be seen again. Makes one wonder: all the work of the Red Team was a total waste of tax dollars, filing a whistleblower case is a joke, why bother funding the OSC if government bureaucrats and politicians are allowed to ignore its findings. All the tax money that was dumped on FAA security in the 20 years and more before 9/11 was a total waste. Without the government bureaucracy the aviation industry would probably have behaved the same but at a fraction of the cost to the tax payer (or more appropriately the flying public).

And people wonder why we have the worst government debt since World War II; walking a shaky tightrope, according to some economists, that could collapse the entire world economy. And this is what we're paying for. And no one is ever held accountable. It also made me question the increasing "globalization" of politics and the melding of independent country's economies. I'm estimating that there were no more than fifty key managers and senior staff that were responsible for the direction the Tombstone Agency was heading – in spite of all the evidence that FAA was misdirected, and of which they were all very much aware. If our government couldn't or wouldn't control the fifty managers and senior staff in FAA, imagine the infinitely larger bureaucracy of the increasingly global government and industries.

Well, life continued nevertheless. My graveyard shift job gradually morphed into a rotating shift as TSA hired more folks to staff this already over-staffed operations center, doing pretty much the same thing I was doing. I lasted nearly a year in this position before they got rid of me.

During that time we had one particularly harrowing experience. In the middle of the night we were watching some action movie on the big screen plasma TV as one of the computer geeks was moving equipment around. He accidently unplugged the cable TV hookup and the screen went dead right in the middle of the action. For a frenetic ten minutes everyone was spazing out trying to find out what happened and re-plug the appropriate plug to watch the rest of the movie. A crucial segment of our nation's air defense systems was down for ten minutes. But our intrepid security experts soon had the system up and running again and everyone stayed awake for the rest of the shift. That was the most exciting thing that happened in that one year prison sentence.

As I mentioned previously, our elected officials were adamantly opposed to conducting any type of investigation into the who, what, when, where, how and why of the 9/11 attacks. But once the initial shock of the attacks started to wear off a bit, the victim's families started to organize themselves and demanded that the government institute a formal investigation to include an examination into why the government failed in every single program area that should have warned of and/or prevented the attacks. This encompassed the collective multi-billion dollar failure based agencies of our intelligence, law enforcement (primarily FBI) and security agencies combined.

None of our unaccountable politicians were going to face down the wrath of the victim's families so they acceded to having a special commission. Initially President Bush appointed Henry Kissinger to head the Commission, but the families protested as no normal person trusted him (I suspected), and his name was rescinded. According to press reports, he supposedly withdrew his own name from consideration for a possible *conflict of interest*. Being somewhat slow, let me see if I understand this – he's withdrawing his name because of *a possible conflict of interest* concerning the 9/11 attacks? Like maybe, he should be investigated to determine what this interest is! So, anyway, the 9/11 Commission commenced its dog and pony show and our elected officials were still able to avoid stepping into the fertilizer and dirtying their shoes. From the get-go the Commission failed to ask the essential questions of: What did you know? When did you know it? And what did you do about it? They blatantly stated that their purpose wasn't to point the figure or lay blame blah, blah, blah – why bother wasting more tax dollars.

In mid-May of 2003 a Commission staffer called me up and asked me if I wanted to testify at the next official public hearing focusing on aviation security. Of course I accepted. But the hearing was only in about six days and I had to submit my written testimony two days ahead of time. I figured if I made too hard hitting a statement they'd un-invite me, so I watered down my critique a bit to make it palatable to the bureaucracy. Plus I still had my day job (and night) to contend with so it didn't give me a lot of time to write up something intelligible but not too critical to get bumped off the speaker list. Unfortunately, neither Steve Elson nor Brian Sullivan were even invited to testify and collectively we could have buried FAA in the hole I was starting to dig, and probably TSA along with it.

I still had the same goof of a boss to contend with and he wouldn't give me the time off to testify at the 9/11 Commission. I explained to him that this was an official government proceeding and they asked me to testify. "Nope", he insisted, this is a personal thing I'm doing blah, blah, blah. It was pointless reasoning with him and just as pointless going over his head trying to get a manager to get my supervisor to abide by federal regulations. So on the day of my testimony I just didn't show up for work and arrived at the Hart Senate Office Building where they were holding the hearings. If my boss wanted to write me up for insubordination for being absent without leave so be it. I'd deal with that later. As it turned out, however, nothing was ever said about it again. In fact, I had to fight endless little battles like this with my masters in TSA and won every single one of them as TSA, contrary to their own wishes, still had to abide by the blatant façade of OPM regulations at the end of the day, at least to some extent. But every little battle I won just buried me deeper and deeper into TSA's manure pile.

On May 22, 2003, I arrived at the Commission hearings after they had already started – got stuck in the ubiquitous Washington, D.C. traffic, but I wasn't scheduled to testify until late in the day. The last one to testify as it turned out.

One of the difficult things I had to contend with was finding out where the invisible line was that I shouldn't cross lest TSA take official action against me and find some trumped up *legitimate* reason to fire me. These rules of government whistleblowing aren't exactly clear.

On top of that I hated public speaking and even though I had already done numerous live TV interviews, testifying like this in the hallowed halls of Congress just increased the pucker factor. Both Steve Elson and Tom Devine (my GAP lawyer) joined me at the hearings to watch my back legally and physically. So sitting near the back of the hearing room I listened to what seemed an endless droning of government bureaucrats and politicians prattle on about how sorry they felt for the victims. Most of them didn't even have anything to say about aviation security one way or the other. This is what they call an investigation?

On top of this, as each new speaker sat down in front of the Commission and commenced their dribble – none of them were required to take an oath affirming to the truth of their testimony. An oath isn't just a polite gesture to kick off a Perry Mason TV cross examination. In theory, the reason behind it is that if the one providing testimony is later found to have lied then they would be subject to severe legal sanctions. In these special government investigations, from the get-go they make it clear that the testifiers can say whatever they want and no effort will be made to corroborate their testimony, and even if they are later found to have lied there are no legal consequences whatsoever.

So the day dragged on with one bureaucrat or official droning on an on saying little if anything about the failures in aviation security which contributed directly to the ease of the terror attacks. Even Hillary Clinton got face time in front of the Commission prattling on about how sorry she felt for the victims – she had absolutely nothing to say about aviation security. This was absolutely the craziest investigation I ever participated in. The one big exception was Mary Schiavo, the former DOT Inspector General. She presented a dynamic and scathing critique of FAA Security providing more relevant information concerning the problems in aviation security in her fifteen minutes on the stage than everyone else combined during these two days of hearings, myself included. Wow, I was really impressed, and grateful that I wasn't the only one in the line-up that actually had something relevant to say.

At some point earlier that day – I believe it was shortly after Ms. Schiavo's speech - Commissioner Kean made some dictatorial comment that this commission is not going to get involved in internal personnel issues of FAA; meaning that not only was no one going to be held accountable for maintaining the highest traditions of the Tombstone Agency, they weren't going to be called to account for their actions or decisions they made, or even substantively mentioned in their final report.

I couldn't believe what I had just heard, in just one sentence the Commissioner guaranteed another major whitewash of an investigation. These high level government bureaucrats and politicians make it sound like the federal bureaucracy is some kind of benevolent, non-thinking entity of nature that no one is ever responsible for. It's like a cloud or a fog, it rolls in over the countryside, behaves according to its nature and moves on. Except these bureaucratic fogs never dissipate, they just keep getting bigger and bigger, absorbing more and more tax dollars, becoming more and more powerful, and less and less accountable. The FAA Security Tombstone Agency was theoretically killed off after 9/11. However, a large slice was cut off and allowed to morph into the TSA – adding its own distinctive mark to the emerging bureaucracy. Most of the managers and staff of FAA security transferred to TSA – with promotions. The rest were allowed to stay with FAA and finish their careers, unscathed.

What the 9/11 Commission should have done is ask, and demand answers (under oath) the three little questions I brought up before: What did you know? When did you know it? And what did you do about it? The senior FAA managers should have been asked why they did nothing when confronted with the scathing reports of the sorry state of aviation security from the Inspector General, the General Accounting Office, and especially its own Red Team; not to mention the icing on the cake, the very own study conducted by the Appropriations Committee of the House of Representatives. If they admitted to being morons who had no idea what to do about it, then at least corrective actions could have been taken to eliminate or at least minimize the hiring and promotions of morons in government agencies.

If they were the least bit honest they would get into the issue that federal agencies don't work in a vacuum. That our elected officials (namely the President and Congress jointly) pull the strings of these agencies and the agencies do exactly what the politicians dictate. Exactly what kind of influence did this political pressure have on the bureaucrats maintaining the Tombstone Agency methodology in spite of all the warning indicators that terrorists were going to light off something big and that security was a joke. What did the Appropriations Committee do with their report, or rather, why didn't they do anything as a result of the report? The finger of blame would eventually point directly at the Congressmen (and President) themselves.

This in turn, I believe, would stab at the very heart of how our political system has developed. Our elected officials get millions of dollars annually from industry lobbyists. This is nothing short of bribery. Every

Congressman on the various committees that had oversight responsibilities over FAA and the airline industry should have been, and still should be, subpoenaed to testify under oath, as well as the lobbyists and their bosses. The last question the Commission should have asked is what influence this bribe money has on our elected officials, who in turn pull the strings of the political appointees that head the various agencies, who in turn engender a cultural mystique that encourages an incompetent sycophantic army of managers that, like in FAA's case, was responsible for this Tombstone Mentality which allowed for the ease of which the terrorists executed their attacks. And the attacks themselves, were used, in large part, as a motivation or excuse to engage in wars (not sanctioned by the Constitution) which in turn threw more billions of dollars into the military industrial complex which in turn threw more money into the pockets of our elected officials through the legalized bribery of this lobbying.

This is the can of worms that my Congressional contacts warned that our elected officials did not want to open. This is what zipped through my mind as I'm sitting there listening to the 9/11 dribble testimony.

I literally almost just up and left to go home. Working through any kind of official government proceeding was proving to be as pointless an effort as everything else we attempted in the lead up to 9/11 proved to be. My written statement was already part of the official record, since I sent it to the Commission two days prior, they made copies and put it on a table in the back of the room, available to the press and anyone else that wanted a copy. It has since been made available on the internet. Speaking in front of the Commission was just to contribute too and provide some legitimacy to this dog and pony show. On the one hand, I was thinking, since this was the biggest charade of a government joke since the Warren Commission left so many unanswered questions resulting in endless conspiracy theories and contributed greatly to a general distrust of government. What alternative was there? The last resort was to engender and cultivate the press and hopefully their coverage would force some changes.

So I gave my two cents worth in open testimony and answered some of their lame questions. My verbal testimony is available on C-SPAN. This moment was the culmination of years of work on the part of a lot of people who tried to prevent 9/11 by working through the system. It wasn't just Steve Elson, Brian Sullivan and myself that worked on this, but there were at least a score of other FAA folks that worked in a support role for us, providing valuable documentation. Elson and Sullivan had already quit FAA before they really got rolling in this effort. I was the only current employee that was dumb enough to think that something positive could be achieved by getting more actively involved in this circus.

In their final report, the Commission didn't include any of my relevant testimony, written or oral. More importantly they didn't include any documentation I (or Elson or Sully) gave them or offered to them. They didn't even want to see this documentation. I am listed as a witness though on page 441 of their manuscript. The commission did mention in general terms the obvious inadequacies of FAA and used that as justification for creating the TSA which corrected all those problems, or so they claimed. So let's let bygones be bygones and move on with things. That was it.

Well, I thought at the time, this pretty much wraps up this chapter of my travels down the river of life. I did everything I could. But I soon found that the current opened up into a much wider river and propelled me onward down the same path in spite of my efforts to swim ashore and get out of this stinking river and plod toward a different life path.

My first public criticism of TSA occurred in my written testimony to the 9/11 Commission in which I stated that TSA is beginning to show some of the same warning signs as the failed FAA bureaucracy. I also made some comments about the lack of a TSA Red Team. TSA had a group of people that *tested* security which I referred to as a "Pink Team." You can get any idiot to run around testing security, TSA proved that. But the real value of a Red Team is developing the expertise in the team to the point where they can think the way terrorists do and project the next most likely attack methodology so that appropriate steps can be taken to deter that attack. But this was way beyond the TSA's Pink Team's capabilities, and way over the heads of TSA's bureaucrats to do anything about it even if they had the information delivered to them on a silver platter.

Instead, what TSA did was establish a bureaucratic mindset that everyone was a potential terrorist until they proved themselves otherwise – at least in theory. If you think my analogy of the federal government adopting the same frame of mind as Hollywood is a bit of a stretch, read this: According to a *Congressional Quarterly* June 13, 2007 article titled, *Appropriations Show Support for DHS Red Team Scenarios*, by Eileen Sullivan, the government spent millions of tax dollars on Hollywood script writers to dream up every conceivable type of terrorist attack. This was a worse than useless exercise and expenditure of tax dollars. Planning for every conceivable attack, no matter how unrealistic, is worse than the non-information coming out of the TSA Pink Team. At least the money could have been spent on more productive programs, or better yet, not spent at all. But the government did use it to further its aims to treat the whole country as suspect and extend its ever growing tentacles into the fabric of daily life. In these Hollywood movie infinite scenarios, your 90 year old wheelchair bound grandmother could engage in a terrorist attack, and that is something we have to guard against – using their reasoning. Before 9/11 the bureaucratic mantra was "we must be doing something right, we haven't had a terrorist attack since the last one." After 9/11 the bureaucratic mantra is, "we have to be right all the time, the terrorists only have to be right once." Hence everyone is suspect. Instead of reasoning the situation out, its just easier to make everyone a suspect until they prove themselves otherwise (which doesn't make any sense anyway – you may not be a terrorist today, but what's to change your mind-set tomorrow).

My testimony to the 9/11 Commission, however, was another little victory of mine against the TSA bureaucracy and also resulted in the bureaucracy burying me still deeper under their growing pile of manure. At the same time, the press went through another round of interest in my story and now, especially since I opened the door on comments about the TSA, they were very interested in getting little sound bites of my opinion on whatever the latest garbage that surfaced in the news about TSA.

My attitude at the time was if TSA is going to treat me like this, assigning me work that a monkey could do, then I'll make their lives as miserable as possible (while staying within the law), and my public comments about TSA became increasingly critical.

A few months after my testimony to the 9/11 Commission the tiny TSA operations center I was assigned to was moved from a small section of the huge FAA operations center near Dulles Airport to a massive new facility specifically constructed for TSA which was also located near Dulles. They had the nerve to call the place *The Freedom Center.* They have a crumpled piece of iron from the World Trade Center buildings in the foyer as a monument with the words of Edmund Burke above it, "The only thing necessary for evil to triumph is that good men do nothing." I thought I was going to heave, again, when I saw that. Looks great, but is nothing more than the typical Hollywood based illusion government. It turned out, and for good reason, that my TSA chain of command didn't want me to set foot in the place. A year or so later another employee of the Freedom Center filed a whistleblower case against TSA alleging gross expenditures of tax funds on fancy decorations and other improprieties, all of which the subsequent investigation confirmed. Had a brief flash in the news and that was about it.

On the first day I was scheduled to report to the Freedom Center, I arrived at the security guard's shack and discovered that my government ID wouldn't allow me into the building. I used the front desk phone to call my supervisor. This guy was a first class jerk. The previous few months he appeared increasingly sickly, probably from a heavy dose of cognitive dissonance. When TSA was treating me this way I threw it right back in their face. If they couldn't take it then too bad. I made sure I did the BS they told me to do so they couldn't fire me for cause. But I pushed their buttons as often as I could. I was slowly shifting my focus from fighting terrorism to fighting the TSA and unaccountable government – which I viewed as a much more serious threat to the people of this country than terrorists could ever hope to be. If I could do this by causing these clowns to get ulcers then maybe they'd eat themselves to death. I always looked to my oath of office for intellectual inspiration: "to defend this country from all enemies both foreign and DOMESTIC." Foreign enemies are easy, the *domestic* enemies are a much more insidious group. They're a cancer that leeches off the legitimate efforts of the government, slowly strangling it, and one had to be careful not to kill off the good with the bad.

So my supervisor told me that I'm no longer assigned to this unit. Apparently the management there didn't want me to see all the new stuff and gadgets they had there out of fear of me reporting this to the press. I wasn't even allowed in the building. It took about two hours for the boss to get around to telling me that I was now assigned to the Airports Division at TSA headquarters near downtown DC. This job change had to be in the works for weeks, if not longer, but they didn't bother telling me till the morning of my reassignment. By this time, my anger about being treated like this gave way to gallows humor and I just learned to expect the worst from these people. They were so pathetic they were laughable. My only choice was to ride out this little trip down this segment of the river of life until I could extricate myself from this mess. In the interim, I was enthusiastically, spending my free time trying to fix this broken system continuing work with Elson and friends, as well as a new batch of like-minded folks that popped up.

After I got situated in my brand new cubicle life at TSA headquarters, the first job I was given was to update the TSA phone directory. This turned out to be a monumental task. On 9/11, FAA Security consisted of a little more than 1,000 employees, 150 of whom were based at headquarters and the rest scattered around the country with a few overseas. A few years after 9/11 the bureaucracy exploded to several thousand people at headquarters and untold thousands scattered all over the place. This didn't include the airport screeners which numbered some 60,000. The thousands I'm referring to consisted of TSA inspectors and an army of staff members and managers that it took to *manage* a huge bureaucracy. And the numbers would continue to grow. I heard reports that there were some 5,000 people assigned just to TSA headquarters. I, as one of the junior staff members, making well over $100.000 per year – the costs for this monstrosity were astronomical.

After I finished that little endeavor my next task was to go through an old FAA airports security manual and every time I saw the word "FAA", I was instructed to cross it out with a red pen and scribble in the name, "TSA." This was the intellectual limit of doing things better than the FAA.

After I finished that assignment, a former FAA manager, now in my chain of command, asked me to write up a "Lessons Learned" document from my Red Team days and apply it to the current TSA situation. He gave me about a month to write this up. I had to tone down my rhetoric a bit from what I was thinking at the time. The best thing TSA management could do to kill off the Tombstone Agency way of doing things was pour gasoline over themselves and light themselves on fire. But that recommendation wouldn't go very far in my report. Still, I was grateful to the manager asking me to do this – it beat the hell out of the other crap I was assigned to do. So I made a serious attempt at producing a document that government bureaucrats could understand and digest while being of some use. I submitted my twenty-one page report on September 26, 2003 and it was very critical of how TSA was evolving. Stating that all TSA was doing was using the rotten foundation of FAA to build a massive sky-scraper and it's just a matter of time before the structure implodes in on itself. As I reviewed this in June of 2015, yet another major news report surfaced about the 95% failure rate achieved by the TSA's latest Pink Team efforts, corroborating everything – all over again.

As I mentioned previously, the TSA has a small army of thousands of inspectors, staff weenies, lawyers, supervisors and management personnel to over-see the whole process. Effectively they aren't doing anything differently than the small army of the hundreds of folks from the old FAA days, and we all know how well that worked. A person can spend an entire thirty year career doing TSA security work and by the last day before their retirement have no better understanding of how terrorists interface with the security environment than they did on their first day on the job. FAA proved this point – it never evolved, instead being content to stay within its own playpen.

What TSA needed to do, I emphasized, was to look at security the same way terrorists do, or essentially how a real Red Team would operate and think (not the TSA Pink Team). It requires an operational knowledge of the capabilities of terrorists, apply that to the security systems in place and come up with the most feasible methodology that terrorist will most likely use in their next attack. In effect, drum up a probability table on the most likely means of attack, and prioritize limited security resources to thwart that attack. While it might not be practical to have the entire agency operate like a Red Team, it was certainly do-able to have them *think* like a Red Team and develop a bureaucracy that would act on this Red Team assessment way of thinking. Do this through appropriate training and leadership.

In theoretical physics, going back to Einstein's days, physicists, when they couldn't come up with a real world experiment to explain a complex physics equation, would instead conjure up a "thought experiment" in which, using the best of the knowledge and logic they have would project a series of events that would logically lead to a certain irrefutable outcome. There is no reason why this type of methodology couldn't be applied to Red Team applications in TSA, starting with the agents on the front lines and extending into senior management. But alas, looking back on those times, the only thing that really astounded me is my endless naiveté of the workings of the government.

    I submitted my report to the manager that requested it, he seemed to like it and passed it on to his boss who was one of the new senior bureaucrats in the agency with no background in security. Well, my report didn't exactly fit within the normal bureaucratic way of thinking. Ten days later I was transferred out of the Airports Division and sent to the General Aviation section. This is a tiny little backwater part of the agency that didn't even exist pre-9/11. It was just one of the many cancerous tentacles that metastasized out of the government hysteria after 9/11. I've been assigned to the same unit since then. At the time of this writing (late 2014) my salary is approximately $130,000 per year – to do a job that would take me about two hours to train the average high school graduate to do. It requires absolutely no knowledge of security or terrorism, basically just servicing various computer data bases and bureaucracy maintenance chores. Advancement in his or her career would depend entirely on their manipulation of the bureaucracy, and he or she would have no more understanding of security or terrorism at the end of their thirty year career than they would have today. And I'd wager that the vast majority of the field agents and staff at various levels are as equally and productively employed as I am.

    Aviation Security is the type of work in which there are only two methods to ascertain whether its effective or not. The first method is the success or failure of an actual terrorist attack. The Tombstone Agency adopted the attitude that the absence of an attack means the system is working. The second yardstick measurements are the results and conclusions of a real Red Team. And TSA has proven they'd rather not know how things are going, and instead rely on the old Tombstone Agency methodology.

Well, the life of a federal government whistleblower is, if one is lucky enough, about the dullest time of their career. Most whistleblowers are fired or quit out of exasperation. But I wasn't going to give them that satisfaction. For the first few years after 9/11 I received about a dozen letters in the mail with no return address. I opened the first couple of these and discovered a sheet of paper with a curse word cut out of letters from a magazine, given the glossy texture. I just tossed these away and didn't give it a second thought. If these gutless wonders were too wimpy to confront me directly I wasn't the least bit concerned.

On one occasion though I received a large brown envelope with no return address in the mail. The postal stamp was illegible. I didn't open it but could tell from just feeling it that it contained a half inch thick or so of some pliable material. With just a preliminary non-intrusive examination it had a similar texture to, and size, of sheet explosive, which I had some familiarity with. I put this item on a corner table in my basement and didn't give it much thought for a month or so. Occasionally, when passing it while doing house chores I'd just give it a passing glance looking for any sign of discoloration or leakage of oils. Something that might indicate a possible explosive or other chemical. But all it was doing was collecting dust.

After a month my curiosity overcame me and I carefully sliced open the package and discovered the

Fortress of Deceit

December 2003 issue of the *National Geographic Society Magazine* featuring an air force cover story. There was no note, no sign of tampering, just a right off the magazine rack magazine. Well, I had an insatiable appetite for reading, whenever I had down time, like sitting in a doctor's office or riding the commuter bus to work, I'd always have a magazine or book with me to read. So I started lugging this magazine in my backpack and over the course of the next few weeks would read a few pages when I had the time. Always curious, whenever I opened it, why anyone would bother sending me this, and anonymously at that. I read the magazine occasionally at work during lunch and on the occasional break and would have it on my desk waiting to see if any of my colleagues would give off any sign of recognition upon seeing it. None what so ever.

Half way through my reading began a story about the *Samurai*. I, of course, knew something about this Japanese warrior, what with my long term and continuing interest in martial arts. The Samurai were a fearsome and highly disciplined warrior. A lone Samurai would, without hesitation, face off against a thousand enemy soldiers, knowing he was going to die, but would do so out of an over-riding sense of duty and honor. This was a well written and researched article typical of National Geographic. One of the main things I learned from the article was that the name Samurai meant "to serve." In the third last paragraph of the article it mentioned that contemporary Japanese consider whistleblowers to be the modern day Samurai.

Wow!

A big flash of light, or maybe enlightenment, hit me. First, I was impressed that someone actually went to the trouble of sending me this. And second, I never really looked at my whistleblowing as anything special. I was just doing my job (fighting all enemies both foreign and DOMESTIC). My oath of office mandated that I take these steps. But now I stepped back and started looking at this from an intellectual or maybe even a spiritual point of view.

The article also reminded me of one of my first direct exposures to the Japanese culture. It was late 1978; on this particular Friday I spent eight hours working in the shipping and receiving section of a major downtown department store. By the time I got off shift I was covered with black newspaper print from the newspapers we used to pad the merchandize we'd ship out. After work, I went to my evening law school class, not exactly fitting in with my fellow classmates, most of whom were dressed in business attire, and I always received the evil eye from the professors by showing up not conforming to the image of a prospective lawyer. As much as I tried to clean up at the school's restroom, layers of newsprint only wear off from repeated abrasive erosion. So I was sorry sight.

After class I'd get something quick to eat at a fast food joint then go to my second job as a bellhop at a hotel in downtown Cincinnati. This was a very posh hotel, and still is, and I'd scrape more newsprint off my face and hands before my shift to try to make myself a bit more presentable. There was a lot of downtime on the graveyard shift and on most of these nights I'd spend every extra minute reading through one of my law books. On this night, however, a couple of Japanese businessmen (part of a large group of them) approached me while I was standing at the front desk leaning over a law book. The taller one, well over six feet tall, explained that his colleague (a short elderly gentlemen) left his camera bag in a taxi and he asked if there was anything I could do to track down the bag emphasizing that they were leaving the next day to fly home. The elderly gentleman muttered something in Japanese and the taller guy, who had perfect English, explained that the individual that has the bag can keep the camera equipment but he would like to have the numerous roles of exposed film back. Through the interpreter I questioned the elder gentleman to find out which cab company he thinks he left the bag with, he couldn't remember the name, so we had to go by descriptions. He was of little help, not paying much attention to the ride, so I knew I had to check out every taxi company.

I had a real mystery to solve here, spent the rest of my shift calling up every cab company in the phone book and even flagging down taxi's passing the front of the hotel to interrogate the drivers. Even walked around the immediate blocks peaking in the windows of parked cabs to see if there was anything in the back seat. This was turning into something of an adventure. While the hotel was probably the best hotel in the city – frequently having rock bands and campaigning politicians as guests (including the President); the night time atmosphere around the hotel was dark and spooky. Hookers, pimps, drug dealers, drunks and speeding cop cars were a common sight. I knew it was pretty hopeless when I started, but I had to try, it was apparent that somebody absconded with the camera bag.

Shortly after the Red Sun rose, literally, the tall interpreter approached me at the front desk. At his questioning, I explained in some detail the efforts I took to find the bag but that it was my belief that whomever found it probably kept it for himself. Still, I stated, there is a chance that someone might turn it in to the lost and found and that I'd check with these cab companies over the next week or so to find out if the bag was turned in. If he cared to give me his address in Japan, I'd be more than happy to ship him whatever I found. He gave me his business card and

Fortress of Deceit

thanked me profusely for my efforts. Turned out the interpreter was not only the official interpreter of the group but also the CEO of their company.

With the morning slowly passing by, hotel guests were waking up and were ringing for bellhop assistance to lug their crap out to waiting cabs, buses, or personal cars. Developing into a routine busy Saturday morning. As I turned away from the CEO to go about my other duties, he said, "Wait a moment, I'd like to introduce my associates to you". I explained that under the circumstances I can't wait here, my boss will be quite upset with me just milling around while other guests fume from lack of hotel support. He went to the front desk and talked to the duty manager for a few moments and I heard him explain that his company just spent a small fortune at the hotel and he would like my services for the next half hour or hour. The duty manager nodded at me, giving me the OK.

So I'm standing in the middle of the large hotel lobby with the CEO. Every time one of his party moseyed down to the lobby to get some breakfast, the CEO would introduce me to the individual and jabber on for nearly a minute explaining who I was and what I was doing; my only knowledge of Japanese was from my judo instructor, but I could pick up on the inflection and body language. Then each member of the party would bow his head toward me, some would shake my hand. I always made a point of bowing lower than the other person as a sign of respect (since I was the junior member in this drama) – think I saw that in the old *Kung-Fu* TV series. The bowing seemed to come naturally to me; in judo, combatants would bow to each other before knocking each other senseless, but I didn't really comprehend the deeper meaning of this at the time. Forty-five minutes later I was introduced to all thirty or so members of his party, and I went off to get some long overdue sleep.

I never did find the camera bag and notified the CEO via letter. Weeks later he responded in a like manner, thanked me again for my efforts, and told me to look him up if I ever get to Japan and his company would take care of me. I subsequently did make it to the land of the Rising Sun, as an Air Marshal, but never had the chance to look them up – what with the cloud of secrecy we operated under.

The above situation did, however, cause me to pause and reflect. I couldn't explain it, but I understood that a current in the river of life was tugging at me, pulling me away from the course of life I originally longed for, some semblance of normalcy. But I quit law school shortly thereafter and continued my pre-ordained journey downstream, in the direction the karma indicated.

Since 9/11 I've met over a hundred federal government whistleblowers from a score of federal agencies including: the CIA, NSA, FBI, the military, HUD, CDC, VA, FDA, and many other agencies. But they were all special people, they had something in them that most people lacked. They witnessed a grievous problem in government, and against impossible odds sacrificed themselves to try to correct the problem. Some were motivated by a sense of religion or their personal sense of ethics, or some combination of these and/or other traits or values. But they all shared one common ingredient: they took their oath of office to abide by the United States Constitution seriously and their sense of personal honor forced them to take this action. In this current atmosphere, when one files a whistleblower disclosure against a federal agency, it's not just the agency that you indict, it's the entire federal bureaucracy that is called into question.

Most of these federal whistleblowers were either fired outright or quit their jobs which were made untenable by the same people that were the object of their whistleblower disclosures. While I was leaning in this direction already, this National Geographic article helped put things in perspective, in a more cosmic sense. I read up even more about the history of the Samurai and while they certainly had a brutal side, their sense of honor was inspiring. I even incorporated some of their martial training into my own daily martial arts conditioning, particularly the boken or wooden sword. Even felt the spiritual or ZEN aspects of using this weapon.

It even helped transform my demeanor at work. Instead of arriving at headquarters every morning expecting to butt heads with some other idiot manager or supervisor – typically winning every fight, but continually losing the war; I realized that I was driving management nuts just by showing up every day and not lowering myself to their standards. I adopted a sort of mental akido – a Japanese martial art that uses the force of an opponent against himself rather than engage in yet another endless pugilistic round every day. The resources of the federal government are effectively infinite, and one gets worn down engaging in a boxing match every day – even if you win, eventually you'll get too worn out to continue.

By December of 2004 I realized that I will never again engage in any counter or anti-terrorism work. My last entry into my terrorism data base was the last day of that year. I don't even pay attention to the news worthy terrorism anymore. Oh, I see the headlines and occasionally scan through an article, but it's hardly even a passing interest. I reached the conclusion that terrorism and the government's response to terrorism was merely a symptom of a much larger disease, but wasn't the disease itself. Still, I felt compelled to do what I could to prevent the next major terrorist attack.

By the date of my last terrorism entry in my data base I had already made the determination of what was going to be the next major terrorist attack that would potentially kill thousands of people, and the moronic bureaucrats in TSA and DHS had no more clue, or interest for that matter, on what was going on in the world or in their own bureaucracy than the morons in FAA exhibited in the lead up to 9/11. There's a certain bureaucratic way of doing things and it doesn't matter how many people get killed so long as the procedures are adhered too.

The problem was though, what to do about it. I already knew from previous experience that working through the Inspector General's Office was a total waste of time and effort. While they might investigate minor cases of waste and fraud they didn't have the gonads to take on a whole agency. And even if they did, they didn't have the legal authority or power to make sweeping changes in TSA. The GAO was little better and they had no more authority to make changes than the IG did. It all rested on the shoulders of Congress and the President. But as the good government employee I figured I'd at least go through official channels and do things the way the bureaucracy liked. So I sent letters to both the IG and GAO concerning TSA's malfeasance to try to get them to do some semblance of an investigation. I received no response whatsoever.

What I was slowly discovering is that Congress set up a formal process where-by a federal employee could make allegations of gross waste, fraud, abuse of authority, and threats to public safety resulting from government mismanagement (the word "gross" being part of their formal statement – not just everyday waste, fraud, abuse of authority and threats to public safety caused by government mis or malfeasance), have these issues investigated and a formal decision made on the allegations and evidence. Then the employee is allowed to be made persona-non-grata by the same bureaucracy. In my case I didn't even file a whistleblower disclosure against TSA and they treated me as if I had the plague. But I was really surprised that both the IG and GAO refused to communicate with me anymore.

As a test I went to the IG's public website and submitted a form alleging some relatively minor example of waste that I witnessed in my own little shop just to see if some low level staff wienie or investigator would follow through with their own procedures. Even followed up with a phone call. No response whatsoever.

While all this was going on I was contacted by a number of TSA employees who wanted to provide me with examples of corruption and stupidity that they were exposed to. They wanted me to forward this documentation to my contacts in the press and/or Congress. Some of these employees were so afraid of getting caught just talking to me that we had to arrange subrosa meetings with each other. Occasionally, after arriving at my cubicle first thing in the morning, I'd find a sticky note on my computer screen with a number or letter on it. A signal that someone needed to talk to me, and we'd meet at a prearranged location and time. This was later complicated when TSA installed a tiny CCTV camera near my desk. Then we shifted to signals left right outside the TSA buildings. A rock leaning against one of the numerous little garden boxes outside, as an example.

After a while I'd have to explain to my TSA colleagues that my Congressional contacts were dying off, with the exception of a few die-hards that would only talk to me using similar subrosa methods to communicate – even my former Congressional contacts were afraid of being seen with me. And the press, while they were interested in the little tidbits of information and documentation that I provided them ultimately wouldn't do anything with the information knowing that it came from a third person. I even started receiving phone calls and emails at home from TSA employees around the country and even from different agencies asking me for guidance on how to file a whistleblower disclosure without committing career suicide. Ultimately, I'd have to explain to them that if they expect to file a whistleblower disclosure and actually accomplish something productive they'd be better off waiting for a cold day in hell. On the other hand if they are doing it out of a sense of honor or abiding by their oath of office, then they should go for it, and I spent some time explaining how the bureaucracies were most likely to react to them.

After talking with these good folks from around the country I became convinced that literally half of our federal tax dollars are a total waste of money. You might as well burn this money in your fire place and the government would accomplish just as much. Another 40% of our tax money was wasted on programs, equipment and people that were so poorly managed that you might as well get rid of it, although they were salvageable with appropriate leadership (not management). That leaves about 10% of our tax dollars that are effectively and constitutionally used and of some benefit to the taxpayers.

Ok, I thought, if they want to play like this, so be it. I sent a letter to the Secretary of Homeland Security, no response. I then sent correspondence to our main elected officials in the House and Senate who were on the respective committees that had oversight responsibilities over the DHS and TSA bureaucracies – no response, from any of them. After Lying Loy, I'd wait a few months after a new TSA

Administrator was appointed, give them time to settle in and send them a letter – no responses whatsoever. Perhaps the funniest situation was the administrative tenure of Kip Hawley. I had absolutely nothing to do with it, but some intrepid citizen set up a web site where one could buy T-shirts, coffee cups and other miscellaneous paraphernalia emblazoned with an etching of Hawley's face with the caption, "Kip Hawley is an Idiot." There was even an article in the news about some passenger who tried going through a TSA checkpoint wearing one of these T-shirts who was pulled off to the side for extra screening because of the T-shirt.

One of Hawley's inner circle of managers bore a striking resemblance to Miss Piggy of the Muppet's fame, and just as her name sake, had an over-active sex drive. According to rumors the manager had a number of EEO cases filed against her costing the tax payer a small fortune to *resolve* these issues. Just a continuing list of rip offs of the taxpayer (and which parallels the Hollywood theme, cartoonish as it is in this case).

There is no end to this nonsense when Congress just washes its hands of its oversight responsibilities over the executive branch. At the same time, when one files a whistleblower disclosure, one is made persona non grata from the whole federal government, including the Congress which made these screwball laws.

CHAPTER TWELVE
A Gathering of Samurai

+

"It is not the oath that makes us believe the man, but the man the oath."
Aeschylus

+

+

So this, and the everyday BS of my assigned work – which a monkey could do, and probably do better – was my life in TSA up to about 2006. During this time frame, however, a lot of other things were going on too. After 9/11 the whole federal national security bureaucracies were hit with a rash of whistleblowers who witnessed major malfeasance within their own agencies. This included disclosing torture of prisoners, NSA misdeeds, FBI and CIA incompetence as well as in a score and more of other agencies.

Perhaps one of the more prominent of these whistleblowers was Sibel Edmonds. Sibel is a petite woman of Persian ancestry whose brain was wired in such a way that she was fluent in a mess of foreign languages; having struggled with just learning English I was very cognizant of her gift. After 9/11 she was hired by the FBI to translate a large backlog of surveillance audio tapes, some of which may have given the FBI a further hint of the impending terror attacks. In the course of her work she was hit with the usual bureaucratic misfeasance and malfeasance and was fired just for doing her job. She also came across surveillance tapes implicating a number of US Congressmen and other high government officials in certain wrong-doing. Sibel's story was widely reported in the news and several movie documentaries and books. She fought a legal battle to get her job back which went all the way to the US Appeals Court in Washington, DC; one step away from the Supreme

Fortress of Deceit

Court. Everything came crashing to an end though when THE President invoked the "state secrets privilege" which gives our chief executive the power to classify any information that is embarrassing to the administration and his lackeys in Congress. Everything about Sibel was classified as a national secret, even her date of birth and which languages she speaks.

But this didn't deter Sibel, she formed an organization called the National Security Whistleblowers Coalition (NSWBC). I'm proud to say I was one of the first of her many recruits. You can still find it on the internet.

Sibel organized several meetings of national security whistleblowers in which we shared our individual stories and went directly to Capitol Hill (as a group) to petition Congress to enact some laws that actually protected whistleblowers, instead of the still current joke of laws which are little more than window dressing.

The first time I walked into a large room full of these whistleblowers I was struck by the energy in the atmosphere. This wasn't a boisterous pep rally but a quiet, dignified assembly of seemingly *normal* folks who exemplified the highest degrees of integrity and courage that I've ever been around. I could sense it in the atmosphere and was frozen in awe. It was another WOW moment in my life. Most of these folks did not have the fortune of grabbing the attention of the news media; instead, quietly and anonymously suffered the indignities and retribution of an evil and unaccountable federal bureaucracy that they reported against. Many had their careers and even families destroyed.

Later (or possibly simultaneously), the GAP and the Project on Government Oversight (POGO, another whistleblower advocacy group) sponsored large gatherings of whistleblowers. Over the course of these few years I had the pleasure to meet a number of nationally prominent whistleblowers too, including: Daniel Ellsberg, who pointed out our government's deceit in expanding our involvement in the Vietnam War; Colleen Rowley, the FBI whistleblower (and Time Magazine person of the year); Anthony Schaefer of *Able Danger* fame, Ray McGovern of the CIA, Mike German of the FBI; Joe Carson of the Department of Energy, Russell Tice of NSA, Martin Andersen of the Department of Justice, Robert MacLean of TSA and scores of others. I met a personal hero of mine from my high school days, Frank Serpico, who highlighted rampant police corruption in New York City. We were even joined by folks from various scientific and medical whistleblower associations. This was nothing short of a gathering of Samurai.

Ultimately, however, these gatherings and our attempts to influence Congress had no effect to change the laws. From my observations, what I discovered was that when the republicans were in charge, the democrats were extremely receptive to listening to us and promised to support legislation that would substantially enhance the whistleblowers laws, but it would have to wait until they became the dominant party. Then when that happened, all of a sudden the communication between us and the democrats died off and their promises fell off into the proverbial government black hole. Remarkably, all of a sudden, the republicans became our friends and promised all kinds of support only to have this fall through once the tables were turned again. Then the democrats became our friends again. After a few rounds of dancing with these hollow parties it became clear that working with our elected officials was just as pointless an exercise as working through the various bureaucracies proved to be, and this group effort slowly died out, out of despair. Our one short coming was that we didn't have millions of dollars to throw on their laps to bribe our way through to force effective changes in the national interest. We stopped talking to both parties. It was around this time that I realized that drug pushers and smugglers weren't the scum of humanity that I previously assumed – my apologies to them; that distinction belongs to a different class of people.

In 2004, I was nominated by the head of the U.S. OSC to be the Whistleblower of the Year, which included a $25,000 cash award. Her tenure expired shortly after that and President Bush appointed his own political hack who immediately rescinded my nomination. But that was only the beginning. Things got so bad in the OSC that its own lawyers and staff members ended up filing whistleblower cases against their own organization. But this wasn't the end either. In his first campaign, President Obama pledged to have the most open government in American history and made some statements about how government whistleblowers are essential to this process, blah, blah, blah.

The reality turned out to be a bit different. Obama's administration has prosecuted more government whistleblowers than all the prior Presidents COMBINED. In this atmosphere, a conscientious federal employee who witnesses gross incidents of waste, fraud, abuse of authority or threats to public safety due to government mismanagement would have to be crazy to file a whistleblower disclosure. This is the atmosphere we worked in, and still work in. Welcome to the Banana Republic of the United States of America.

Even the routine of day to day existence as a whistleblower was rarely just routine. During this time frame, a few years after 9/11, I went to the dentist for my routine periodic checkup – destined for a minor intersection with another life's path in the river of life. When I was finished in the chair, I left the clinical part of the office, swinging through the door to the waiting room and was greeted with the spectacle of one of the FAA Security managers sitting there awaiting his turn. During the pre 9/11 days he was one of the key managers that helped propagate the Tombstone methodology of security operations. I had no respect for the guy as a human *bean* much less his management skills or sense of integrity. And I know he didn't like me, having seen some of his emails that were passed to me by concerned insiders.

He was the only one sitting in the waiting room, and he looked absolutely terrible. I'm not saying that just because I couldn't stand the guy, he really looked sickly. My first impression was that he must be suffering through some life threatening cancer type illness and is just hanging on to some routine of normalcy for the increasingly limited duration of his life.

We just stared at each other for a few long moments – neither one moving. He seemed too weak to stand up spontaneously. Then I noticed his lips moving, almost a trembling rather than an effort to mouth any words. He was silent but I could tell he was struggling to say something. Then with some effort he lifted his hand up, slowly I extended mine and we grasped each other's hand in an awkward, formal, but friendly handshake. I immediately started to withdraw my hand but he held onto it. He was struggling to say something but nothing came out. At that point I realized that we just exchanged some intense non-verbal communication.

I had the unequivocal feeling that he finally came to grips with his own responsibility for thriving in and supporting the Tombstone Agency and was tormented by

Fortress of Deceit

the 3,000 innocent lives snuffed out on 9/11, not to mention the thousands of unnecessary US servicemen lives destroyed or lost in these bogus wars using 9/11 as a pretext. As I tried withdrawing my hand again, he grasped it tighter as if he was begging for some token of forgiveness from me. Not only for his own culpability concerning 9/11, but for his attitude and actions toward me. With the competing emotions of pity and revulsion wafting through me, the former won out. I tried to say something but I had as much difficulty with speech as he seemed to have. I just slightly nodded in as positive a manner as I could, he eased his grip, and I left.

As I walked to my car I couldn't fathom the extreme feeling of guilt, remorse, if not even personal torment he must have felt due to his own culpability. He's the only FAA manager or employee that I'm aware of who came to grips with their own responsibility. The rest of the managers are too stupid to realize what they're responsible for, or too amoral to care. May God have mercy on his soul, I thought at the time, for he's living through his time in hell now. The rest of the FAA managers, not so much. Their time in hell will come.

Later that day, I went to the local post office to pick up a package. As the postal clerk handed me the package she said, "Thank you". I responded, "No, thank YOU". She then explained that she knew who I was and what I did and expressed her gratitude for my efforts. Explaining that they always keep tabs of "famous" personages in their mail routes.

The next day, the battle continued. Whistleblowers are by their very nature a resolute group and not liable to give up or be intimidated by the clowns responsible for the mess the government is in. Steve Elson continued badgering

Congress and even the office of the President. He sent numerous reports to them condemning the TSA on the millions of dollars they wasted on different technical security systems and explained why, and how easily these could be circumvented. He effectively used the Red Team version of the physicist's "thought experiments" to describe how to easily beat TSA's multiple level security systems. One couldn't argue with his methodology or reasoning. He also explained how to fix these systems, or do away with them altogether and replace them with a more effective system, or just do away with them as they served no useful function whatsoever. Ultimately none of our elected officials did anything with his repeated in-depth analyses. But that still didn't stop Elson. He occasionally would get a nibble of feedback from one of our elected officials and engage in some back and forth communication. Ultimately though, the elected official would back off and stick his head in the sand. Remedying the problems he brought up couldn't be fixed by tweaking the system a little, but rather required stabbing at the heart of how things work in the federal government and no elected official was going to upset that gravy train. If they terminated a multi-million dollar contract for some security equipment that a half-witted terrorist could tap dance around, the bribe money in the form of lobbying would start to dry up, and this is the heart of the problem. Another factor in this equation is that in this time period of self-inflicted government paranoia concerning anything to do with terrorism, no elected official (with rare exception) wanted to go on record for negating security programs no matter how poorly it functions – in the event something happens they don't want to be blamed for it and lose votes as a consequence, and be labelled as weak on terrorism.

Elson would give these clowns a reasonable chance to provide an intelligent response and when that failed to come forth he'd start sending them *hate mail* and calling them a "traitor" to the country by their failure to abide by their oath of office, and filled with a lot of four letter words. He was even investigated by the Capitol Hill Police, the Secret Service, and the FBI for allegedly making threats against the President and members of Congress. All of which was a bunch of hooey. Typically when the investigators completed their latest investigation of him they'd leave him with their tails dragging between their legs and being in somewhat of agreement with Elson and his motivations for sending these inflammatory emails, letters and phone calls to our elected officials; but only after bombarding them with documentation supporting his allegations. He even got on a first name basis with some of the investigators after they had to make repeated calls to him.

The reality is, if Elson had any intention of taking any physical action against the clowns we elect into office – the SS and company wouldn't know about it until well after the fact. But this wasn't in his nature, if any of them bothered to examine his documentation and assessments it was clear he was trying to keep people from getting killed and roughly chastised those in authority who had the power and responsibility, and refused to correct the problems.

But Elson was like a sealed boiling kettle of water, getting ready to explode. His wife made him go to an anger management therapist – just for his own health. After a couple of sessions the therapist agreed with Elson's reasoning for getting angry, even supporting his cause and acknowledged that there was nothing he could do to assuage his anger feelings. Elson lasted two visits with his anger management therapist before the therapist angrily kicked him out of the office. Probably had to go to his own anger management therapist.

Fortress of Deceit

Regarding my own situation, I realized that working through any government channels to try to improve security was a totally pointless exercise. I dutifully went about my assigned *janitorial* duties which were little more than symbolically shoveling manure from one pile to another, and the next week shoveling it back to the original pile. I gave them no excuse to fire me for cause. At the same time I'd always try to find some excuse to interject some humor into an otherwise terrible environment.

On one occasion I stepped into the ground floor elevator for the slow ride near the top of the TSA twelve story building. A couple of floors later one of the senior female TSA managers comes aboard followed by several of her sycophantic lap dogs. They were talking shop, trying to impress the little worker bees in the elevator, which is their normal MO. I just rolled my eyes waiting for my floor and slowed my breathing to minimize the chances of being contaminated by their exhaled air molecules; when there was an inappropriate pause in the conversation. I turned my head and noticed the manager giving off the pre-warning signs of an impending sneeze, which gave me a few moments to mentally prepare for this.

She sneezed and before anyone had the chance to give the usual blessing, I blurted out, "Shateahod!"
She said, "Excuse me, what did you say?"
"Shateahod", I repeated.
"What is that?"
"Its Cajun, you hear it all the time down in the Louisiana Bayou!"
"Oh, are you Cajun?"
"Oh no, but I've done a lot of work down there." I lied. I was little more than a bit familiar with the place.
She complimented me on my acceptance of cultural diversity.

Fortress of Deceit

"Oh yes, that's me."

What I was thinking at the time was of the chaos theory of physics; a basic principle of which is that the flapping of the wings of a butterfly could set in motion a series of events that would eventually lead to the formation of a tornado. There was a chance that, in the name of cultural diversity, she'd use that word next time someone sneezed, and that person would use it, and that one, and the one after that. Eventually all the managers at TSA headquarters would be calling each other "shateahod" – the Cajun pronunciation of "shithead". Sha-tea-hod (hod rhymes with cod, the fish). That would be worth all the BS I had to put up with and would have been the crowning highlight of my government career.

I also had the opportunity to interact with a number of TSA lawyers. The first time involved a private law firm out west that wanted me to testify as an expert witness concerning a religious group that the local airport authority wanted to kick out of the airport, claiming they were a security hazard. The law firm sent me a pile of documents to look through. When I finished reading them, my conclusion was that not only were these religious folks not a security threat but if everyone at the airport behaved as civilly as they, there wouldn't be any need for the cops or the security staff. Before I had a chance to testify, however, TSA had to get their nose in this private affair and the TSA lawyers refused to allow me to testify claiming that everything I ever said, did, learned, or was about to testify to concerning anything to do with aviation security belonged to the government, and I couldn't testify without their permission lest I be fired. I found this rather amusing in that up to that time TSA had absolutely no interest in anything I had to say about aviation security and I was condemned to working what was essentially an entry level data input glorified clerk job. The private lawyers could have fought this ruling and probably would have won, but their clients didn't have the tons of money and years to blow on this side issue to their case.

Three times under TSA's leadership I found myself in situations where I had to file EEO cases against my bosses. The whistleblower protection laws were such a joke that I had to resort to whatever laws I could get my hands on to give me some respite from their repeated attempts to try to get me fired. I couldn't follow through with any of these cases though. Without a competent lawyer to battle the federal bureaucracy it can be another pointless exercise. When confronted with violations of the whistleblower protection laws the government lawyers would acknowledge some possible misdeeds on the part of management but would state they most likely would fall under violations of the EEO laws so they didn't apply under this venue. When the venue changed to the EEO side the government lawyers would acknowledge some problems with management but said these were most likely violations of the whistleblower protection laws. My third and last EEO case TSA just out right dismissed my case because I failed to respond to some important documents they sent me in the required time frame. After back tracking this, I discovered that TSA sent these documents to the wrong address. I never received them. When I complained about this they nonchalantly said that if I wanted to continue to pursue this case I need to fill out another form and send it back to them for consideration. This was crazy, actually, they were crazy.

At this point I went to a law firm to see what options I had. First off they told me it will cost me $50,000 to $100,000 up front for them to process my case. And since my situation has elements of both the EEO and the whistleblower laws, it would probably cost me a bit more. After some heated discussions, the lawyer informed me that if the government really doesn't want to confront the issues they can just continually delay the proceedings. I could spend another ten years in litigation and I'd have to fund their services ahead of time. These lawyers were as crazy as the TSA lawyers. They were all part of a corrupted system, designed primarily to benefit the lawyers and bureaucracy rather than the employee or the tax payer.

    I did have some back and forth email exchanges with one TSA lawyer in particular. She was burying me with a ton of *legalese*. I don't recall what the issue was, but I do remember that even when this was going on I had no idea what she was talking about and I wasn't about to waste time researching all the legal citations she coughed up. Time to fight fire with water. For years I had been collecting those little security caveats that frequently appear on the bottom of emails. Things like: "The information in this email is confidential and intended only for the recipient of this correspondence, blah, blah, blah." Most of these are quite wordy and very legally sounding. These things were also so stupid that I started collecting them, copying and pasting them into a regular word document. This was probably one of the more intellectual things I accomplished working for TSA. By the time of my dealings with this lawyer I had nearly five pages of these caveats using the tiniest font that my computer could muster. How mankind survived without these lawyerly inputs for so long is beyond me.

    So when this lawyer finished trying to impress me with her legalese emails, I responded with a one or two sentence email followed by five pages of these caveats pasted to the bottom of my email. I figured I must have really pissed her off, not taking these latest allegations seriously or something, as I didn't receive any correspondence from her for three days – and we were going pretty hot and heavy there for a while. When she did get back to me via email, she apologized for the delay and explained that she had to read through each of the little caveats at the end of my email and make sure she was in compliance with the referenced directives, took her two days to do this. I responded back, "You must be kidding, that was a joke." Another thirty minutes went by. She then explained that she was laughing so hard at herself for twenty minutes that she couldn't type, then she had to go the lady's room to compose herself. Well, I had to give her credit for having a sense of humor. That was the last I heard from her. In fact, that was the last communication I had with any TSA lawyer.

Since then I learned that TSA has had one of the worst records of employees filing EEO cases out of the whole rest of the federal bureaucracy combined. Forking out tens of millions of [tax] dollars in settlements not to mention funding a whole army of bureaucrats, lawyers and staff whose sole job is to process these EEO cases. One TSA lawyer told me that in addition to the staff lawyers, TSA contracts out to at least one highfalutin law firm in the DC area – at great cost to the taxpayer.

I fully understand from the American Indian's perspective why they referred to the white man as the "forked tongue devils", as they would say one thing and mean something else – not abiding by treaties etc. Of course, this trait isn't unique to the white race or even to people in general; however, I think it is a common attribute of people in power, who are accountable to no one.

In the federal bureaucracy, on one side of their mouth they speak of their commitment to abide by the spirit and technical components of the EEO laws. On the other side of their maul, when an employee does file an EEO complaint against his manager all of a sudden it becomes an adversarial process in which the agency defends its action at great costs to the tax payer. If the litigant has the resources, patience and a half way decent lawyer the case eventually makes it to an administrative judge which can result in additional payout to the offended party – all at tax payer expense.

Of course, its made an adversarial process because you can't expect management to make a fair appraisal of itself, given that the ethical, moral and even legal standards of management are so low. I would suggest that a way to cut down on this waste, fraud, and abuse of authority would be for the managers to be held personally accountable for their own actions. When an EEO judge does find fault against a manager for failing to abide by the EEO laws then an automated system of punishment be dealt out to the responsible manager(s). A sentence commensurate with the severity of the offense.

After repeated violations of the EEO laws a manager should be heavily fined, fired or even criminally prosecuted. I guarantee that once you figuratively hang the head of a miscreant manager on the front gates of the agency, the rest of the managers will comply with the spirit and letter of the law, saving the tax payer hundreds of millions of dollars annually across the entire federal bureaucracy. As it stands now, a government manager can engage in multiple heinous violations of the law and so long as they play the bureaucratic game they will suffer no consequences.

It's a crazy system, and it kept getting nuttier, because its allowed too by Congress.

Fortress of Deceit

On July 28, 2008 at precisely 4:36 PM; TSA sent out a system wide email to all its employees with the subject line: *TSA has a Zero Tolerance of Retaliation Against Whistleblowers.*

Maybe all this pain and hard work finally accomplished something. The email explained that any supervisor, manager, or other person in authority who retaliates against an employee for filing a whistleblower disclosure will be subject to disciplinary action up to and including dismissal from federal service. Wow, again, I……..thought at the time. This is exactly the type of leadership I was talking about. You just hang one of these managers for retaliation and the rest of them will be too afraid to engage in illegal and retaliatory action against an employee for reporting behavior that violates the provisions of the whistleblower laws. The managers would be more inclined to run a taut ship and make sure they didn't have any hidden dirty laundry to air in the first place out of fear that one of their own *disgruntled* employees would rat them out. It would probably encourage more folks to report these activities who were straddling the fence on whether to report mis and malfeasance in the government; basically a lot of good folks who witnessed the worst in the government and wanted to do the right thing, but were afraid too.

In one swipe of the pen (pushing computer key board buttons, in this case) this new policy directive had the potential to transform the federal government. I didn't have any illusions about suddenly achieving peace, love, and harmony or even eliminating waste and fraud etc, but this would be a massive step forward in making the federal government accountable to *We the People*, especially since our elected officials completely washed their hands of the matter and were indeed a big part of the problem.

Fortress of Deceit

At the bottom of the email was the usual POC (point of contact); a name, email address, and phone number of a senior manager responsible for issuing this policy directive. I waited a few days, so as not to appear too over-eager in this matter and to calm down a bit. I called up the number and a gluttonous sounding lady picked up the phone. The conversation went like this (to the best of my recollection):

She said, "Hello, Office of Human Capital , Mrs. _____ speaking."
I said, "I'm a TSA employee and I recently read your amazing zero tolerance of retaliation against whistleblowers policy directive."
"Oh yes, we're quite happy with that one."
"Well, I'd like to speak with Mr. _____ , whose listed as the POC for this directive."
She explained that Mr. _____ isn't available at the moment, and that she is tasked with handling any inquiries about this email.
"OK", I said.
"My name is Bogdan Dzakovic and I'm a TSA employee and an official federal government whistleblower and I'd like to report retaliation." There was a pregnant pause on her end.
"I…, I don't understand." She didn't quite whimper.

I re-explained that I'm an official government whistleblower, had a ruling reached in my favor by THEE United States Office of Special Counsel, and I've suffered retaliation by various TSA managers for engaging in this totally legal process.

There was another pause on her end. The tone of her voice lowered a couple of octaves and with a brief but noticeable pause between each word, she said:
"You……….don't………understand……., TSA…….has……a….. zero…. tolerance… against.. retaliation

317

policy, so you can't have been retaliated against" – speaking her words faster after she regained her required pat footage response again.

"I beg to differ", being somewhat slow, but starting to realize that this was just another jerk off government office. This manager was too stupid to know that she worked in a jerk off government office, thinking that just producing a well-written, *Magna Carte* type document meant she earned her pay.

I went into a brief history of the TSA retaliation finishing with the fact that I was one of the few people in the entire federal government who actively tried to prevent 9/11, tried to hold managers accountable who could have prevented it, but didn't, and as a consequence TSA has had me do idiot work that you could train a monkey to do, and the monkey could probably do it better. It was clear I was starting to get a little heated.

She said, "Why don't you go to the [TSA] Employee Assistance Program Office."
"What for?" I questioned.
She belched, "Well, they can provide psychological counseling."
"You've got to be kidding, I don't want counseling."
"They would probably pay for it, under the circumstances."
"Your policy states, (and I read directly from it to her, summarized here), that any manager that engages in whistleblower retaliation will be 'subject to disciplinary action including the possibility of being fired' blah, blah, blah; and I'd like to report this retaliation and the names of the offending individuals included my entire chain of command going all the way to the Administrator's Office of TSA and especially Lying Loy."

Fortress of Deceit

Eventually she admitted that they don't have anybody assigned to take my official statement nor even initiate an investigation into my allegations, much less have any intention of actually holding anyone accountable for their illegal actions.

Near the end of the phone call she was sounding less like a pompous, over-paid government gelatinous drone moron and more like some body that really wanted to help. She suggested a number of different routes for me to take, all of which expectedly led to dead ends.

Finally she said I should file an EEO complaint, which I did. And the bureaucracy quickly rejected the complaint admitting that while I may have been retaliated against for whistleblowing, this does not fall within the legal boundaries covered by the EEO laws – after several months and thousands of tax dollars in man hours. Case closed.

I had a number of email exchanges with the Human Capital office. The last thing they suggested I do was contact the TSA Ombudsman. By their own propaganda the Ombudsman is an independent, impartial bureaucracy within TSA setup to help resolve employee issues – among other things. I had several face to face visits and email exchanges with a senior manager of that unit and the best suggestion she could cough up was that I should quit TSA and get another job. I informed the manager that that doesn't quite work either.

And I'm sure TSA presented this Zero Tolerance policy memo to Congress (especially since Congress loves to be lied too) and our elected officials reasoned that there is no need to enhance whistleblower laws since the agency itself has a Zero Tolerance policy against retaliation. This place was crazy – Washington, DC is probably the most expensive insane asylum in the world, all at tax payer's expense.

I did, in fact, do job hunting starting even before the TSA Ombudsman admitted my career was toast in TSA. Starting a couple of years after 9/11; when it was already looking pretty grim that my federal government career was over, I started looking for other employment. A few years later the Washington Post reported that over 800,000 people were working as government contractors in the intelligence/security field just in the Washington DC area. Doing what? – I doubt if anyone really knew, there is less oversight over government contractors than there is for government agencies.

This paranoia was crazy, and extremely lucrative to the contractors. Congress ladled out billions of dollars of contracts to the beltway bandits with greater ease and enthusiasm than soup was ladled out at a soup kitchen. I'm sure they weren't doing anything more substantial than regular government work, but it at least might be my *out* of the nonsense I was currently doing.

I had several interviews with various beltway bandit companies. They were all very interested in picking my brain about my Red Team experience. Most of these companies were interested in developing a Red Team training program and sell it back to the government for another multi-million dollar contract.

The more computer savvy of the companies were working on developing some algorithmic computer program that would evaluate security systems to reach Red Team type conclusions; well, at least they understood the value of real Red Team work. None of these contractors did anything on the cheap. The more expensive a system, the better it must work is the only criteria for the government awarding these contracts, it seemed.

Well, this certainly seemed like a silly way to do things. The government had their own in-house Red Team "expert" (namely me), but didn't want anything to do with me. Even Steve Elson offered to help them free of charge except for expenses. He continued to look at this as a public service and not a money making adventure. The government preferred to spend billions of tax dollars to have beltway bandits tell them what do. The amazing thing to me was that just based on my interviews, these contractors had no idea what to do and were just making stuff up, package it up real nice (which was their real expertise) – and sell it to the government, who just looked at contractors as being experts in the field, otherwise they wouldn't be contractors. This was crazy.

This wasn't even free enterprise at its best. Eating out of the government trough like this was little more than corporate welfare. Still, I thought at the time, if I get my foot in the door with one of these highly respected beltway bandits I might be able to tweak my work toward providing Red Team services to the numerous international companies or even foreign friendly governments – who had more of a vested interest in protecting their people and property – and were particularly paranoid to boot, in this increasingly bizarre environment.

What I discovered, however, that within a couple of weeks after my very positive interviews with these companies I'd receive a phone call from them apologizing profusely but stating they were not able to hire me after all. My 6th or 7th, and last interview, was arranged through a mutual friend between myself and a middle level manager of that company. They were very excited about the prospects of bringing me on board. He even showed me the office I would have if I joined their company. A very nice corner office in one of the ever growing sky-scrappers overlooking Dulles Airport at a distance.

And then a week or so went by and the manager calls me up saying they can't hire me after all. The mutual friend informed me that while the management and staff wanted to bring me on board; when my name got to the vice-presidential level of the company, they had a big debate amongst themselves and decided that if/when the government finds out that I'm now working for them, it could affect their getting additional contracts with the government.

The hatred and fear of government whistleblowers went this high.

My options were shrinking.

I even gave half a thought to applying to McDonald's restaurant for a management trainee position just to get out of the poisonous TSA atmosphere. I could at least say that when I worked at the busiest McDonalds's in Cincinnati when I was in high school that the manager put me on grilling Big Mac burgers because I was reliably fast (one has to make twice as many burger patties per sandwich).

I gave thought to going into private practice as a security consultant for the security companies that had the lucrative contracts with the government. It was clear, just based on my limited exposure to them, that they were just guessing on how to *do* security; but that was good enough for Uncle Sam, who couldn't get two brain cells to fire off at the same time. It was easier to pay someone else to do it's thinking for them. But this would most likely be subject to the same informal blacklisting.

My only realistic option was to gut out working for the government until I could afford to retire. So I kept my day job shoveling manure and after hours continued doing the more important work. Even five years after 9/11 I was still engaged in doing sporadic press interviews. But this was the time of more in-depth reflection on 9/11 and the production of the TV and movie-like documentaries of that era.

I was interviewed by Stone Philips of *Dateline*, but they never aired the show. A producer kept telling me to be patient; that they really liked the show, but it never aired. Roger Cook, who was an interviewer of a popular British TV news magazine (their equivalent of 60 Minutes) flew to Washington to interview me and Elson for his last show before retirement. It received rave reviews in England. I even received a phone call from a producer of the Oprah Winfrey show that wanted to fly me to Chicago to appear as a guest on the show. He explained that they were going to have 6-8 "heroes" on the show and wanted to get into their personal stories. I told him I don't want to talk about my personal travails but rather the still un-fixed problems in the unaccountable federal government. I suggested he bring Steve Elson, Brian Sullivan and myself on the show and we'd blow people's socks off. Well that never materialized, and I declined to participate in the show. I recall his last plea when I refused the show: "But this is Oprah Winfrey!"

By this time I was growing weary of doing interviews with the news media, and contributing to the *Hollywood* sound bite, short attention span productions. I'd spend an hour or more being interviewed and the final product would be a one sentence sound bite. It wasn't worth the effort anymore.

But along came producers of the documentary *On Native Soil*, a show subsequently narrated by Kevin Costner. I was interviewed for nearly three hours for this production, but in the final product they only had a few seconds of my interview. Even these things were becoming increasingly pointless. *On Native Soil* did have, however, an extended transcript on their website of the joint interview they conducted of me and Steve Elson and they kept in the names of some of the high ranking officials we identified. One anecdote of mine that they included on their website concerned an informal meeting I had with a Special Agent who worked for the Department of Transportation's Office of Inspector General and who was heavily involved in the IG's investigation of my whistleblower case against FAA. We went to get a coffee and sat down at a table in the local cafeteria. I kept pushing him to find out who was responsible in the IG's office that came up with such a lame investigation of my whistleblower disclosure.

He refused to tell me. So I mentioned the name of the supervisory agent that was running this case; he paused for a moment then pointed his index finger straight up in the air. Implying that it was someone above his head. I mentioned Todd Zinzer (the official Elson and I previously briefed), and he pointed his finger up in the air. I mentioned some no-name bureaucrat above Zinzer's head, and he pointed his finger straight up in the air. I then asked if it was the Secretary of Transportation Norman Mineta, and the agent gave me the thumbs up sign. That's how high this nonsense went, and the DoT Secretary's immediate supervisor is, of course, the President of the United States. Even though the IG's case did agree with the gyst of my allegations, I felt it should have been a lot stronger. The *On Native Soil* website was something anyway.

Later I was interviewed by the *National Geographic Society* for their movie documentary *Inside 9/11*. I literally spent some 7 or 8 days working with them (took leave from work to do this). They even sent me to Hollywood to participate in some annual festival of upcoming TV shows. Stayed at the Beverly Hilton Hotel. We, myself and others who were interviewed for the show, were even interviewed by *Entertainment Tonight* as part of this dog and pony show circus. Well, if this is what it takes. I was interviewed by ET for about fifteen minutes but their final production had only three or four second sound bites from each of us. Here we all were, talking about things of national and even international significance but if you sneezed at the right time while watching these shows you'd miss everything we were saying. Even the final version of *Inside 9/11* only had seconds of my participation.

The funniest thing that happened at the Beverly Hilton occurred when I was walking down one of the halls on the way toward one of their large auditoriums where we were going to joint staged interviews of the *Inside 9/11* interviewees. One or two reporters would glom onto each of us speakers for a quick interview about our particular involvement in this circus. Then Bo Derek came around the corner and all the reporters dropped what they were doing and swam toward Bo like hungry piranhas; taking photos and trying to get a sound bite out of her. She reminded me of the baked potato I had for dinner the previous night. Without all the make-up and special effects, all these people looked pretty normal in person.

One of my fellow interviewees for *Inside 9/11* was Peter Lance, a very meticulous investigative author. Mr.

Fortress of Deceit

Lance impressed me as being the most genuinely intellectual person I ever met in person – a giant in his field. Gave me a signed copy of his latest book, *1000 Years for Revenge*.

Hollywood is an interesting place, like one of those strange planets the crew of the Star Ship Enterprise would beam down to; but it was too weird for me. I was glad to leave.

The general river of life theme always manifested itself when I least expected it too. So I eventually made a point of being aware of its nature. As life went, just as a canoeist learns to read the river while paddling downstream to avoid capsizing, avoid rapids that were just too dangerous or noticing the ripples caused by shallow rocks that could snag the boat or rip out the bottom, and avoiding the dangerous eddies which could suck under an unwary river-man, not to mention man-eating predators; I was becoming somewhat agile in just avoiding the noxious government forces railed against me and managed to paddle past them without getting emotionally involved in this poisonous situation. Let them stew in their self-made swamp. I had better things to do than play their stupid games.

And then along comes Fred Gevalt. Fred made a sizeable fortune, at least based on my standards, working in the aviation publishing industry. He was as fed up with the government and its pre and post 9/11 insanity, particularly concerning aviation security, as a lot of us were. Out of his own pocket he financed a professional film crew directed by Rob DelGaudio, and interviewed Steve Elson, Brian Sullivan and myself in some depth regarding pre-9/11 activities; and Jeffrey Black as well as others more involved in TSA post 9/11 activities. The final production is called *Please Remove Your Shoes* and has been shown on national cable TV as well as in Europe and elsewhere. Working with these fine folks was the highlight of my entire post 9/11 federal government sentence. Just everyday decent Americans trying to make a positive difference. This is the best Hollywood type production made on the subject, and received several awards.

Jeffrey Black's situation was unusual even under contemporary whistleblower standards. He was one of the thousands of FAMs that were hired after 9/11. He never was a whistleblower but was suspected of being one by the clowns in TSA management who retaliated against him in a blatant display of arrogance and stupidity. So he subsequently filed a whistleblower retaliation case against TSA. Watch *Please Remove Your Shoes* if you want the seamy details.

Over the years I was interviewed by a number of major periodicals including *Mother Jones, Consumer Reports, Penthouse, Vanity Fair, Salon,* countless newspapers, internet news services, and others. Even got a few articles and editorials published including a symposium in *Front Page*. *Al Jazeera* picked up some of these news articles and copied them on their website. One of my idiot managers at the time thought I was talking directly to terrorists and threated yet another round of disciplinary action against me – till I explained how the internet news works and that *Al Jazeera* is a news service and not a new terrorist group; he is another of the up and coming intellectual elite of the agency. *Vanity Fair* wanted a photograph of me but they didn't send a photographer, they sent an *Artist*. This guy had me standing in a thicket of weeds at an airport for over two hours while being eaten alive by bugs. How we suffer for our art. Must have taken scores of photographs but couldn't get the lighting and atmosphere right I guess. Alas, the *Penthouse* article was written by a free-lance writer, and I wasn't interviewed at THEE penthouse.

What I found curious is that the New York Times nor any other local New York City news services expressed any interest in talking to any of us to shed some light on a situation that smoked their city, with some minor exception.

While all this was going on I was still concerned about what I perceived to be the next major impending terrorist attack, and found myself equally powerless to do anything to prevent it. By this time I was clearly enmeshed in the *Casandra Syndrome* - a concept originating in Greek Mythology in which one perceives the future but can't get anyone to listen or prevent the impending disaster. And it hurt, deeply. Not out of any offense to my ego, but I dreaded the unnecessary loss of innocent lives – all over again. I felt like I was in one of those science fiction movies in which the protagonist goes back in time to prevent a major disaster, but can't.

Then I was interviewed by the author Bill Katovsky for an anthology book he was compiling which he named *Patriots Act*. He interviewed some twenty individuals whom he considered to be "patriots" and published the book in 2006. In this book he quoted me as saying (summarized here) that the next most likely terrorist attack will be a massive bombing effort directed against commercial aviation, about twenty terrorists operatives, and TSA's knee jerk reaction would be to take away everyone's toothpaste. On July 9, 2006 *The San Francisco Chronicle* published a follow up article Katovsky wrote of me titled, *Flying the Deadly Skies*. I was so confident of the probability of this attack, that in that same article I was quoted as saying, "I have never in my life been around more gutless, inept and outright ignorant people than I have at TSA headquarters, most of whom are in management." I thought I threw in a few choice four letter words to emphasize the point, but I guess he cleaned it up for the newspaper.

About a week after the article was published I happened to bump into a TSA manager that I would occasionally have off the record conversations with. One of the few. He informed me that TSA was contemplating serious disciplinary action against me for the comments I made in the *Chronicle* article and stated that I might even get fired. I just shrugged my shoulders and went off to get my daily dose of coffee at Starbucks. By this time I was fully ingratiated into the river of life concept, or ZEN, Divine intervention, or whatever one wants to call it (I can't explain it, but I know it's there): That life isn't just a random sequence of events, but there was some kind of force involved with the direction in which one's life was destined to go. You could fight it, and be miserable, or at least be misdirected, or recognize this energy and direction and follow the path you were meant for, or just change directions altogether.

On August 10, 2006 a month and a day after Katovsky's *San Francisco Chronicle* article was published, it was reported in the main stream press that the British government had just foiled a terrorist plot in which the terrorists were going to blow up twenty US flag commercial aircraft on the same day while they were flying over the Atlantic Ocean towards the US. The plot would have killed another two to three thousand people. The explosives were liquid based explosives, and that same day TSA announced that it was restricting the amount of liquids and gels (including toothpaste) that passengers could bring onto commercial aircraft. Almost exactly what I had predicted and what I was so concerned about the previous few years.

Fortress of Deceit

Well, TSA would have looked pretty stupid in the eyes of the press and even the blindfolded eyes of Congress for disciplining me for something I was just quoted to have predicted weeks earlier, with my personal comments about TSA as an aside. Thousands of innocent lives were saved by the Brits and nothing our government was doing would have prevented it, and certainly nothing TSA was doing. In fact, it was TSA that guided the terrorists to attack in this manner. TSA was in the habit of informing anyone who would listen via its news releases and on its own website, exactly how its security systems operate. Best I can figure is that they did this to assure everyone that they were behaving politically correctly and to demonstrate that they actually knew something about security by divulging the technical details of its various security systems. The result was, however, that TSA essentially provided a *how to* manual to the public – including would-be terrorists. In this case, how to by-pass it's infamous layers of security and bomb commercial airplanes. Prior to 9/11 I used to state that FAA's version of security resulted in *zero security*. But TSA's version of security was actually less than zero. How could one possibly trump FAA's malfeasance? TSA's managers figured out how to do it by blabbing about it's security systems to make sure no one took offense to it. And they haven't gotten any smarter since then.

I also had other aids in helping me predict this latest attempted massive bombing effort. North Korean agents destroyed (south) Korean Air flight 858 on November 29, 1987 killing 115 people, using liquid based explosives as the main charge. Even the *Bojinka* operation involved liquid based explosives. This was old stuff, but TSA apparently never heard of it before. In the Korean situation, when the two suspects were about to be captured they swallowed poison, the older man died but the younger female survived. Based on my own limited exposure to the police and military in South Korea, both very disciplined and steeped in martial arts, I expected the surviving terrorist to undergo grueling incarceration and interrogations. The Koreans didn't torture the survivor but treated her somewhat kindly, and she subsequently blabbed in great detail of the entire mission. This might have been something to emulate by our own government as a better way to obtain information from captured enemies – since most reputable sources report that torture rarely provides actionable information.

It was clear that our government would rather be dead wrong (so long as the dead meant somebody else besides themselves) rather than do a search internally to find out what they were doing wrong. Instead, their approach is increasingly to treat everybody in the country as a potential evil doer until they prove themselves otherwise rather than focus on what the real threat is. Using every new terrorist attack, no matter how lame, or every new would-be terrorist arrested by the FBI (in my day in law enforcement most of these FBI operations would have been considered entrapment, and illegal) as further justification to destroy the Constitution and further their aims toward Orwell's Big Brother syndrome.

All this is connected: While others previously opened the door on the un-Constitutional behavior of the National Security Agency, Edward Snowden ripped the door off its hinges. In early 2014 a reporter chastised the head of NSA for not knowing about the "probable cause" government restriction of the 4th Amendment, concerning how it conducts searches; give the man a break, he was never required to read the Constitution. I suspect the NSA used as a model of operating the 2006 movie *The Lives of Others*, which depicted sleazy Stasi (east German secret police) agents conducting surveillance wherever they wanted – all in the interests of state security. The only difference between then and now is the technology involved, but its just as sleazy.

As an act of desperation in April of 2008, I filed a whistleblower disclosure against TSA- in spite of the anti-whistleblower hysteria of our government. It has the Office of Special Counsel case number (OSC File No. DI-08-1931). It is a 40 page long narrative with a couple of hundred pages of documentation. I thought the evidence I presented against TSA was more damning than what I offered in my FAA disclosure and unlike in my FAA disclosure I offered solutions to fix the problems I presented against TSA; but some eight years later the Office of Special Counsel still hasn't made a ruling on my case. They never even bothered to investigate my allegations, nor did they officially close it *no action*. For all intents the case is trapped in a bureaucratic black hole – never to see the light of day.

My last *big* attempt to try to do my job occurred on August 20, 2010. Our latest fearless leader John Pistole had been appointed as the new administrator of TSA a few months prior. I gave him the few months on the job to get his feet wet and then sent him a lengthy email outlining some of the major ways TSA is screwing up; with the subject line of: *TSA, a dangerous culture of mismanagement.* I even offered to provide him the methodology I developed that is an infinitely better predictor of the interface between security and terrorism than the entire multi-multi-billion dollar funded intelligence, law enforcement, and security bureaucracies combined. No response from him what-so-ever. Although I did receive feedback from a medium level manager that I sent the document through, effectively chastising me for sending such an email to the god-like Administrator (who apparently knows all).

Fortress of Deceit

I sent a few more emails up through my chain of command attempting to provide some security enlightenment; but management proved again they'd rather be dead wrong rather than upset the ways of the bureaucracy.

One of the goof managers in my chain of command sent me a *Letter of Counseling* threatening to fire me if I send any more unsolicited correspondence to the managers in my chain of command. I guess he learned in government management school that I was supposed to be intimidated by this. But I made about fifty copies of his letter and posted one in a prominent position in my cubicle prison cell. For several weeks after that, every few nights after I left the office someone would rip the letter off my cubicle wall – which I replaced the next day. I would even *inadvertently* leave a copy on the copy machine or in the lunch room so people could see how big a jerk he was. Got lots of hysterical communications from colleagues about this. Even folks I had never talked too before. Eventually he got promoted, yet again.

Within a few weeks of the letter of counsel crisis, I arrived at my cubicle first thing in the morning – per usual. Even before I had a chance to turn my computer on and mosey over to get a coffee the same goof that gave me the letter of counsel arrived at my desk with his boss in tow. The pair reminded me of those ventriloquist comedians that use a dummy as a prop – but I wasn't sure which one of these was the ventriloquist. They told me to drop what I'm doing and they escorted me down to the criminal investigations office of TSA. I was written up for being potentially violent prone in the office and subject to immediate dismissal from federal service if found guilty.

So I found myself in a police-like interrogation room, very reminiscent of my agency days except now I was sitting in the suspect's chair. Across from me were two very intense looking criminal investigators. I could tell by the looks on their faces that they thought they just caught the latest iteration of Charles Manson and they were determined to make me crack under their grueling interrogation.

This lasted for about seven hours (including time to write up the statement)– the longest interrogation I was ever involved in. I didn't know about it until that day, but I discovered that one person, possibly more, in my office since the unit was reorganized about a year previously were taking notes on everything I said or did in the office, and was passing this on to my manager – the same that counseled me on my letter writing. They had a whole litany of specific charges that I had to answer to: making racist comments (my manager was black); talking in detail about killing people with guns, knives, and bombs; buying illegal drugs and bringing them into the office, and a whole lot of other behaviors not appropriate for a government employee.

Well, I thought I was toast. It took TSA about ten years to drum up enough bullshit charges against me to finally fire me for cause – even if the charges were all trumped up. It didn't make any difference if the charges were bogus, I'd be fired and have to spend a fortune on lawyers trying to get my job back, or else I'd just disappear. Even if I won the case, which would cost the tax payer more money, it wasn't money out of their pocket. So they had nothing to lose and everything to gain. I had no faith in any TSA employee (especially any manager) exhibiting any sense of honor or integrity and expected a lot of false testimony against me. Nor did I trust the two investigators, I figured they were specially selected lap dogs that management could *trust* to do the *right* thing. It was not un-noticed that this occurred under the Administrative tenure of an FBI bureaucrat.

If they were going to be this way I was going to throw it right back in their faces and come clean on everything – just to make it a matter of record. Even if that record disappeared down the government black hole.

The first thing they hit me with was my purchase of drugs and use of same while on the job. I responded that that was true and their faces brightened; and I explained that almost every morning after I turned on my computer I would ask everyone in my cubicle area if they wanted some drugs as I was going out to get some. Some folks would take me up on the offer and twenty or so minutes later I'd return with a load of coffee cups filled with Starbuck's coffee. Caffeine is a drug, I emphasized, as I noticed the muscles sag a bit on my two inquisitor's faces. Oh, so the drug charges were bullshit. This would explain, however, why I was always *randomly* selected to undergo the indignity of the drug tests whenever these events occurred at headquarters.

They had me on the next charge, however, based on their demeanor. I was overheard talking about guns and bombs and killing people.
"Yeah, that was true too", I responded.

And they perked up again. I explained that a number of folks in my office asked my opinion on what type of gun they should get for home defense and I explained to them the various advantages and disadvantages of the guns they were contemplating buying. Uh oh, more bullshit charges look on their faces.

Fortress of Deceit

Regarding talking about killing people. Yes, that was true too. As the new guy in my office (which was recently reorganized), I was drilled on what my qualifications and background were. In office discussions my Red Team experience was a popular topic – which was basically replicating how terrorists would kill people in the aviation environment.

The lead investigator asked me why they'd come to me to talk about guns etc, figuring there was more to this than just my innocent explanation. I explained that Uncle Sam spent a small fortune (not to mention what I spent myself) teaching me how to kill with guns, bombs, knives and unarmed when I was an air marshal, and when I was an Air Marshal Team Leader I taught other people how to kill. Going through a whole litany of the training. If they had a problem with any of this they should contact the people that sent me to this training. More bullshit, and they moved sluggishly on through the charges.

By this time, the primary investigator still did a pretty good job of keeping a mean but deadpan face, the secondary investigator, however, kept rubbing his eyes, forehead, and temples and looking at his watch as the day wore on. But they were thorough, and persisted in trying to find a weak link in by rebuttals.

As to the racist comments I had no idea what this was about and asked them to explain the background of this charge, which they did.
"Oh yes, I recall the situation now."

I explained that on one particularly boring day as I was sitting in my cubicle, I commented to my cube mate about when they fix the transporter they're going to beam me out of here as I don't belong on this planet. My cube mate and I then engaged in a brief discussion about *Star Trek*. He asked me which of the TV series I liked best. I told him I really liked the original *Star Trek* series with Kirk, Spock and company but couldn't stand the follow up shows because they were so nauseatingly politically correct. I explained, as an example, that in the original series the Klingons were the dregs of the universe and went into an inventory of their nastier and unsavory traits. In the latter series, all of a sudden the Klingons were respectable and honorable creatures, even interbreeding with humans. When the investigators realized I was written up for making racist comments about Klingons, even the lead investigator started to crack under the strain.

My favorite charge, however, was yet to come. I was accused of being a cannibal. In the course of normal bs sessions in the office with my fellow cube mates, someone started talking about the importance of political correctness – and particularly concerning acceptance of other religions. Not one to shy away from some verbal jousting over philosophy, I interjected that that is crazy and this political correctness is a diseased way of thinking.

I brought up a legal case from Florida, in the not too distant past, involving the religion of *Santeria*, which is a Puerto Rican version of *Voodoo*. Apparently, according to the news article I read, the Florida Supreme Court stated that the torture and killing of animals for religious purposes is protected by the Constitution. This is crazy reasoning, I emphasized, which everyone reluctantly agreed with and based on the quizzical looks on their faces, were starting to question this political correctness which is drummed into their heads by the government and most of the news media, and which almost seems to be their own new religion. If these insane principles don't apply to everything then there is some serious flaw in this reasoning. (I was once chastised by one of the TSA managers for not talking and behaving politically correctly; my response to her was that she wasn't politically correct either for not accepting me because I thought differently than she – she avoided me like the plague after that.)

"Let's take this a step further", I stated. Under this line of reasoning, I argued, if I adopt the religion of *cannibalism* (which actually is or was a religion in certain 3rd world countries), I should be able to kill and eat anyone I choose too – all in the name of religion. Of course, no one would accept this. But it is precisely this type of reasoning which is destroying the Constitution and the Judeo/Christian foundations of this country blah, blah, blah.

By this time I was on a roll with the investigators and could have continued yammering about their charges for the rest of the week. But they pretty much had it with me and let me go. They didn't quite apologize to me but shook my hand and told me not to worry about this mess. I was actually quite impressed with their integrity. Doing their jobs professionally and ethically and not buckling under any command pressures. Later I discovered that everyone in my office that they interviewed corroborated my side of the story. I came away with a much heightened respect for my colleagues, especially since we all worked in this toxic atmosphere.

What's even more peculiar about this is that (according to my recollections from early on in my career) in the federal government OPM rules, there's a clause that if an employee makes false charges against another employee then the accuser is subject to the same disciplinary action as the would-be perpetrator would have been if the charges were true; including dismissal from federal service. Instead, both of the two clowns that escorted me to the criminal investigations office were promoted – one within government circles, the other without. They released the hounds on me on a fishing trip, just hoping they'd be able to find something that they could hook on me. They probably each made, at that time, upwards of $150,000 per year of tax dollars not including cash awards and were up and coming rising stars, some more of the intellectual elite of the agency.

This was just another of those little continuous strings of battles that government whistleblowers have to fight - and win. But still the war is lost. And if one wonders how and why there is so much non work discussions going on in a federal office – well, that's just the nature of the beast. There was no point to any of this anymore. It reminded me of the situation Elson once described to me in which the entire office filed grievances against their manager for incompetency and abuse and the manager eventually received a big cash award for "having to deal with difficult personnel problems", and was repeatedly promoted, including within TSA. Looking over my history in TSA as a whistleblower, it seemed that all I was doing was getting overpaid, incompetent assholes promoted. I was done with this crap, it was time to paddle my way out of here and continue my journey down the river of life, but down a different fork of the river. Being under criminal investigation on bogus charges was the seed that motivated me to write this book – as a last resort, since everything else we tried was a pointless waste of time.

(I wasn't involved in this situation, but its relevant to the story of waste, fraud, and abuse: Under the federal government retirement rules, one's retirement benefits are based in large part on the three highest paying years of one's federal service. For most federal employees, their career involves a gradual progression of pay and usually the last three years of employment are also the highest paying. When I worked at FAA headquarters there was a lady whose main job was dispensing cellular phones and pagers to headquarters personnel. Under TSA, however, she apparently became one of their intellectual elite, and was promoted to an assistant division manager position – a high level job. She then completed her mandatory three years at this massively increased pay grade, and retired; making a lot more money in retirement than her career merited. In March of 2016, Wikipedia reported that the median HOUSEHOLD income in the United States in 2014 was $53,657. You should know that the managers in TSA make, or will make, more in retirement benefits than most Americans make during the most productive years of their working life. All at taxpayer expense!

   Shortly after this I submitted a very blunt letter through my chain of command requesting an in-house transfer to Ohio. I explained that since TSA is allowing more and more folks at headquarters to telework from home (ostensibly to cut down on office expenses) that this would be easily accomplished. I explained that TSA has so dummified the work we do that I could do this crap on the moon and no one would be the wiser. I also pointed out that TSA doesn't particular like me and its obvious I can't stand TSA – so a little parting of the ways would do us both some good. Well, of course they denied my request.

   About a year later, however, my latest supervisor, sympathetic to my cause, re-awakened this effort and told me to re-submit my letter but tone down the rhetoric and emphasize the hardship component of my request – the need to be closer to my sister who was going through a particularly severe bout of cancer. Not long after that, my request was approved and I found myself teleworking in my hometown; mucho thanks to my supervisor.

The bottom line of all this is that there are some really decent folks in TSA, all of whom are responsibly trying to do a job in service to their country. I believe they are a minority – particularly in management, but they are there. The system is completely broken, however, starting at the top with our elected officials.

Epilogue
+
I tremble for my country when I reflect that God is just.
Thomas Jefferson
+
+
On a strategic level:

On July 20, 2014 there was a full page add in the New York Times paid for by the *Aspen Institute Justice Society* and *Annenberg Public Policy Center* harping on the fact that there are 92 Congressional committees and subcommittees that "oversee" the Department of Homeland Security. This is a perfect government model to avoid any accountability.

One of the new bureaucratic entities that burst into life as a result of the poorly thought out knee-jerk reactions of 9/11 was the establishment of so-called *fusion centers*. The Department of Homeland Security website lists a fusion center in every state of the Union and another twenty plus smaller fusion centers scattered about. The US Senate conducted internal reviews of these centers and discovered they produced nothing relevant to thwarting terrorism as well as documenting massive management problems by Department of Homeland Security bureaucrats, and yet they continue to fund them – on the taxpayer's dime, of course. (Ref: The October 3, 2012 report by the United States Senate, Permanent Subcommittee on Investigations, Committee on Homeland Security and Government Affairs, Chairman Senator Carl Levin – titled, Federal Support for and Involvement in State and Local Fusion Centers.)

Fortress of Deceit

I don't believe there were more than fifty managers and senior staff in the Federal Aviation Administration that were responsible for orchestrating the Tombstone Agency method of operations. Starting from the Administrator on down this included not only those personnel at headquarters, but also the senior management teams at the respective regional offices. Not more than fifty! The rest of us pretty much did what we were told to do – more or less. Literally ALL the appropriate offices in the federal government that had any interest in aviation security matters knew that FAA was a failure based agency. And yet the combined resources of the Executive Branch of the federal government, which includes the President, the Secretary of Transportation, the Office of Inspector General, the Senior Executive Service (SES) (which by its own words, takes responsibility over the federal bureaucracy); as well as the combined resources of the Legislative Branch, which includes the entire House of Representatives and the Senate, the numerous committees and subcommittees that had oversight responsibilities, the individual Congressmen that received our personal briefings on the subject, the General Accounting Office, the Surveys and Investigations Unit, and the all-powerful Appropriations Committee; couldn't or wouldn't control the malodorous behavior of just fifty senior bureaucrats. In keeping up the tradition of rewarding failure based individuals and bureaucracies not one person was held to account for their actions. In fact, many of these people were rewarded for maintaining the tombstone standards, and I'd wager all of them.

From my own direct experience and observation, the TSA makes FAA Security look like an elite organization by comparison. The bigger they are, the more severe the bureaucratic problems, and the less chance of any accountability.

Fortress of Deceit

We have the worst national debt since World War II and what I presented in this book is just a microcosm of government waste, fraud, and abuse. This doesn't even include ill-begotten wars that don't meet the minimum criteria of the Constitution, and which destabilized much of the middle-east and middle Asia resulting in untold innocent casualties, as well as sparking off the worst refugee crisis since World War II, not to mention thousands of our own servicemen and women needlessly killed and wounded and many thousands more suffering PTSD with shoddy treatment from the VA.

I attended numerous congressional C-SPAN covered hearings of FAA Security before 9/11, and TSA after. These were all kind of like watching a family picnic version of a tennis game in which mom and the kid are just trying to lob the ball over the net to keep the action going. Every once in a while, one player or the other would spike the ball and everyone would have a good laugh. The last Congressional hearing I went too was about ten years after 9/11. Per usual, there were a few moments of some seemingly serious questioning and pressuring on the part of a Congressman. In every single previous hearing I went to I filed out of the room like everyone else as soon as the hearing was over. In this case, a reporter that I had previously worked with noticed me and we were just chewing the fat in the back of the hearing room. Once the cameras were off and most of the audience left the room, I observed the very same 'hardball playing' Congressman approach the bureaucrat, shake his hand and gave him a friendly pat on the shoulder like they were old buds, laughing and carrying on. I was too far away to hear them, but it looked like they were making plans for a golf outing – just based on the Congressman's motion of hitting a golf ball. This was all just a big joke. I stopped going to these hearings after that. It wasn't worth the cost of the metro ride. Based on my own observations, the Congress feels its doing its oversight job just by having hearings and getting some TV coverage, and behind the scenes they support whatever the trend that profits them the most.

At a press conference I attended a few years after 9/11, a reporter asked Sibel Edmonds (one of the many FBI whistleblowers); "Why do government bureaucrats treat whistleblowers like this?" Sibel's simple and insightful response was: "Because they can!" There isn't anything sophisticated or complicated about this. At best the President encourages this behavior by ignoring the problems within his own executive branch agencies, the SES has a vested interest in protecting its own, and Congress allows it all to happen. Congress set up the United States Office of Special Counsel – a bureaucracy through which a government employee can report "gross" malfeasance of executive branch activities, and even if one follows their procedures to the letter of the law, the same government persecutes whistleblowers for following these procedures.

Even when Congress does hold C-SPAN covered hearings of the latest improprieties in the government spotlighted by whistleblowers, they treat the situation as an isolated incident. If we're lucky they apply bandaids as a fix, when, in fact, there's a pandemic of waste, fraud, and abuse in the federal government.

Even the Founding Fathers of this great country had a more prescient attitude concerning the importance of whistleblowers in keeping the federal government clean. That Continental Congress voted to pay the legal bills of two individuals who reported federal misconduct and were being prosecuted on the state level. And its been downhill ever since. Compare that to today, where federal tax dollars are used to persecute whistleblowers, even those who follow whistleblower laws to the letter. President Obama has prosecuted more federal government whistleblowers than every other President combined. A few years back, Senator Grassley was instrumental in passing legislation making July 30 National Whistleblower Appreciation Day, which is the anniversary of the 1778 Continental Congress' passage of what is most likely the world's first whistleblower protection law. While it's a symbolic step in the right direction, its nothing but that - symbolic.

    In late 2014 a colleague referred me to the website *stuffaboutnames.com*. I ran my first name *Bogdan* through their search mechanism and discovered an interesting cache of information on the name. The latter portion of the site had a listing of famous persons with the same first name in various categories including: soccer players, writers, architects, saints, diplomats and nearly a score of other categories. I was somewhat perturbed to find that my name was listed in the category of *criminals*, sharing the space with one of Stalin's henchmen. I tried to contact the *owner* of the site to ask them, if they want to use my name, then provide the evidence that I'm a criminal or delete my name from that category; but there's no one to contact. Embedded in the internet forever? I would expect this type of treatment (as well as what I previously identified) if I lived in the former Union of Soviet Socialist Republics or some third world dictatorship, but not in the US.

    It also made me realize that federal government whistleblowers share the same light as political prisoners are bathed in, in communist countries and dictatorships. The Soviet Union had psychiatric hospitals loaded with political dissidents. Mildly reminiscent of the TSA manager that suggested I receive therapy, and my immediate managers that tried to fire me for being violence prone – just because I wrote them correspondence they didn't like. In China they arrest people for *disturbing the social order*, which can be anyone that criticizes the communist regime. In the United States, the government just ruins one's ability to make a living if you dare criticize the bureaucracy. As late as May of 2016, the TSA was back in the news for engaging in retaliation against it's employees that attempted to correct various mismanagement practices that directly impacted national security. TSA issued "directed re-assignments" on these good people; forcing them to continually move around the country till they quit. One of my TSA colleagues was allowed to move herself from headquarters (in DC) to California to be with her husband who is a manager in TSA and who rattled the cage by trying to improve things; a month after she arrived in California she was directed to move back to headquarters. At the same time TSA doled out massive monetary bonuses to its failure prone managers on a scale that the former FAA managers could only drool over. Pin-headed, unaccountable bureaucrats and politicians are the same everywhere, no matter the political system. It's no wonder parts of the world are in such a mess.

One of my exasperated and burned out looking Congressional staff contacts pulled me off to the side when I was wandering through the hallowed halls of one of the many Congressional office buildings, and told me that the real reason Congress doesn't pass meaningful legislation protecting federal whistleblowers is that they're afraid their own Congressional staff members would eventually demand the same type of protections – and their little house of cards would come tumbling down.

On a tactical level:

Which brings me back to aviation security. The last head of TSA (as I write this) was a former FBI bureaucrat, John Pistole. According to TSA's own website, it states that Pistole was the longest serving TSA Administrator (by inference, has some responsibility for the status and direction the TSA has taken) and will continue TSA's approach of being a "risk-based, intelligence driven counter-terrorism agency." Sounds good; but the problem is that aviation security has ALWAYS been a risk-based intelligence driven bureaucracy, that's a major reason it failed so miserably on 9/11, politics aside (I'll get into the counter-terrorism nonsense shortly). Our collective intelligence agencies (namely the FBI, CIA, NSA etc) that provide this risk-based driving force are remarkably inept at predicting anything (I previously went into this history). And there is a bureaucratic advantage to using this intelligence driven approach – when the inevitable cataclysm occurs, the TSA bureaucrats can just blame the intelligence community for not providing them actionable intelligence rather than accept the blame on themselves, where it rightly belongs; and the intelligence community will argue that if only Congress would have given them more money and allowed them to increase spying on everyone, then they would have been able to prevent the attack.

Typically the intelligence community finds out about a new attack when everyone else does – after it happens. Which is why Congress continually dumps more tax money on these failure based bureaucracies, hoping they'll eventually get it right. To base the whole transportation security sector on the oft proven failure based intelligence bureaucracies is just bone-headed stupidity. Even before 9/11, Steve Elson would argue before our Congressional contacts and other bureaucrats that your local bank doesn't wait for the police to tell them that they should beef up security as the threat of bank robberies is now high. There will always be that unknown factor. Instead, banks always have a high level of security based on reasonableness and prudence, and the security is incorporated into their everyday business environment and done so without infringing on anyone's Constitutional rights.

TSA should have long since based its security on the same standards – reasonableness and prudence based not on intelligence, but on Red Team assessments (or how vulnerable the systems really are to even a half-wit evil-doer), a heavy dose of common sense, and of course, be creative enough to work within the confines of the Constitution. But to make matters even worse, TSA (under Pistole's management) has now incorporated this "intelligence driven risk based" philosophy into employee's fitness reports, so an employee officially questioning this nonsense can lead to a failing performance review and lead to an employee's dismissal. Effectively taking this bureaucratic tombstone mindset a step further than the FAA dared too. (When I responded to my own fitness report appraisals, I'd explain why this risk based intelligence driven nonsense was doomed to failure; but as the good little TSA employee, I fully support TSA's program no matter how many people it kills (loaded with sarcasm). It was apparently enough of an explanation and acceptance of this crap to satisfy my chain of command so as not to suffer any official retribution on my performance appraisals).

As to the term "counter-terrorist": For anyone who actually worked in this type of environment, the term *counter-terrorist* refers to the type of people that jump behind enemy lines and shoot terrorists in the back of the head, or calls in an air strike. The term "anti-terrorist" refers to folks engaged in security operations designed to deter or thwart a terrorist attack. Even when I was an air marshal, this type of work is ANTI-terrorism. But it sounds cooler, I guess, to call oneself a counter-terrorist rather than an anti-terrorist. This isn't even security based on intelligence, its Hollywood based security. It is not just a matter of semantics, its an indication of delusional thinking on the part of senior management.

However, the bottom line of all these problems is that the current state of aviation security, just as it was before 9/11, is designed primarily to keep honest people honest and keep dumb people from hurting themselves or others, but does little to stop a terrorist. It's a big mistake to judge security based on the lack of a terrorist attack. Only a proper Red Team assessment can determine that vulnerability, and TSA would rather have us learn things the hard way – all over again. (In June of 2015, the press reported the latest version of the TSA Pink Team identifying 95% failure rates in their testing – nothings changed since before 9/11; except for the expense involved and the erosion of the Constitution).

As part of my whistleblower disclosure against TSA in 2008, I took a random sample of the job announcements for senior staff positions and managers. Not one of these job announcements had any educational requirements whatsoever. According to Wikipedia, the US Department of Education had a $70 billion budget in 2013. Apparently the senior managers in TSA think so poorly of our government run educational system that they have no educational standards for its own senior staff and managers (this might be the only intelligent decision these bureaucrats made). But there is a downside, this little omission allows TSA to hire and promote people with no requisite background in security – basically the system gives management the flexibility to hire and promote people based on cronyism, whomever is in good standing politically, as well as the over-riding cloud of diversity (which by definition turns a blind eye toward competency in favor of the latest political expedient) – the latter which the agency proudly touts. With rare exception TSA was no more successful in hiring and promoting qualified minority people into management than their abysmal tract record of hiring and promoting competent white people into these positions. Frequently, government managers and Congressmen state that one of the big hurdles to effective bureaucracies is that managers can't fire bad employees. The problem isn't the occasional bad employee, the problem is the routine hiring, promotion and retention of incompetent managers whose only bureaucratic strength is blind loyalty. In these same job announcements I reviewed there wasn't a single one that required any knowledge or experience in security either. Becoming a staff member or manager in the TSA is probably the only job in this country other than being a pimp or a prostitute in which one can make well over a hundred thousand dollars salary with absolutely no experience or education requirements. This breeds a bureaucracy which revels in its mediocrity, at best, and its unconstitutional behavior at worst. (One of my TSA supervisors only had a high school diploma as his highest level of education and never worked a day in his life in security, while all his subordinates either had a graduate degree or were working on one; selected for management as he was the one least likely to question dangerously stupid policies, and he is on his way up the management chain. He excelled in the diversity department, however, even surpassing those other minority candidates who did have a graduate degree.)

And, credit should be given where credit is due. The bureaucracy within THE bureaucracy: the Senior Executive Service (SES), about which the rest of the entire federal bureaucracy revolves. The United States Office of Personnel Management website states: *"….as the keystone of the civil service reform act of 1978, the SES was established to '…ensure that the executive management of the government of the United States is responsive to the needs, policies, and goals of the nation and otherwise is of the highest quality.'* These leaders possess well-

honed executive skills and share a broad perspective on government and a public service commitment that is grounded in the Constitution." And later: *"They operate and oversee nearly every government activity in approximately 75 federal agencies."* I'm not sure what the phrase "and otherwise is of the highest quality" really means. But based on my experience should be rephrased to reflect that, "we cater to the least common denominator", just based on their performance. And, "grounded in the Constitution", I seriously doubt that SES level civil servants are required to even read the Constitution. From my observations, the SES is more closely aligned with a cult rather than a public service "grounded" in anything.

I had some discussion with Coleen Rowley (one of the many FBI whistleblowers and a Time Magazine person of the year), concerning the appalling behavior of our intelligence, law enforcement, and security agencies – all of which failed miserably in the lead up to 9/11. Even if they deliberately tried to, how could every single facet of these agencies fail like this? The [SES led] government's appalling behavior led to the beginning of all the conspiracy theories that have sprouted up since 9/11. But Coleen came back with a brilliant retort: "It was a conspiracy of stupidity!" And these government bureaucrats make more in retirement benefits than most Americans make during the prime of their working life – all at taxpayer expense.

The solutions to this mess:

First; the Constitution must be reestablished as the working document of how this government is supposed to function. Without this, the rest is pointless. The oath of office many of us have taken as federal civil and military servants should actually mean something, with certain and specific obligations, with penalties for lack of adherence to the rules. Adherence to the Constitution will, at a minimum, reduce the volume of blatantly stupid, costly, immoral, and dangerous programs that our government engages in.

Second; get rid of the Department of Homeland Security, save the outrageously expensive overhead costs and hire *leaders* to run the agencies that currently fall beneath its umbrella rather than the *managers* they currently have, with some possible exceptions.

Third; get rid of the Transportation Security Administration, they've had about fifteen years to get their act together but can't and won't. A child born the same year as TSA has learned a lot more about life than TSA has learned about security. Put security back on the shoulders of the aviation industry, only hold them to appropriate legal standards of accountability. The industry CEOs would be clamoring to hire real security professionals that would help keep their business in business and keep them out of jail. Managing security and the terrorist threat is no different than managing the other unique risks associated with the aviation industry – but it has to based on science or at least rational thought, not lobbying or political correctness.

The single biggest deterrent against aviation related terrorism is that now flight crews and passengers are very much aware of the potential of a terror attack; and unlike the government, they are not wearing politically correct blindfolds – when survival is at stake, the gloves come off. Installing double-hulled doors to the cockpits of commercial aircraft (in which one door has to be closed before the other can be opened) would effectively eliminate hijackings. The current single hulled doors are just a sloppy fix.

Fourth; there are some serious issues with the federal government's Senior Executive Service. They enjoy the perks of their status and claim responsibility over the running of the federal government, but are no more accountable than anyone else has been. If they won't discipline their own, then someone else needs too. Or get rid of the SES entirely as an organizational entity.

Fifth; end the persecution of government whistleblowers. Make the government bureaucrats personally accountable for retaliating against these folks with severe consequences. A dedicated federal employee shouldn't have to fear for his livelihood for reporting gross malfeasance in the government.

Sixth; there are only two ways to determine whether a given security system works, the first is the success or failure of an actual attack, and the second are the assessments of a Red Team. Its essential to incorporate Red Team operations into the security infrastructure of this country. It works, if properly led and executed.

Seventh; use red team tactics against the terrorist organizations themselves, apply asymmetrical methodologies to undermine their own organizational structure.

On a personal level:

I'm reminded of the ancient Roman dictum, "bellum nec timendum nec provocandum", or, "war must be neither feared nor provoked." While I fully support a strong military in this increasingly bizarre world, I lament how our elected officials routinely misuse our military personnel and sacrifice their lives over BS; using the avoidable 9/11 attacks as a pretext for its latest round of malfeasance. Then they have certain elements within the Veterans Administration treat the surviving wounded like dirt, until the press gets hold of the latest and endless scandals and mismanagement of that agency – almost all reported by whistleblowers. Official neglect of our veterans has occurred after virtually every war our country has engaged in, and yet the talking heads in government make a big hypocritical show of honoring veterans at every appropriate holiday; these folks deserve a lot more than lip service from our illusion based politicians and bureaucrats. And how many of our dedicated military servants are allowed to wither and die in the meantime? The federal bureaucracy won't change until its forced too.

In 2012, some very decent individuals in my TSA chain of command arranged for me to get out from under the heel of TSA headquarter's boot and move myself to my home state of Ohio and telework from there. With a change of management attitude in late 2014, this was rescinded and I was ordered back to headquarters in a "directed reassignment). (This is just one of the ways management screws with employees.) I opted to quit instead. With a taste of freedom, no way could I stand being in that toxic atmosphere again. On my last day of work, images of the final scene of *Papillon* where Steve McQueen floats away from the prison island wafted through my mind. "Hey you bastards, I'm still here!", he muttered. This will forever be the last remembrance of my Hollywood/Government/Cartel career. So I took an earlier retirement than I was planning on, in early 2015.

Just pondering my journey down the river of life: Both my parents lived through the middle of the war between Nazi Germany and the Soviet Union. Each, as far as I can tell, were on opposing sides of the war just based on the political boundaries of the time. While they survived the war I'm convinced the hardships they endured contributed greatly to their early deaths. As time went on I grew up with an instinctive desire to spend my life doing what I could to minimize man's inhumanity to man. I turned that desire into action in my career. Unfortunately, failing miserably.

On my first day of retirement I picked up a couple of roses from the local market and went to my parent's graves, which aren't that far from my current house where my fiancée and I now live. I placed the flowers on the headstone and sat down in the cold, damp grass, not really thinking of anything, just zoning. I had long sense lost my own thousand yard stare, but the scars were still there.

My thoughts drifted to 1962. I was living at the orphanage and one of the nuns pulled me out of the daily routine of orphanage life and told me I was going to see my mother. This was a big treat, just getting out of the routine, but seeing mom was icing on the cake. My older sister then took me to the house where we lived when my mother wasn't in the hospital, and she was sitting on the back porch. We spent a lot of time just talking.

At one point my mom asked me if I was being treated OK and how I was doing – knowing her influence over her children was waning, and that she could do nothing to protect us anymore, or help direct our lives. I didn't want her to feel bad so I said that I was doing fine. She asked if I missed her, and again, not wanting to make her feel bad, I said, "no." But I immediately recognized the pain in her eyes and realized I said the wrong thing. So I changed my answer to "yes." We hugged each other for an interminably long time (for an eight year old). Right before I left to go back to the orphanage she gently caressed the side of my face saying something I can't remember now, I was too choked up knowing I had to leave her again. She died a few days later. (I didn't know it at the time, of course, but our home town was one of the cities where the federal government was conducting radiation and other experiments on poor people without their consent during this same time frame. My efforts to contact the applicable federal government offices to find out if my mother and/or father were victims – no response.)

While I was still sitting at the gravesite I couldn't help but think of the two funerals, but they happened so long ago and my memories are a mix of both of them. I recalled, however, during one of the burial ceremonies that a bird was chirping away on a nearby tree and I looked in that direction and noticed that the same tree was still standing there – 52 years later. I hadn't noticed it before but another bird was chirping away in the same tree, and I wondered if this bird was the progeny of the bird I saw there half a century before. As I stared at it, I felt a gentle caress on the side of my face, was it the breeze or something else? I pondered for a just a moment. Life taught me to keep an open mind to the possibilities, and an involuntary smile came over me. From somewhere outside, it was acknowledged that I endured, and then some. On one level anyway, I won.

Its time for someone else to pick up the gauntlet, perhaps yet, another damn orphan.

Fortress of Deceit

AFTERWORD

By

Tom Devine

A gonzo book about whistleblowing is long overdue. Bogdan Dzakovic's story overflows with experiences that make a reader want to laugh, cry and yes scream at the same time. This is the professional autobiography of an everyman trying to serve the public in the too often insane world of government national security bureaucracies. It is as darkly entertaining as it is educationally insightful. While reading and rereading it, I could not help but flash back to Kafka's *The Trial,* Monty Python's movie *Brazil,* and all of Hunter Thompson's *Fear and Loathing .....*

As Bogdan's lawyer for his Federal Aviation Administration Red Team whistleblowing, I had to become too familiar with the FAA's passive aggression against its consumer mission. This betrayal of the public trust made it possible for 9/11 to happen. But his experiences with the reality behind a popular TV show like *NIS* demonstrated there is no depth of self-caricature too low for government military bureaucracies like the Naval Investigative Service or even the Coast Guard. He wonders why all employees take an oath to the constitution about which they never are taught or trained. He describes censorship to erase the embarrassing failure of a test against sabotage later akin to what sank the U.S.S. Cole. He details how bureaucrats sabotaged the opportunity to catch a drug smuggling mothership, because preventing a rival office from getting credit in an agency turf war was a higher priority than the agency mission. All while employees spent up to 25% of their time padding "success" statistics, because the top agency priority was justifying more money and power.

But it gets better/worse. Consider priorities at the NIS. Bogdan was assigned to a five day, multi-state investigation costing thousands of dollars and leading to a barren Native American Reservation where he was attacked by dogs but no suspect in sight. The point? Allegations that a Native American had stolen $20 prior to his military discharge. Or there was international investigation that spent $10,000 to recover a missing junk fiddle which had disappeared before being thrown away. When I finished the chapter on NIS, the book's setting was clear – a darkly humorous version of the Twilight Zone.

Fortress of Deceit

But this is not a nightmare novel, satirical movie or television program. The tragedy is that Bogdan's story is about the reality of life in the national security institutions charged with keeping America safe. That reality? A basic contradiction between public service as the official mission, and bureaucratic self-interest of the agencies charged with that mission.

Most of the insanity Bogdan discloses reflects bureaucratic attitudes so deeply ingrained that they have become akin to instinct. Some reflect a structure whose rules cannot withstand scrutiny. For example, he describes military justice procedures that permit a service member guilty of a brutal rape to continue attending classes, while his victim remained in the hospital. In terms of consequences, though, it doesn't matter whether the cause was attitude or structure. Either way the public loses.

What is worse is that these abuses are not limited to national security agencies. To a greatrer or lesser degree, they are a knee jerk reaction common to all bureaucracies -- government, corporate, nongovernmental organization, media left or right. The first reaction is to threaten retaliation if employees even ask hard questions. The second is ugly personal abuse. The third is to destroy them in a highly visible way as a warning to others. For example, Bogdan describes how his supervisor angrily cussed him out for suggesting a rape prevention training program would be healthy. An FAA aviation safety whistleblower with whom I've worked got the same treatment when she suggested that flight attendants should be trained in how to use emergency rear exits, an inexplicable oversight that would render the doors irrelevant if needed.

I'm speaking From personal experience. Since 1979 I have worked at the Government Accountability Project, and have formally or informally helped some 6,000 whistleblowers during that period. GAP is a non-profit, non- partisan public interest organization whose reason to be is service for whistleblowers, those employees who exercise free speech rights to challenge abuses of power that betray the public trust.

We help in four ways. First, we defend them against retaliation through conventional lawsuits in national courts up to a recent successful Supreme Court appeal. We also represent whistleblowers in international tribunals such as at the United Nations. Often the best defenses are more informal, by recruiting support from political figures more powerful than the bullies, or through action by government whistleblower protection agencies. Second, we help them make a difference by investigating their charges and then waging legal campaigns around the truth, often integrated with the reprisal defense. For both aspects, the magic word is solidarity. GAP's strategy is to act as a matchmaker between isolated whistleblowers and all the groups in society that should be benefiting from their knowledge. Through the investigations we create a record of documents and sworn statements from other whistleblowers, so that the initial falling rock becomes a landslide for the truth that cannot be ignored. Then we share the information with all those who are affected by the cover up – affected communities and citizen groups; law enforcement agencies and regulatory bodies; legislative members and committees to seek broader investigations and hearings; the media as the lifeline to society; investors; and even competitors. When that occurs, instead of a corrupt organization surrounding the isolated whistleblower, society surrounds those who are abusing their power.

Third, we advocate enactment of stronger laws protecting whistleblowers' free speech rights, and then monitor their implementation. We have been a leader in drafting or campaigns for passage of 33 whistleblower laws or policies. They range from Washington DC's law, to nearly all national whistleblower laws in the United States, as well as Intergovernmental Organizations (IGO's) including the United Nations, World Bank, Organization of American States and African Development Bank.

Whistleblower rights are one of the world's most dynamic areas of law. When I first came to GAP, the U.S. was the only country with a whistleblower law. Now 30 nations and six IGO's have whistleblower laws or policies, with 60 more proposed globally. Our duty when advocating whistleblower laws is the most important principle: first do no harm. As a result, we often oppose fraudulent whistleblower proposals with supportive titles that actually are traps to identify political threats and then rubber stamp any ensuing retaliation. We check whether whistleblower proposals or laws are "metal shields" (creating a fighting chance to survive) or often gaudy "cardboard shields" (guaranteeing doom despite their appearance). To help choose, we have prepared research you can find on our website, www.whistleblower.org, listing whistleblower laws globally, as well as the 20 best practices for rights that are metal shields.

Similarly, one of our primary lessons learned is that passing even credible whistleblower laws on paper is only the first step in a long journey for freedom of speech. Without ongoing efforts, in practice rights that are solid on paper may disintegrate into traps that discredit their purpose and victimize those who take them seriously. Even good faith laws inevitably lead to cycles of trial

⁻ntial to act on lessons learned. For example, in
⁻er law for federal government workers is
⁻ with passage of the Whistleblower
⁻ment Act of 2012, after a thirteen year

⁻o share our lessons learned, so that rights sink in
⁻ledge and training. We publish law review articles,
op-eds, and books to share all the details of new laws,
⁻s the painful lessons of experience. Our most recent book,
⁻rporate Whistleblower's Survival Guide: A Handbook for
⁻ ⁻mitting the Truth, recently won the International Business
Book of the Year Award at the Frankfurt Book Fair. Since 1979
we have operated a law school clinic, currently with the D.C.
School of Law, and regularly have college or law school interns in
full-time apprenticeship roles. For practitioners, we offer
continuing legal education courses and videos. We teach at training
programs for government investigators and ombudsmen on how to
work more effectively with whistleblowers. GAP also has worked
with university and law school professors to develop academic
programs on whistleblower rights, and has sponsored
whistleblowers on college tours to share their experiences.

While GAP has been in business for almost 40 years,
whistleblowers have been in business since the dawn of organized
society. As long as institutions have had power, it has been
abused. I think of power as being like the ring in the Tolkien
trilogy. As a rule humans can't handle it, and it can destroy those
who possess it. But sooner or later, the bravest always have
challenged the abuse strongest personal risk. Those who do it with
weapons are revolutionaries. Those who do it with words are
whistleblowers. I think of Jesus as a whistleblower against the
corrupt church Pharisees. Martin Luther blew the whistle on the
Catholic Church.

There is nothing magical about the term "whistleblower." In the
Netherlands, these same individuals are called "bell ringers," after
those who warn their communities of danger. Other nations refer to
whistleblowers as "lighthouse keepers," after those who save ships
from sinking by shining the light on areas where rocks are both
invisible and deadly.

No matter what we call them, whistleblowing is freedom of speech
when it counts the most, and therefore is the most dangerous. It is
easy to have freedom of speech in a soccer stadium to say almost
anything about a referee who calls a penalty on the wrong athlete.
One reason is that it is hard to retaliate against tens of thousands of
dissenters. Another is that the wrong decision is not a secret. It

likely was televised. It is different for whistleblowers. They are challenging secrecy enforced by repression, and may be one of only a few who know the truth.

Whistleblowers exercise freedom of speech in three different contexts. We usually think they are exercising the freedom to protest. In this setting their speech is the lifeblood of justice, essential to hold those responsible who abuse their power.

A second, even more important context, is the freedom to warn. Here whistleblowers seek to prevent avoidable mistakes or disasters, before it is too late for anything except damage control and finger pointing. In this setting, they can be like the bitter pill that keeps an organization from getting sick. I view institutional leaders' response to whistleblowing as a test of their management maturity. Most organizational problems get buried in the middle of bureaucracies, and a leader may not even know about them until getting blamed for the consequences. Whistleblowers should serve as their eyes and ears. We regularly advise corporate leaders that it is bad business to silence or kill the messenger.

The third context may be the most fundamental – the freedom to create, by challenging conventional wisdom. What do I mean? Less than a thousand years ago we all believed the earth is as flat as a table, and that the whole universe revolves around us. Thanks to Copernicus and Galileo, we know better. They received the whistleblower treatment. Galileo spent the rest of this life under house arrest. But they made a difference as the founders of modern society, and they keep the scientific profession honest.

In the end, whistleblowers are people who make a difference as the living histories who refuse to be rewritten. Whether they are right or wrong, noble or self-serving, they are essential to keep power from corrupting absolutely. By challenging conventional wisdom, they keep society from being stagnant and are the pioneers of change.

Why do they do it? Whatever we call them, these are individuals at the intersection of valid but conflicting values. We like team players and find cynical troublemakers and are resentful of naysayers. But we also admire rugged individualists and have contempt for bureaucratic sheep. Similarly, no one wants to be viewed as a squealer or tattletale. A common synonym for informant is "rat." But we have equal contempt for those who look the other way, do not want to get involved, or make a conscious choice to see nothing.

Transparency triggers another valid contradiction. Any citizen in a former dictatorship cherishes the right to privacy. But a cornerstone of democracy is accountability through the public's right to know. Sometimes it's necessary to choose, or have the choice imposed on us.

The most difficult choices force would-be whistleblowers to answer the question: loyalty to whom? For almost all of us, the loyalty is to our family. Getting fired threatens our capacity to support children and other loved ones. The common slogan not bite the hand that feeds you is both a cultural norm and can be a necessity for economic survival. Similarly, there is loyalty to our co-workers, who may be among our best friends, and often feel as defensive or threatened as the whistleblower's institutional target. Loss of family and friends are common consequences for breaching this loyalty. But what about loyalty to our communities, which can be victimized by corruption?

Should we remain silent and passively join cover-ups that could kill our neighbors through contaminated food or a poisoned environment? What about loyalty to the law, and to our nation? The latter is called patriotism.

After weighing these conflicting values, two factors consistently tip the scales. First, whether their motives are idealistic or self-serving, whistleblowers are being true to themselves. As one explained, "I want to be able to keep looking at myself in the mirror." If they didn't act on their knowledge, the "what if's" would haunt them.

Second, all of us want to make a difference, for the world to be a better place because we were here. Most of us try to do it through our families. Whistleblowers broaden the circle, sometimes to the extreme. And repeatedly they have succeeded in changing the course of history, in settings ranging from their communities to the world.

One of my primary teachers and most effective clients, Ernest Fitzgerald, in the 1980's exposed the world's most expensive nuts, bolts, coffee pots and toilets seats, all purchased by the U.S. military at taxpayer expense. In 1968 he exposed lies to Congress that were covering up a $2 billion cost overrun on construction of Air Force cargo planes. Ernie calls whistleblowing "committing the truth," because those who do it are treated like criminals. That is ironic, because these eyewitnesses are the Achilles' heel of bureaucratic corruption by thwarting secrecy, its breeding ground. They are the lifeblood of anti-corruption campaigns, which are lifeless, empty symbols doomed to failure without testimony from those who bear witness. Consider how they made a difference challenging corruption in the U.S. and Europe. They have --

* increased the government's average annual civil recoveries of fraud in government contracts from an average less than $10 whistleblowers at telephone companies, the Department of Justice and the National Security Agency (NSA), exposed and led to controls on blanket, illegal domestic government surveillance of all electronic communications.

* exposed government orders to abandon Federal Air Marshal (FAM) defenses during a confirmed, more ambitious 2003 rerun of the 9/11 suicide attacks targeting not only U.S. cities but also the Australian and European capitals. FAM coverage was restored, and the mass hijacking prevented.

* caused creation of a national milk testing program after exposing suppression of a test that after approved demonstrated 80% commercial milk was contaminated with illegal animal drugs.

* forced the resignation of World Bank President Paul Wolfowitz, who took office pledging a campaign against Third World corruption, by exposing that his own practices were indefensibly corrupt.

* exposed failure for a year and a half to deliver purchased and tested vehicles capable of protecting U.S. troops from landmines. After their delivery, landmines dropped from 90% of casualties and 60% of fatalities, to 10% of casualties.

* reduced from four days to two hours the amount of time racially-profiled minority women going through U.S. Customs could be stopped on suspicion of drug smuggling, body cavity-searched and held incommunicado for hospital laboratory tests, without access to a lawyer or even permission to contact family, in the absence of any evidencethat they had engaged in wrongdoing.

* sparked a top-down removal of top management at the U.S. Department of Justice ("DOJ"), after revealing systematic corruption in DOJ's program to train police forces of other nations how to investigate and prosecute government corruption. Examples included leaks of classified documents as political patronage; overpriced "sweetheart" contracts to unqualified political supporters; cost overruns of up to ten times to obtain research already available for an anti-corruption law enforcement training conference; and use of the government's visa power to

bring highly suspect Russian women, such as one previously arrested for prostitution during dinner with a top DOJ official in Moscow, to work for Justice Department management.

    * acted as catalyst for resignations by all European Commissioners, after exposing systematic EC procurement fraud organized by the EC President.

    * convinced Congress to cancel "Brilliant Pebbles," the trillion dollar plan for a next generation of America's Star Wars anti-ballistic missile defense system, after proving that contractors were being paid six-seven times for the same research cosmetically camouflaged by new titles and cover pages; that tests results claiming success had been a fraud; and that the future space-based interceptors would burn up in the earth's atmosphere hundreds of miles above peak height for targeted nuclear missiles.

    * exposed accurate data about possible public exposure to radiation around the Hanford, Washington nuclear waste reservation, where Department of Energy contractors had admitted an inability to account for 5,000 gallons of radioactive wastes but the true figure was 440 billion gallons.

    * inspired a public, political and investor backlash that forced conversion from nuclear to coal energy for a power plant that was 97% complete but had been built in systematic violation of nuclear safety laws, such as fraudulent substitution of junkyard scrap metal for top-priced, state of the art quality nuclear grade steel, which endangered citizens while charging them for the safest materials money could buy.

    * forced a new cleanup after the Three Mile Island nuclear power accident, after exposure how systematic illegality risked triggering a complete meltdown that could have forced long-term evacuation of Philadelphia, New York City and Washington, D.C. To illustrate, the corporation planned to remove the reactor vessel head with a polar crane whose breaks and electrical system had been totally destroyed in the partial meltdown but had not been tested after repairs to see if it would hold weight. The reactor vessel head was 170 tons of radioactive rubble left from the core after the first accident.

    * bore witness with testimony that led to cancellation of toxic incinerators dumping poisons like dioxin, arsenic, mercury and heavy metals into public areas such as church and school yards. This practice of making a profit by poisoning the public had been sustained through falsified records that fraudulently reported all pollution was within legal limits.

* forced abandonment of plans to replace government meat inspection with corporate "honor systems" for products with the federal seal of approval as wholesome - plans that could have made food poisoning outbreaks the rule rather than the exception.

Whew! These whistleblowers have proven over and over that an individual *can* make a difference, and they have more than ever before. It is a copout to say you can't fight city hall or big business.

Unfortunately, unlike these whistleblowers Bogdan will have to be satisfied with being true to himself. Initially his persistence appeared to be making a difference. The U.S. Office of Special Counsel, the federal whistleblower agency, found a substantial likelihood that FAA misconduct suppressing its Red Team created a substantial and specific danger to public health and safety that contributed to 9/11. A subsequent Transportation Department Office of Inspector General report confirmed that conclusion, and the FAA made numerous corrective actions commitments to restore an effective Red Team. The Department of Homeland Security settled a retaliation case with Bogdan in part by assigning him to prepare a "lessons learned" document so that the pre-9/11 mistakes would not recur.

But the agency reneged *en masse* on its reform commitments. The Red Team remains, as Bogdan calls it, the Pink Team. Most telling, within days if turning in his "lessons learned" report, the agency reassigned him to administrative duties needing only a high school degree. The report was marked secret and ignored.

He's in good company, however. There has been a legal revolution in whistleblower free speech rights, and a cultural revolution in their acceptance by society. But it has not taken root inside most organizations, and the national security bureaucracy least of all.

Bogdan wisely decided to stop beating his head against the wall. Consider the ongoing adventure of one who hasn't, Federal Air Marshal Robert MacLean. In 2003 his disclosure prevented DHS from going AWOL by canceling all relevant Air Marshal missions during a confirmed Al Qaeda hijacking plan for a drastically more ambitious rerun of 9/11 – this time targeting Washington DC but West Coast cities, European capitols, and even Canberra the capitol of Australia. After a congressional outcry and within 24 hours of MacLean's disclosure, DHS said it had made a "mistake," restored coverage and the hijacking was prevented.

How did the agency react to Mr. MacLean likely preventing a national tragedy by exposing its "mistake?" It retroactively pseudo-classified the relevant text message canceling the missions as "Sensitive Security Information," and then fired him for endangering the country by exposing pseudo-classified information. After a nine year legal battle the Supreme Court held 7-2 that Mr. MacLean's freedom to warn was legally protected by the Whistleblower Protection Act, and from the bench Chief Justice Roberts praised his service to the country.

How did the agency react to the Supreme Court's mandate for freedom of speech? It assigned him to FAM undercover missions on flights to the Mid-East. But Mr. MacLean is the most publicly visible Air Marshal in agency history, having appeared on the Internet over 50 times, including national and international television news shows, as well as congressional testimony. DHS took this action despite intelligence that ISIL has been researching the Internet to identify Federal Air Marshals and target those flights. DHS might as well have been painting a big red X on every flight MacLean was assigned to protect. I wondered if the agency was willing to endanger the public to pursue deadly retaliation against Mr. MacLean. We filed another lawsuit with the Office of Special Counsel. Again the agency had to reverse itself, and ended the flying missions.

Did DHS get the message? As Bogdan would say, Noooooooo. It placed Mr. MacLean under retaliatory investigation, reassigned him to an empty room without any duties, and is trying to block his security clearance based on the financial consequences he suffered due to getting illegally fired. Will it ever end?

This Alice in Wonderland world is the reality for national security whistleblowers, more than anywhere else. As a rule the national security bureaucracy's response to them, especially when publicly vindicated, has been the short-sighted strategy of intensifying retaliation. The bureaucratic imperative is to sustain and expand power as the first priority, at all costs. With that paradigm, the strategy is to make an example of people like Bogdan or Robert MacLean. Others must get the message: You're going to lose, even if you win. Otherwise, questioning or even challenging authority might become contagious.

The far sighted alternative would be to view whistleblowers as what Senator Grassley calls them, -- the "canaries in the coal mines" who serve as advance warnings of preventable misconduct, problems or disasters. But most seldom at national security agencies, that type of mature management approach is the exception, not the rule. They remain on the frontier of transparency and whistleblower rights in particular, and government accountability in particular.

This is dangerous and unacceptable. The lessons learned from Bogdan's book and other whistleblowers like Mr. MacLean all lead to the same conclusion. Bureaucratic breakdowns sustained by secrecy and enforced by repression are a clear and present danger to national security.

By contrast, whistleblowers are a win-win to make us safer for everyone except those missing their power. Many proposals to make us safer are very costly, both in terms of money and liberty. But it doesn't cost any money to listen, and whistleblower protection relies on strengthening freedom instead of threatening it. It is no coincidence that freedom of speech is the first amendment to the U.S. constitution.

This book tells shares the surreal adventure of a person who actually tried to live the constitutional duties to which government employees swear an oath of allegiance without any government training in what they are. If you want to know whether to trust the government, read this book. If you want to know why you shouldn't, read this book. If you think the answer to government misconduct is more authority for managers over front line employees, read this book.

If you distrust all government employees because of bureaucratic abuses, please read this book. As the human wild card, whistleblowers are the Achilles' heel of bureaucratic corruption. As Bogdan's story proves, the most inept, abusive agencies can generate the most heroic public servants.

Bogdan and other whistleblowers' spirit cannot be suppressed. Based on always learning about the dark side, I should be one of Washington DC's most cynical pessimists. Despite knowing the worst, however, I am probably one of the most idealistic and optimistic. Because in every example listed earlier, they were the Davids and the powerful institutions they defeated the Goliaths. Whistleblowers are the human lifeline to turn information into power. The bottom line lesson I've learned from working with them is that nothing is more powerful than the truth.

Fortress of Deceit

COVER

By

Rob DelGaudio

Fortress of Deceit

Made in the USA
Middletown, DE
28 July 2016